To Jimmy Finn,

You will always be my hero!

#10
Rex Kern

Full Endorsements for

THE ROAD TO THE HORSESHOE AND BEYOND

It was fun to read the comments of friends, from before my days at Ohio State, during my days there, and several after leaving the university. Obviously, there would be outstanding quotes for the back cover of the book.

Then reality hit. There were enough great quotes and reflections for a library of books, but only one back cover. It was pure torture to cut and cut to fit the space with the picture of Woody and I planning to beat USC at the 1969 Rose Bowl.

Please excuse the numerous omissions. It is now a pleasure to provide the full comments of many friends, mentors, and heroes from my life.

★　★　★

"I think the race chapter was very well done. Hopefully, others will read the book and realize race issues are not rocket science. It's about compassion and caring for your fellow man. Glad to endorse the book."

ARCHIE GRIFFIN, Ohio State football, 1972-1975, All-American 1973-1975, Heisman Trophy winner, 1974-1975.

"Once a Buckeye, always a Buckeye!

"No matter where I've traveled or lived, my roots always stretch back to my home state of Ohio, often with some tie to The Ohio State University. I prided myself on being a Buckeye football fan since the age of six and missed only one game until the age of twenty. My love for OSU football never died, nor did the memories of the greats who played there. Any such list is not complete without Rex Kern, the three-sport star who was the Buckeyes's quarterback in the late 1960s and was later inducted into the College Football Hall of Fame. Rex took OSU to an undefeated season and national title in 1968, punctuated in the Rose Bowl, where he famously beat O. J. Simpson's University of Southern California team.

"Just as my life was impacted in many ways by OSU's legendary football coach Woody Hayes—a great friend to our family when I was growing up—so too was Rex's life influenced and shaped by Woody.

"While Rex and I went to Ohio State at different times, our paths crossed many times throughout the years. I have always had great respect and admiration for Rex, for both the way he handled himself and the way he was revered by all Buckeye fans.

"There are so many common threads in our respective lives, but if there is one important one that binds us, it is that Rex and I have allowed our lives to be shaped and inspired by family, faith, our love of country, and yes, our love of being Buckeyes. In his book, *The Road to the Horseshoe and Beyond*, Rex takes us on the journey of his remarkable life. Along the way, you might learn a little about leading a life well lived, but also, when you reflect on your own life, what you should appreciate and hold dear."

JACK NICKLAUS, Buckeye great and PGA legend with an unmatched 18 major titles.

"I really enjoyed this book on many levels. The obvious backstage pass to his playing days in high school, college, and the NFL . . . especially the magical 1968 Championship season . . . the Woody Hayes stories that shed light on the legendary and yet complicated man . . . Rex's love and devotion to God and his family . . . and the countless examples of mental and physical toughness, love, compassion, empathy, and selflessness."

KIRK HERBSTREIT, Ohio State quarterback and football analyst at ESPN.

"Rex has many fine qualities but the first word that comes to mind when I think of Rex is INTEGRITY. Rex has been a great friend to our family and that friendship is reciprocated.

"I enjoyed reading *The Road to the Horseshoe and Beyond*. It gives the reader a glimpse into Rex's whole life, not just his time as an athlete. He didn't pull any punches, which brings me back to that word INTEGRITY.

"I had no idea that Rex was such a gifted writer. So Rex, can I suggest a departure to fiction? Perhaps a football mystery? With great affection,"

STEVE HAYES, son of Woody and Anne Hayes.

"This book is much more than a dissertation about sports. Yes, you will enjoy many entertaining and fascinating sports stories, especially those about the legendary Woody Hayes. But, as you read this book, be ready for a battle— actually, be ready for several battles. Not only will you learn about Rex's personal battles in sports and life and how he overcame them, but you will learn how his life experiences, which are built upon the foundation of faith and the bedrock of 'being your best in everything,' can help all of us navigate life's many battles.

"So, put on your battle gear and enjoy an inspirational story about an all-American kid who became an All-American example of a life worth emulating."

JERRY LUCAS, Ohio State basketball, 1960-61-62, champion at every level of basketball, two-time NCAA Player of the Year, Memory Expert.

"I have long admired Rex Kern from the time I met him in 1990 as I assumed the presidency of The Ohio State University. Kind, thoughtful, devoted to family and the Buckeyes. I started to read his book out of friendship and obligation. I finished his book with a real sense of joy and inner peace. This book is worth reading because it is an American story, forged in the heartland of this country and buttressed with compassion, steel, and common sense."

E. GORDON GEE, President, The Ohio State University, 1990-1997.

"Rex Kern's Buckeye roots run deep into his soul, but I'm a former Baltimore Colt, and we claim him too. Rex is a champion, a leader, a man of epic character and integrity; every one of those ingredients was apparent from the first day he reported to the Baltimore Colts.

"He had an aura. He was special, as a person as much as an athlete. He led Ohio State to a National Championship, but he had a fine NFL career as well.

"Reading this book of his life's experiences was a joy."

ERNIE ACCORSI, General Manager, Baltimore Colts, Cleveland Browns, New York Giants.

"Take Woody's advice this time—don't PASS on this book! Dr. Rex Kern, by all accounts, has had a fascinating and consequential life. Ohio State University sports fans are very familiar with his heroic efforts in that arena, but his experiences prior to that, as well as off the field and after his football career, lend themselves to insightful and very interesting stories. This is a fun read which also is most instructive in terms of life's lessons!"

JEFF KAPLAN, former member of Coach Hayes's coaching staff, then his "brain coach," OSU Senior Vice President/Executive Officer, and current OSU trustee.

"What an extraordinary gift! What started out as a recollection of stories has turned into a jam-packed book full of unforgettable basketball and football moments played at the highest level by a gifted young athlete from Lancaster, Ohio, and so much more. This book is also a refreshing reminder of what is important in life. As one of Buckeye Nation's most celebrated athletes, family, friends, and fans will enjoy reading Rex Kern's remarkable tales of incredible wins, painful losses, and excruciating injuries. Fortunately for us, Rex takes us on this journey and in doing so passes along the wisdom of faith, humility, character, honor, and trust that were passed along to him by his family, his teammates, his coaches, and his staunchest supporters."

ELLEN HAVENS HARDYMON, daughter of Jack Havens, business partner, and friend for life.

"The chapter on race is worthy of a Pulitzer Prize."

LARRY HISLE, two sport prep All-American, thirteen-year MLB player, two-time All Star, Director of Youth Mentoring, Milwaukee Brewers.

"Due to personal issues as a junior, I was late going out for the football team. My teammates had run their mile in qualifying time. I had to run alone, except when I arrived, Rex was there to pace me. He ran a second time so I only had to run once. That meant the world to me. I made my time by four seconds."

TIM BAILEY, Lancaster High School football teammate.

* * *

Thank you all for your thoughts and insights. I wish we had a dozen back covers.

REX KERN
OLE #10

www.amplifypublishing.com

The Road to the Horseshoe and Beyond:
How a Small-Town Athlete Benefited from Ohio State Football to Build a Life

I have tried to recreate events, locales, and conversations from my memories of them. I may have changed some identifying characteristics and details such as physical properties, occupations, and places of residence.

For more information, please contact:
Amplify Publishing, an imprint of Mascot Books
620 Herndon Parkway, Suite 320
Herndon, VA 20170
info@amplifypublishing.com

Library of Congress Control Number: 2021917072

CPSIA Code: PRFRE1021A

ISBN-13: 978-1-63755-295-7

Printed in Canada

Dedication

To Nancy, John-Ryan, and Michael and to all future generations of Kerns.

To Lancaster.

To all my coaches and teammates who inspired me, in competition and in life.

And to the greatest mentors a man could ever have.

THE ROAD TO THE
HORSESHOE
AND BEYOND

How a Small-Town Athlete Benefited
from Ohio State Football to Build a Life

REX KERN

WITH **LEE CARYER**

amplify

CONTENTS

PREFACE

This book may or may not be as successful as a *New York Times* bestseller, but that type of success is not the primary goal. The goal is to find a way to pay forward *and* pay backward at the same time.

In 2019 our son John-Ryan and his wife, Heather, gave me a writing book for Christmas and asked me to use it to tell my stories. I intended to do it, but there never seemed to be time.

That same year George Chaump, my quarterback coach at Ohio State, and Earl Jones, my high school football coach, both passed away. My college coach, Woody Hayes; my high school basketball coach, George Hill; and several high school, college, and NFL teammates had preceded them. As I began writing the book, I lost others who had a profound effect on my life, such as my close high school friends Joe Edwards and Ed Klinker.

It was time for serious thought and action.

My first decision was to write something for my grandchildren and their children about the life lessons I learned growing up in Lancaster, Ohio, just down Route 33 from Columbus. Woody called that "paying forward." Our sons know my wife, Nancy, and I are faithful in our giving. It made sense to pass on ideas and experiences as well.

After considering how to do that, I decided the best way was for our relatives, present and future, to know about the people who had influenced me throughout my life. That gave me the chance to "pay backward"—to say thank you to the many people who had meant so much to me in so many ways. I immediately jotted down eight priority contacts. Eventually, that list became several dozen.

I had written a doctoral dissertation, so I felt comfortable writing a book. As months went by, however, there did not seem to be any time to write it.

Lee Caryer and I had talked several times over the years. He wrote *The Golden Age of Ohio State Basketball: 1960–1971*. I thought he did a great job with that book, and I enjoyed several articles he had written about recent Buckeye basketball teams. I thought he had the interest in sports and the writing skills to share the responsibility of completing this book.

The first thing Lee said was, "Rex, I think what you have in mind is an interesting idea, and I would like to do it. But if it is good enough for your relatives, why wouldn't many others find it valuable? Besides, there is a large group of Buckeye fans, like myself, who fondly remember the Super Sophs and would be interested in new stories about them.

"Let's do this," he continued. "Let's begin with the idea to provide stories and lessons for future generations of Kerns by introducing your friends, coaches, and teachers, and we'll stay true to that. As we proceed, if we want to include experiences and people at Ohio State, we have that latitude."

So I gave him the eight names, and I called them to ask permission for him to call at a convenient time. To give each person an identity, we decided for each to have a write-up as well as excerpt parts of their stories in other chapters.

It was fun to read their thoughts, and it was even more fun to hear how much they were enjoying the conversations. We initially titled the chapter "Living Legends." This was going well.

Soon it was obvious we needed to include those who had passed on, so I told him about them and arranged calls with their relatives. He did research and added valuable information. Thus began a chapter we tentatively named "Fallen Heroes."

A chapter on faith was necessary, and Lee suggested we discuss my injuries in detail. "I know you have had many," he said, "but only you, your wife, and your doctors know how many."

Like phone numbers of friends, I kept adding injuries for a while. The injuries were tied closely to my Ohio State and NFL careers. While working on this Preface, a friend reminded me of one operation I had forgotten. Hopefully the list is complete.

"The subject of race is something we must address for the future," Lee said. "You went from an almost all-white community to captain of a high visibility, highly successful mixed-race team. The problem has not been solved in four or five centuries; you can't do any harm."

I was skeptical, but the approach we presented made more sense than some I have seen. Most important, a few of our African-American friends gave their approval.

The 1966 basketball season stood out for its impact on the Lancaster community. Lee believed he could discuss my role more objectively than I could, and he already had valuable input from two starters on that team, Captain Paul Callahan and Bill Grein, and other students who remembered it. I liked the result. Of course, we wanted to touch on the other sports seasons, which we combined into another chapter.

The chapter on leadership and mentoring seemed a good way to discuss how so many people have contributed so much to my life in so many ways.

We settled into a pattern of talking twice a week for two hours, usually on multiple chapters. He wrote drafts, I corrected misunderstandings, and we discussed alternatives. After a couple of those cycles, we had something to put away as a semifinished product and went on to another chapter.

The Woody chapter is quite long. We both wanted to shorten it, but there is just so much to say about the man in order to present the full picture.

Somewhere along the line, I realized the book could be used to raise money for some of my favorite organizations: Buckeye Cruise for Cancer, which helps fund cancer research; the Archie Griffin Scholarship Fund, which offers Olympic sports scholarships at Ohio State; the Fellowship of Christian Athletes in Columbus; and the Ohio State Athletic Department came to mind immediately. There may be others.

As I neared the end of the book, a conscious decision had to be made: Did I quote everyone directly, even if unacceptable words were involved, or use something like "*unprintable*?" It seemed clear that teaching young people that certain words are not necessary was preferable.

One more thing: As we were completing the book, I read this quote: "Do not follow where the path may lead. Go instead where there is no path and leave a trail." It was written by one of Woody's favorite writers, Ralph Waldo Emerson.

That's me, I thought.

I thought about my first idol, my brother Keith. He was three years ahead of me in school, though only two and a half years older, and an outstanding athlete. During high school, he became a star guard in basketball and a great second baseman in baseball. He would have played football if he had been bigger. Since sports dominated my world as a child, I wanted to beat him at everything, and I worked hard to do it.

Too many people to count have helped me take a serious look

at my faith, and they have guided me as I've developed my relationship with God throughout my life.

Through sports, I met many men who believed in the importance of education and a true princess who convinced me to seek excellence in that world. "Being your best in everything" became our mutual goal, which we passed on to our children.

As I was failing to achieve my career goal of becoming Ohio State Athletic Director I met a man who saw a physical education graduate with the potential to become a businessman. Due to my admiration of him, my desire not to disappoint him, and his direct guidance, he was correct.

It is a pleasure to invite my relatives, my friends, and anyone else who would care to join me in thanking the many people who have taught me so much and guided me in so many ways. Also, it is the intention of my wife, Nancy, and myself to provide some thoughts, beliefs, stories, and ideas for our young relatives—present and future—to consider on their way to becoming outstanding men and women. We love you dearly.

While you learn from all these individuals as I did, consider the words of Danish philosopher Søren Kierkegaard, who wrote, "Life can only be understood backwards, but it must be lived forwards."

My prayer is that they help you look backward and forward as they have me.

—Rex Kern
Ole #10,
OSU football, 1968–1970

FOREWORD

For those of us who were blessed to grow up in Ohio in the 1960s and 1970s, and if we happened to love sports, we were most certainly touched by the legendary Rex Kern.

The Ohio State Buckeyes, and the extraordinary accomplishments on the gridiron and on the court, were the lifeblood and pride of every Ohioan. But when Rex Kern burst on the scene, it was taken to a whole new level.

As a high school sophomore, I had Rex Kern's photo from *Sports Illustrated* laminated on my course folder so that I could carry my idol with me in every classroom. As a young high school quarterback, I visualized his ballhandling magic, his knack for the big play, and his ability to lead his team to victory every weekend.

Rex Kern became our football hero, but more importantly he became our spiritual North Star. If Rex Kern reads the Bible, then we should read it too. If Rex Kern demonstrated humility, we needed to as well. If Rex Kern believed we must serve others, we will too.

Rex will be the first to tell you that he was shaped by an amazing family, a wonderful hometown, the opportunity to be an Ohio State Buckeye, and a loving God. Get ready—you are about to participate in his magical journey of success, adversity, and lessons learned. His story will rekindle memories and remind us how fortunate we are to live in this nation of freedom and opportunity.

YEA OHIO !!

Jim Tressel
President, Youngstown State University
former head coach, Ohio State University, 2001–2010
106 wins, 22 losses, 2002 national champions

CHAPTER 1

LANCASTER EARLY YEARS

"Wait until you see my brother. I knew Rex was going to be special."
Keith Kern

W as there more pressure to play in the Rose Bowls or the Michigan games? More pressure in college or the NFL? More pressure in the NFL playoffs or when the Super Sophs played mighty Purdue, who had beaten Ohio State 41–6 the previous year?

People have asked those questions and others like them for as long as I can remember.

If I do not know the person very well, I usually just pick one or the other and try to tell that person something he or she may not know in explaining the answer.

Since this book was written for dear friends—past, current, and future—and anyone else who decided to read it, I want to give the most complete answer I know: the most pressure I ever felt was not in any of those situations.

As soon as I could throw a football or hit a baseball, and long before I could shoot a ball through a basket, I loved to play. Long before kids my age were interested in sports, I pestered my brother, Keith, to include me in games with his friends. Keith was three grades ahead of me, (only about two and one half years older!), but he and his friends welcomed me even though I was by far the smallest. They taught me to throw a spiral, catch a punt, turn a double play, throw a bounce pass, and other life necessities for a young would-be athlete.

The joy of playing never left me, but soon it had competition. I am referring to the joy of winning. As soon as I felt accepted by Keith and his friends, I wanted to beat them. I had a passion for learning about the games and practicing the games that never left me. For Keith, sports were a hobby, so he did not want to practice as much as I did. When my badgering fell on deaf ears, I learned there were some things I could practice on my own. Eventually, the kids at school became interested, and I could play with them. Mom and Dad liked to play catch with me. Mom would hit me ground balls, and Dad would tell me how to field them. Some days I actually got to play enough.

When I was in fourth grade, I played on my first actual team: a basketball team for our elementary school. There were eight elementary schools in Lancaster, so the eight teams got together every Saturday, each with an adult coach. In my mind, it was big time. I had trouble sleeping Friday nights before a game. Scores and standings were kept. I was proud to play for West School, and I played to win. My coach was another voice helping me learn to play—and to practice.

At first I was a catcher in baseball, which put me in the middle of the action on every play. In American Legion, playing with older guys, I might be in the outfield. When I began to play football in seventh grade, I became a quarterback. That kept me in the middle of the action, but when I went to high school my father suggested

I change my position in baseball. He had seen catchers whose fingers were disfigured by foul tips, and quarterbacks handle the ball every play. I moved to third base. When I played American Legion with older guys, I still played outfield.

In grade school, I had coaches who cared about their players and cared about teaching their sport. In junior high, I had coaches who knew more about the sport and deeply cared about the players. In high school, I had three coaches who were very well qualified and were hall of fame coaches and people in my book. At Ohio State, I played for Woody Hayes, a Hall of Fame coach. Several of his assistants were very accomplished as well. In the NFL, my favorite head coaches were Don McCafferty and Lou Saban, and my favorite assistant was former Colts All-Pro Bobby Boyd.

I will go into all of that in the book, but it was important to present an overview to justify this statement: I felt that my teammates and I were prepared to play every game of every sport I ever played at any level. Before any game, I was confident we were going to win. That did not always prove to be true, of course, but I felt prepared.

Pressure

Chuck Noll, coach of four Super Bowl–winning teams with the Pittsburgh Steelers and member of the Pro Football Hall of Fame, famously said, "Pressure is something you feel only when you don't know what the hell you are doing."

Because of my passion for each sport and the quality of coaching I received, I never felt the kind of pressure fans referred to before or during a game. I was glad to be there and busy thinking about what we had to do to win.

Pressure for me came in social situations, which I had not encountered, meaning almost all of them. Like when I went to my wife, Nancy's, home for dinner the first time and saw her mother had put two forks at every seat. Well, I knew not to use one for the soup, but which one was for the salad, and which one was for the main course? Was I supposed to take one home as a souvenir?

Imagine, some people thought there was pressure when we played Southern Cal for an unbeaten season and number one ranking!

Obviously, I got through that experience, as Nancy and I have been married for forty-eight years. I was nineteen at the time, so I had learned to wait, to watch, and to not ask potentially embarrassing questions. There had been many awkward social situations before, and there have been a few since. Realizing they were going to be a part of my life, I bought an etiquette book back in Columbus.

I knew I was making progress because I still remembered an early significant social experience in my life, when I felt the most pressure and completely choked. It was in junior high, and it helps me introduce my home: Lancaster, Ohio.

As I mentioned, there were eight elementary schools at the time. Kids from the four schools on the west side of town—the "poor" side—went to General Sherman Junior High, where I attended. Kids from the "rich" families went to Thomas Ewing. The first time we had social contact with each other was in junior high, when there were dances at the YMCA.

The dances were easier than I expected. I was interested in meeting so many new girls, and I already knew many of the kids from elementary school. I could hang with my friends, venture out to investigate, and return to safety as needed.

Then it happened.

Ann Taylor, a cute girl from Thomas Ewing, said she was going to have a summer pool party before we started high school. She wanted me to come. I thanked her and said I would let her know.

I knew these Thomas Ewing people knew stuff I did not, but I had no idea what they knew or how I could learn it. Mom and Dad had raised me to live in the General Sherman world, but I knew nothing about the Thomas Ewing world. This would be so embarrassing! *How could I fit in? Should I just wear my swimsuit and a T-shirt, or take a change of clothes? Or wear regular clothes and take a swimsuit? What were regular clothes for a pool party? Should I take a gift? Food? Did I need a haircut?* Finally, a question I could answer, since my father was a barber. I had no idea what I was doing.

Too much pressure

The whole thing was so overwhelming I did not go.

I saw Ann at our fiftieth high school reunion in 2017, and I wanted to say something, but things did not work out.

Fortunately, I did make some progress in high school.

My lab partner in physics class senior year was Mike Vaughn, covaledictorian of our class with my basketball teammate Warren Ticknor. Warren was my other lab partner. If they could not get me through that course, no one could.

Anyway, one day Mike said he was going to the school dance that weekend. It was going to be his first date. He was going with a very intelligent sophomore; he was nervous and wondered if I would double-date with him.

"Mike," I replied, "I have a baseball game Saturday morning at nine and need a good night's sleep, so I am not going to the dance."

He seemed disappointed, so I said, "How about this: I'll pick you up, we'll get your date, and I will be your chauffer for the evening. How would that be?"

"Oh, Rex, that would be perfect," he said. Apparently, no one had told him about me being afraid to go to Ann Taylor's party.

So I picked up Mike in my 1951 Plymouth. We drove to his date's house, and he said, "What do I do now?"

"Well," I said, "you walk to the door, knock, and introduce yourself to her parents. You both get in the back seat, and we go to the dance."

Always thinking ahead, Mike said, "What about after the dance?"

"Most of the people at the dance go to Frisch's Big Boy on Memorial Drive," I said. "She might like a hamburger, fries, and a milkshake."

When they came back to the car, she was talking excitedly about something she had learned in school. When I heard the word *theorem*, I knew my work was done and turned up the radio.

That is the way it goes. One day, you don't know what is going on; the next, you are a fountain of wisdom. My social skills were improving, though there was room for growth.

Not only is that story about the party in a better part of town a commentary on the different meanings of the word *pressure* to different people of different ages, but it is also a true reflection of the class structure of Lancaster, Ohio, in the late 1950s. There were two groups of people: the wealthy ones and the other ones—at least that was the view of our Kern family. To this day, my high school friends identify themselves in part by the junior high they attended.

I have been blessed to travel the world and even sit with the president of the United States with Nancy and my parents because of my faith and athletic ability. As is the case with everyone who has ever lived, I started as a small child with much to learn. As may not be the case with very many people, I had dozens and dozens of friends, mentors, guides, and coaches along the way.

It is a pleasure to have you join me as I recognize the people who meant so much to me so far in my life. For those still living—thank you! For those whose parents, siblings, and friends have passed away—they were dear to me as well.

Lancaster, Ohio

I was born May 28, 1949, in the all-American city of Lancaster, Ohio. Adults referred to it that way. As a youngster, I believed what adults said.

The reason for the designation was a cover story on the city in the November 15, 1947, issue of *Forbes* magazine, complete with a picture of the intersection of Main and Broad Streets and the declaration "This is America."

It seems that in 1941 *Forbes'* founder and editor, B. C. Forbes set up a weekly Lancaster paper, the *Fairfield Times*, for his son Malcolm to run after graduating from Princeton. Soon Malcolm launched the *Lancaster Times*, another weekly publication. Both failed to compete with the *Lancaster Eagle-Gazette*, which had roots beginning in 1809, and young Malcolm went to serve in World War II. When he returned, there were stories to be written about postwar America and Malcolm had good memories of Lancaster. If Malcolm initially had been sent to Keokuk, Iowa, or Waxahachie, Texas, the results might have been different.

In thinking about Lancaster, my memories are of the people.

Certainly, much has been written about the largest employer in the city during my youth, Anchor Hocking, a rare Fortune 500 company in a small town. Many of my friends worked for the manufacturer of glass tableware and glass containers, as I did one summer. In the 1980s it was the victim of multiple corporate take-overs, which took employment from 5,000 to 800. This is not the place to learn that story, or about history, economy, weather, or political issues. People are the subject which interests me: remembering them, thanking them, learning from them, and staying in touch with them.

My First Lancaster

My earliest definition of Lancaster was our nuclear family—Mom, Dad, and my older brother, Keith. Slowly relatives, neighbors, and friends of neighbors joined the group, loosely defined as "my world."

After six years of elementary education at West School, the group expanded quickly. No, we did not have kindergarten. American Legion baseball, where many of my teammates came from different schools, introduced me to more boys, all of whom loved sports. I attended General Sherman Junior High, named for Civil War general William Tecumseh Sherman, born in Lancaster in 1820, with my former classmates and kids from three other elementary schools. After three years at General Sherman, we went to Lancaster High School with the students of four other elementary schools who had attended Thomas Ewing Junior High. Ewing was born in Virginia in 1789 and later practiced law in Lancaster. He was a US senator and served in three presidential administrations as secretary of the interior, secretary of the treasury, and secretary of war. He is buried in Saint Mary's Cemetery in Lancaster.

Looking back, it is easy to see my world expanding slowly. At the time, I was consumed with thoughts of the next game, practicing for the next game, winning the next game, and in the meantime having fun.

The Kern Family

Jean Ritchie married Trenton Kern and had two sons, Keith and Rex. We lived at 630 Garfield. For as long as I can remember, we were known simply as the Kerns.

Since my older brother, Keith, always had a more mature, experienced view of our lives as children, I asked him to discuss our childhoods. Here's Keith:

"We moved into the house on Garfield when Rex was less than a year old—January, 1950. It had been built in 1906; Mom and Dad paid $6,000 for it. West School Elementary was about twenty feet away—close enough to be considered our extended yard.

"Mother and Dad loved sports. Mom was the athlete—track, softball, and basketball. She was so limber she could bend over and put her palms on the floor in her late eighties. She liked to throw the football with Rex. The year after Rex was inducted into the College Football Hall of Fame (2007), she was inducted into the Amanda High School Athletic Hall of Fame. Dad and I were equally proud of both.

"Dad did not talk much about his playing career. I do remember that he played third base on a service team during World War II. His gift was analyzing, teaching, and coaching—the mental and the physical. He drilled a hole in a baseball, put a rope through the hole, and tied the rope. He would twirl the rope so we could practice our swing for baseball. The older we got, the faster the 'pitch.'

"They came to as many games as possible, almost every one. They were not like some parents, who yelled at the umpire or the coach or their kids. They just watched and cheered. After the games, practice began as soon as we returned home. Dad would review every situation and mistake, then demonstrate the correct play. When Dad's practice was over, we stayed outside and played under the lights. We replaced a lot of windows in the back of the house after errant throws.

"I remember Dad buying us boxing gloves and teaching us to box. He would tell me, 'Don't hit your brother so hard. He is smaller than you.' Later that changed.

"When Mother and Dad were busy, we created games like socks and basketball. We rolled a pair of socks into a ball and tried to land them in an inch and a half space above the door in our bedroom. You got a point if the socks stayed in the space.

"At West School Elementary, we created a game for two people where you tried to hit the wall so the other person could not catch the ball. If he did, it was an out—three outs, new inning. When we got older, we added some kids in the neighborhood and played rubber ball fast pitch. With a rubber ball, it seldom broke a window.

"When Rex and I did not have anything else to do, or there was sufficient reason, we were liable to fight about anything. Dad had taught us to box, but we almost always wrestled. Mom gave us heck for fighting in our room. The rooms in the house were all thirteen feet by thirteen feet, yet we played tackle football on our knees in the front room. Sometimes we bumped into a lamp and caught heck for that. We also had a game in the room where the washer and dryer were kept. I remember wearing our pajamas as warm-ups over our shorts, but I do not remember the rules of the game.

"They also took us to many of the local games, and some farther than that. I remember one trip to Columbus for an Ohio State basketball game. St. John Arena had not been built, and the Buck-eyes were playing at the Fairgrounds. Boy, was Frank Howard big! Howard signed a huge bonus contract with the Los Angeles Dodgers and was later traded to the Washington Senators, where he was nicknamed the Washington Monument. He hit 382 Major League home runs.

"Our family never left Ohio for vacations. For years we alter-nated going to Cleveland and Cincinnati for baseball weekends. If there was a twilight doubleheader on Friday, we saw five games, including the Sunday doubleheader. Sometimes it was only four.

"On Saturdays we walked twenty feet to our basketball court at the school. If you were not there at nine, you had to wait. We did not want to wait and got into games at an early age because we had a ball. In the winter, we shoveled snow off the court and played with gloves, which had the fingers cut off.

"In fifth and sixth grade, I played the trombone. It was fun, but far from a passion. When the teacher said, 'Those of you who intend to play sports in high school should drop out now,' I quit the next day.

"There was no junior high baseball team, but we had American Legion in the summer. There was no seventh-grade basketball team, but I made the eighth-grade team. I played both sports in high school and was captain of the basketball team as a junior and a senior. I liked football but was too small. As I started to make a name for myself in sports, at five seven, 127 pounds, I always told people, 'Wait until you see my brother.' I knew Rex was going to be special."

A Challenging Time

"A time of great upheaval for our entire family began on February 18, 1959.

"I was at school, seventh grade, and felt like my head was burning inside. I went home at noon on a Wednesday. Mom said my temperature was 105 degrees. I was taken to Lancaster Hospital on Saturday, where I went into a coma and suffered convulsions. Two doctors agreed that I had to be taken to Children's Hospital in Columbus, about thirty-five miles away.

"I was unconscious for ten days. The doctors said there were no precedents, so they experimented with me. They packed me in ice and tied me to a bed. Later, Dad said, 'I wish we had taken pictures, but we were too worried to think of it.' The doctors called it brain fever and sleeping sickness. They said it was fifty-fifty whether I would make it through. Finally, the ice took my temperature from 105 to 90 degrees.

"After three weeks in the hospital, I was able to go home. We later found out that the five previous children with similar symptoms had died. In all, I missed about ten weeks of school, and my weight went from 110 pounds down to 89 pounds.

"The community gave us tremendous support. The doctors wanted me to gain weight, so a typical day included chocolate malts and banana splits at Tastee Freez. The following year, when I was not prepared for class, especially for a test, I went to the principal's office, and he always said, 'Lie down.'

"It must have been a rough time for Rex because Mom and Dad were totally focused on me. He must have felt left out, and as a fourth grader, afraid of something he did not understand, because none of the adults seemed to know any answers. The disease turned out to be encephalitis.

(Rex here. Keith is doing a fine job, and it was a rough time. As a fourth grader, my idol was in trouble, and no one could help me understand why. I could not ignore how frightened they were, which frightened me. Sometimes I went to a scary hospital. Usually I was dropped off somewhere so Mom and Dad could go. In many ways, I suddenly had to fend for myself and solve my own problems.

I wanted to help, but what could I do? I decided all I could do was be on my best behavior to make their lives as easy as possible and pray. When Keith recovered, I remembered that prayer had helped, though the feeling of making everyone's life easy faded a bit. The experience did help me relate to the feelings of a child in a situation he or she did not understand. It also helped me learn that difficult times make you resilient and can even serve as stepping-stones on the way to success. Back to Keith.)

"Rex and I only played together on a team once, in American Legion baseball in 1965. I was young for my age, so I was out of high school, and Rex had finished ninth grade. He played in the outfield; I played second base.

"Other than sports, our big family activity was going to Grandpa Ritchie's farm in Amanda, about ten miles away, where Mother was raised. Usually our uncles—Don, eight years older than me, and John, six years older—would take us to the barn so we did not bother the grown-ups. We watched them rope cows and calves, sometimes helped them bail hay, and rode the calves ourselves like horses.

"When I was sixteen or seventeen, we went out to the farm to shovel manure. It was twenty inches deep and crusting on top. We had to shovel it into a manure spreader, then drive the tractor while spreading the fertilizer. I had my driver's license but had never driven a tractor. I had no idea it had dual brakes, much less how to use them. The tractor started to gain speed, and we were headed toward the horse trough. I turned as hard as I could to avoid it. For some reason the tongue of the spreader lodged against the tractor's rear tires, causing it to stop. We were lucky!

"When something went wrong, my strategy was to immediately blame Rex. He knew that was coming, was in no mood to be blamed, and was certainly tired of the smell of manure.

"'I'm not taking this,' he announced. 'I'm going home.'

"He started walking, forgetting home was at least ten miles away. I waited a little while, then reported that he had left, and I was going to get him. He had gone about a mile and a half and was hiding in a tree. I have often wondered what would have happened if I had acted like I did not see him.

"We also collected pigeons on Grandfather's farm. We did not do anything special with them; it was just something to do.

"We both had paper routes as children. We shared a route delivering the *Ohio State Journal*. We had to get our papers at four thirty. That was too early for Dad, so Mother did it with us. We gave up after thirty days.

"Later, we each had a route of about fifty-five papers of the *Lancaster Eagle-Gazette*. I had Washington, Garfield, and Pierce; Rex had McKinley, Roosevelt, and Jefferson. When one of us had practice or a game, which was nearly all the time, the other did both routes. When we both had a conflict, the Bozman brothers, Howard and Rick, delivered for us.

"I also had a *TV Guide* route. They were delivered to me. I paid eleven cents an issue and sold them for fifteen cents. I had about twenty customers. Hard to believe that was less than a dollar a week.

"My senior year was career-oriented, in that I went to school in the morning and worked at Hocking Valley National Bank in the afternoon. I worked there until 1971, when I took a position with the Fairfield County Auto Club. I was with AAA for thirty-one years, then retired.

"We did not think about it at the time, but Rex and I grew up in a rough neighborhood. The people with money lived on the east side of town, east of Memorial Drive, a heavily traveled street that divided the city. We lived on the west side. Dad was a barber, and Mom stayed at home—no money for the country club. Some of our neighbors spent more time in prison than out of it. Many of our friends stood on the top of the fence. Some went the right way, and some went the other. Our parents made the difference for us by teaching us right from wrong.

"Let me give you an example.

"I had a '63 Chevy. One night it disappeared from our garage. The police looked for it for a while without any luck. Then one day one of the women at the bank said, 'Keith, isn't your license plate 3040KK?' It was written on a check, which the thief had tried to cash at the bank.

"The guy who stole my car lived in our neighborhood and was sent to prison.

"A couple of years later, I was in a store downtown looking for some clothes. The guy had been released, saw me in the store, and approached me.

"'I didn't appreciate you sending me to jail,' he said.

"'I didn't appreciate you stealing my car,' I replied.

"'How's Rex? How are your parents?'

"Everything was settled.

"Back to Rex and me. The biggest difference between us was that he liked to work out, and I did not. He would offer to buy the pizza if we worked out together first, and I would refuse—and I liked pizza.

"We had two big similarities: Name the sport, and we were ready to play it. We did not like to study. The second sounds strange because he was so successful at Ohio State, becoming a Ph.D. He will explain that.

"There was no rivalry between us. I went to every game he played at Ohio State, home and away. I remember going to his final graduation at OSU and seeing a headline in the paper: 'Doctor Quarterback.'

"Rex says he put a backboard and rim on the garage, but I thought it was Dad. Dad definitely said, "I don't want other kids horsing around here when you guys are not here." So Rex laid a piece of cardboard over the rim and rigged it so the ball did not go through the rim, but so we could easily get the cardboard off.

(Rex: If I could interrupt, neither Dad nor Keith made or put up the backboard—I did. I also found a way to lock a plywood board in place so kids could not play if we were not there.)

"I did not use it much. When I was in high school, the coach I played for in junior high let me use their gym to shoot anytime I wanted. That same coach came in our house after being overserved, jumped on my bed, with me in it, and broke the bed. As you grow older, you learn things about your teachers you never suspected in class.

"One other thing about Rex was his persistence. No matter how the game was going, he just kept competing. When the injuries piled up, he just kept coming back.

"I know this book is primarily about Rex's days as a youngster in Lancaster, but there is one more story about a time he came back to Lancaster.

"The 1966 basketball team, on which Rex was a junior, was the first Lancaster team to go to the state tournament. For their twenty-year anniversary, almost the whole 1966 team came back to be honored. It was decided that they would play an alumni team during an extended halftime of a varsity game.

"Since I was three years ahead of Rex, we never played basketball together as Golden Gale teammates, but we did oppose each other one time on the high school floor in 1986. I played for the alumni team."

"Keith Kern Steals Limelight"

"Here is an article printed in the *Lancaster Eagle-Gazette* about that game. The headline reads 'Keith Kern Steals Limelight; Helps Alumni Over '66ers.' The article reported that in a fifteen-minute game the final score was 14–11. Keith Kern had nine points, and Rex Kern was 'shut out.' Rex is quoted as saying, 'Here's your headline: we can still make it up and down the floor, but we can't score.'

"Rex had extraordinary athletic talent, but his jump shot could not survive a twenty-year layoff. Yes, I may have made a point of practicing a bit before that game.

"Mother and Dad passed away within a few months of each other in 2012. Mom was ninety-one; Dad was ninety-two."

(Rex again: Great job, Keith. I am looking for a rematch of that game. There are a couple of stories about Mom and Dad I would like to add.)

Mom Was More Than a Fan

When I was quite young, third or fourth grade, Keith Rader, who lived three houses away, was annoying me. I ran after him, ripped his jacket, and handed him ten dollars to get it repaired. He went home and told his older brother Brad, who looked me up and said, "I don't like you picking on my younger brother." Then he punched me in the stomach. I went home crying.

Mom opened the back door. She saw Brad and shouted, "Hey,

Brad Rader, if you touch my son, I'm going to *unprintable*."

Way to go, Mom!

Also, our junior high games were played in the late afternoon. Dad missed most of those because he was working at the barbershop, but Mom came regularly.

One basketball game at Chillicothe Mount Logan, we were kinda getting homered in the first half. After a blatantly bad call, I saw Coach Holland was upset, then saw something unusual out of the corner of my eye. A woman was on the court, wagging her finger at the ref. My first thought was, *That's gotta be a tech.* My second thought was, *That's my mother!* It was out of character for her, but she did know her stuff.

Things settled down without a technical. Mom went back to the stands, and the incident was not mentioned in the Kern household. I probably told Keith, but Dad never knew.

After the season, at the postseason banquet, Coach Holland passed out the usual awards, then said, "This year we have a special award to present called the Golden Whistle Award. The winner is Jean Kern." Those who attended the game laughed. The rest, including my father, were puzzled. The award was not discussed on the way home, but it might have come up behind closed doors.

Did we win the game? I think so.

Most athletes are superstitious, and I vividly remember always putting on my shoes and socks in a certain way before games. During warm-ups, I realized I had not done it. I raced back into the locker room, took them off, did it properly, and got back before the tip. Anyone who noticed probably thought I had to go to the bathroom. That was embarrassing, but I owed it to the team to stay with my lucky routine. Even though I do not remember the procedure, it probably pulled us through for the win. How is that for junior high logic?

Dad grew up on a farm, like Mom did, but it was on the other side of Amanda. I suppose there were class distinctions in Amanda, similar to Lancaster. Mom's father did not like the idea of her marrying Dad. He was the only one of three boys to graduate from high school.

Dad believed your lot in life was fixed. I adopted that attitude without questioning it. Before high school graduation, he took me to a men's store in town, bought me a nice sport coat, and said, "Now, that is your present. It is up to you to make a living in the state of Ohio."

What I heard was, "You are on your own."

When I signed an NFL contract, I intended to use the bonus money to buy a Corvette. When I told Dad, he said, "If you buy that car, do not drive it when you visit. You would not be welcome." He was afraid the neighbors would not approve. They would think we were showing off.

I did not buy the car, but I eventually bought one for Nancy, when we lived in California.

As you will learn, dozens of mentors guided me during my life, helping me grow in ways my parents could not imagine. At times Mom and Dad were uncomfortable with my achievements and felt they were out of place while celebrating them with me. I always wanted them there, but I never found a way to help them truly enjoy themselves.

630 Garfield, my home until I left for the NFL.

This was a Merry Christmas! I may have
worn the uniform to dinner? Bed? School?
That's Keith hoping to borrow it.

The 1961 West Elementary School sixth grade team. I'm standing on the far right. Those are championship charms around our necks.

Hocking Hornets Pee Wee football seventh grade team. I'm on the far right, second row.

CHAPTER 2

INFLUENCERS GROWING UP

"If the Red Head thinks he can do it, we're going to do it."
Coach Dick England, LHS baseball.

Rather than talking about the people of Lancaster, I decided it would be better to ask them to talk about our experiences in their own words. Hopefully I will not regret this decision.

The Bozmans

The Bozman family moved to our neighborhood on the west side when I was in the fourth grade. They only stayed for two years before moving to the next street over into a nicer rental. They always told us what an influence our mother and father had on their lives. Howard, the oldest, will be first, followed by Rick, the second oldest.

"Rex and Keith's father, Trenton, taught me how to pitch. I am left handed, and he was a third baseman, but he showed this third grader the proper mechanics, the windup, and talked about the mental game as well. He was a natural teacher.

"Our single mother raised four boys. There was very little money for the family, and new gloves were expensive. My glove was sec-ondhand, maybe third, and it was right handed. I had to wear it backwards. The Kern family was far from wealthy, but Trenton—Mr. Kern—bought me my first left-handed glove. It was second-hand, but it was left handed, and it was mine. That was a thrill.

"Like any kid, I was so excited that I did not realize Trenton and his family had sacrificed in order to give me that glove. When that sort of sunk in, the glove meant even more to me.

"Every Sunday you saw the Kerns walking to church together, wearing their Sunday best. They never pushed their religion on others, but they lived what they said they believed. Not everyone does that. Now I have a strong faith, which is important to me. In many ways, I got it from them.

"Trenton gave me my first job, sweeping up at the barbershop for fifty cents a week. I did not recognize it at the time, but it taught me discipline and commitment.

"He and his wife, Jean, were both demanding, at least to a boy in elementary school. Now I realize they wanted the best for me, which required the best from me. At times they treated me as the boy I could become, and by doing that they helped me get there.

"Not long before Trenton died, when his health was failing, I spoke at our church about what Trenton and Jean had meant to me growing up. He was home in bed, and Jean was caring for him, but Keith was there. I did not see him or that he brought a tape recorder. He taped what I said and played it for his parents.

"Trenton called me and thanked me for my kind words. Then he said, 'Do you remember the first game you pitched?'

"I did not.

"He said, 'It was a no-hitter.'

"I did not know enough as a young child to realize how important a no-hitter was. He gave me back a memory I did not comprehend at the time.

"We lived on Garfield Ave. The Kerns were one house away. Keith, Rex, my brother Rick, and I lived on the playground. We were all different ages, so our other friends were in four different classes. There was always a group of kids.

"We loved to play fast-pitch rubber ball. Often it was nine-on-nine, like baseball, but we played with less by adjusting the rules. As long as we had a pitcher, catcher, infielder, and outfielder for each team, we could play. A ball hit on one side of the diamond was an out.

"I could not believe how competitive Keith and Rex were. They would disagree, argue, then things got serious.

"In the winter, we used to shovel off the basketball court at West School in the morning, then play all day. We bought those cheap brown jersey gloves and cut off the tips of the fingers to still get a feel for the basketball.

"I started on the 1967 LHS basketball team as a six-foot defensive specialist, but my sport was baseball.

"My hero was Bill Grein. He was two years older and a really good left-handed pitcher. He was very disciplined—everything I wanted to be.

"When Bill graduated, I got to pitch more and earned a baseball scholarship to Ohio U. My sophomore year there we went to the College World Series, which was a big thrill. Plus, Coach England, our coach at LHS, was at Ohio that season, and it was good to be around him again. That 1970 OU baseball team is going to be inducted into the Ohio University Athletic Hall of Fame.

"Unfortunately, I hurt my shoulder in Legion ball in 1968 and spent most of my college career in the bullpen. I just pitched too much, and the shoulder never healed.

"Still, I got to play for the first Lancaster basketball team to go to the state tournament and the best baseball team in Ohio University history! And we won three straight Mid-American Conference championships—1970–1972.

"Thinking back to those days, I know Rex has no regrets about choosing football, but I always wondered how things would have worked out if he had chosen baseball. He was very talented and might have been healthier playing a less violent sport.

"After college I coached varsity baseball and taught. Contrary to the way things are today, I always encouraged my players to play other sports if they wanted to. Now coaches want them to specialize and play and practice one sport. Sports are fun—play all you can. Plus, certain skills are transferable, and all sports teach life lessons.

"One thing that was unique about Rex is that he was always a star yet always a regular guy. He still is. Most stars are not like that.

"After eleven years in the classroom, I got into mortgage banking. I enjoyed that field, and it gave me time to coach Legion ball in the summers and stay on the baseball field.

"Just a lucky guy."

Rex replies: Thank you Howard. Your reflections take me back! Here was my thinking about the three sports at that time.

I liked the idea of being a quarterback and thought I would know pretty quickly if I had a chance to play there. Plus, college football was my first sport after high school. In case football was not promising, I could try basketball. Also, it was very difficult to say no to Woody Hayes. Finally, in my first practice as a freshman, I was in awe of the talent in our class.

The Kansas City Athletics had drafted me out of high school, and they did not want college to interfere with my baseball career. I was absolutely determined to be the first Kern to graduate from college, so that was a negative for baseball at the time. If baseball was the choice, I thought I could go to college, play college ball, and maybe attract some interest after graduation. Also, I had heard stories about Charlie Baughman, Mike's older brother, spending a long time in the minors and never even making the majors. I thought the same thing might happen to me.

Basketball was my favorite sport as a child, and Ohio State head coach Fred Taylor was the first coach to recruit me. I really wanted to play Big Ten basketball for him. He had played basketball and baseball at Ohio State, so I thought I could do that if football did not work out. Due to the overlap in the seasons, and the fact that quarterbacks had too much to learn to miss practices, I feared it would not be possible to play football and a second sport.

Looking back, I think a young teenager did a pretty good job of diagnosing a complex problem. It would have been impossible to mix being a quarterback in football with another sport, but basketball and baseball might have been OK together. Thanks for the great question. Future generations of Kerns might ask the same one.

* * *

When Rick Bozman got the scheduled call, he was at a loss for words. After some deep breaths and two halting attempts at speaking, he said, "It is quite an honor to be asked to talk about Rex and the Kern family."

After explaining his emotions, Rick reviewed a difficult childhood.

"Our mother, Mary, had to raise four boys on her own. She was tough enough to go bear hunting with a switch—babysitting, cleaning houses, ironing, always trying to bring in extra money.

"Before we moved to Lancaster, we lived on the west side of Columbus, on Mound Street, near Jets Stadium. When I was four, we went there for day-old buns. We had no beds; we slept on mattresses on the floor.

Our clothing came from the Salvation Army and was kept in four cardboard boxes. We had no shower. We used a washrag all week, then took turns in a washtub on Saturday night.

"We moved to Lancaster when I was in the third grade. We lived in half a double and paid sixty-five a month rent. Fortunately, we were one house from the Kerns.

"Trenton was a tremendous man, a real gentleman. Jean worked at West Elementary. Some people say the television families of the 1950s, like *Father Knows Best* and *Leave It to Beaver*, were not true to life, but the Kerns were June and Ward Cleaver. They were just as genuine and unassuming as the actors appeared to be on TV. Their house was modest, but neat as a pin. There was no heat upstairs; Rex wore socks to bed in the winter.

"Trenton took a liking to me because he knew I was at risk. My brother, Howard, was calmer and more levelheaded. I was mad, thinking our father had left us, thinking of all the things everybody had but us.

"Everything I have done as a man came from my experiences on the west side of Lancaster. As a child, we never took vacations as a family, because there was no money. I decided my new family would take vacations, which I thought of as getting into a plane and going somewhere together. We did that forty-two years ... it is important to set goals, keep them in mind, and work toward them. They can come true. As a child, our family went to church about once a month. The Kerns went every Sunday. As a father, we went every Sunday. It is important to model people you want to be like—I modeled Trenton, Rex, and Keith Kern, and our coaches, men like John Holland; Earl Jones, the football coach who was a miniature Woody Hayes; and George Hill.

"So I have some Rex Kern stories for you.

"When Rex called yesterday to set up this conversation, he did not say, 'Hello,' or, 'This is Rex.' Instead, he said, 'Hey, want to play a game of marbles?' He taught me to play marbles as well as many other games. He also taught me pass routes. All I had to do was what he told me and catch the ball.

"But back to marbles. He was older and had bigger fish to fry than to play marbles with me as often as I wanted to play with him. So one day I challenged him. He had coffee cans full of marbles he had won in his garage.

"We each started with one hundred marbles, so to win I had to break one hundred. When I did, I said, 'You let me win.'

"'Ever the competitor,' Rex replied, 'You know better than that.'

"Today I live in Lancaster. I often see old friends who like to tell about the time 'I beat Rex Kern at something.' For most of us, it is usually either one or two times or not true at all, but that is my story, and it is true.

"We often had a gang of kids for games, but it was usually Keith and Howard against Rex and me when there were just four of us. Rex wanted to beat Keith, and I did not want to let him down.

"I remember playing touch football with Rex on the pavement. The ball took funny bounces for the rest of us, but it always seemed to bounce straight up for him. It took me a while to realize that his focus, his concentration, and his athleticism were so much different than ours.

"Rex played for the Hocking Hornets in seventh grade. One Friday Rex broke his leg in a game. Saturday at eight, just like every other Saturday, he knocked on our door. We always shot free throws and rebounded for each other, and Rex was not going to miss that. I remember him hobbling around in a cast, banging the ball back to me at the foul line with his crutch.

"No matter what they did, or what recognition they got, Keith and Rex never dominated you, and they always included you.

"There was a Rex Kern Roast in the late seventies, early 'eighties. Governor Rhodes was there, Woody Hayes, Jim Stillwagon, Ron Maciejowski—the whole bunch. When Rick Middleton, a freshman during Rex's senior year and later an NFL linebacker, got up to speak, he said, 'I grew up in Delaware and followed Rex all my life. My first day of practice I asked someone to point out Rex, and there he was—Howdy Doody!'

"We all laughed, and Rex probably laughed the loudest.

"When Rex carried papers, Howard and I subbed for him when he had practice or a game. When he stopped carrying papers, we continued. I will always remember carrying his old route while listening to a radio he gave me as he played a football game at Ohio State. So many memories and hopes, all together at the same time.

"As a junior, I broke my arm in a preseason basketball scrimmage and sat out most of the season. As a senior, I started and averaged ten to eleven points a game.

"In 1969, my senior year, Coach Hill asked us what our goals were. I said I wanted to average about ten points a game, guard the best player on the other team, and win as many games as possible. My highlight was beating Marion Harding, which had a very good team. Their star was Dave Merchant. He scored over thirty points a game and was in the same OSU recruiting class with Allan Hornyak and Luke Witte. They were all first-team All-Ohio. I held him to about half his average: sixteen. My strength was overplaying my opponent, keeping the ball out of his hands. I learned that from guarding Rex. Once he got the ball, he could find a way to score.

"At seventeen I got a job at Snyder Electric Supply about six blocks away. In 1969 I was making $1.65 an hour, less than $100 for two weeks after taxes. I decided the only way to get what I wanted was to outwork people. I learned from people like Rex, Trenton Kern, and John Holland. What respect you had for that man. That's the guy you wanted to be like.

"I took classes, listened to people, and learned how to build houses. I built a home for my family. In all, I fixed up $2 million worth of houses. At fifty-nine, I went to truck-driving school to accept a job with Old Dominion Freight Lines. I retired in June 2021 after ten years. My wife and I raised three kids—all married to good spouses, all good citizens with college degrees—and we have five grandchildren.

"Along the way, something very interesting happened.

"My father, who I thought had abandoned us, had been evicted from public housing. A distant relative informed me that Dad wanted me to call him. He wanted my wife, Mary, and I to visit him. I was *very* hesitant. Mary was one of fourteen children—a good Catholic girl who thought we should go. We talked some more. Finally, she said she was going without me. We went.

"He was seventy-five and looked homeless. He could not read a menu or manage the $800 a month from the Army and Social Security he had to live on. His car was broken down.

"Every Saturday at seven thirty in the morning and every Wednesday at six for five months I went to see him on Marion Road on the west side of Columbus. He was doing well, and I was busy and had to stop the Wednesday visits, but I continued going all day on Saturday for four more months. I set up a savings account for him, and we worked on life skills. After nine months, one Saturday I went to visit, and he was dead in his chair. I thought I was helping him, but he was helping me. It was a happy ending."

*　*　*

Greg Woltz and I have been friends since fourth grade. He likes to tell stories.

"When we were young, we went to Kern's Barbershop and Trenton, Rex's father, paid us twenty cents to sweep up. It took about twenty minutes, then we went next door and bought ice cream bars.

"There was a used car lot cross the street from the barbershop. The building was next to an apple tree, and there was usually a ladder on the back of the building. We would climb the ladder, sit on the roof, and eat green apples. We always took the salt shaker from the Kern house because you have to use salt on green apples. When Mrs. Kern noticed her salt shaker missing, she sent Keith over to get us and the salt shaker. When Keith tried to climb the ladder, Rex would pelt him with apples. He usually popped him.

"In eighth grade, Rex broke his ankle at Circleville, and his dad gave him heck all the way home. It must have been one of his first sports injuries. Mr. Kern wanted him to wear high-tops. Rex said, 'High-tops are for linemen; backs wear low tops.' About the same time, I fell off a motor bike and broke my ankle. The next six to eight weeks we had crutch races in the halls of General Sherman Junior High.

Rex replies: Greg, it was fourth down and short. They went for it, and we stopped them when I broke my ankle. Yeah, Dad ripped me not only all the way home but for the next four years at Lancaster. He thought the high-tops protected my ankles; I was looking for style. The funny thing is, after our senior year, one of the Columbus television stations announced their Central Ohio Back and Lineman of the Year. The winners each received a trophy with a bronze football shoe. Brian Donovan of Bishop Watterson, one of the Super Sophs at Ohio State and my teammate there, had a lineman wearing low-tops on his trophy. The back on my trophy had high-tops.

Back to Greg: "In ninth grade, Rex was ejected. He did not get into fights, but he did have the occasional comment for an official. Coach told the whole team to gather around in a huddle, took number twelve off Keith Spitler, and gave him Rex's number ten. They changed jerseys. Rex went out on the field at quarterback—maybe the only time he wore number twelve. I think we won.

"About tenth grade, I stayed overnight at Rex's house, and we couldn't sleep. He was kind of dating a girl named Vicky English, and he thought it would be a good idea to go to her house and light a cherry bomb. He lit one and threw it on the porch. It did not go off. He assumed it was a dud, went to see, picked it up, and it went off. Either it was powerful, or he was surprised, because he flew off the porch and landed on his back. By the time the family came out, we were way down the street and did not stop to see what happened. I do not remember anything being said.

"After high school I was drafted and sent to Germany as an MP for two years. Shirley, my high school girlfriend, waited for me. We have been married for forty-nine years. Our daughter is a secretary at General Sherman; our son is a teacher and football coach at Cincinnati Colerain. I worked at Anchor Hocking as a warehouse manager for eighteen years before I was downsized, then for eighteen years as a warehouse manager at Value City. I took early retirement but got bored. Now I drive a van at the Fairfield Center for Disabilities and Cerebral Palsy.

"Rex is a great guy. I am honored to be his friend."

★ ★ ★

Dick Daubmire is a lifelong friend and a teammate on five Lancaster baseball teams as well as many Little League, Pony League, and American Legion teams.

"My favorite Rex Kern story happened before high school, in Pony League ball. One of the teams we had played against decided to go up to Baltimore, Ohio, for a tournament and asked the two of us to join their team. When we got there, we were excited because the field had wooden fences. It might as well have been a Major League stadium to us—we were used to open outfields.

"I was pitching, Rex was catching, and there was a runner on third trying to distract us. Rex threw the ball back to me harder than usual, which was a signal for me to look at a runner. I threw to third, and we got him. I should say, 'The ball beat him,' because the umpire called him safe. Rex and I called time and started yelling at the umpire. Rex pulled a pair of glasses frames out of his back pocket, handed them to the umpire, and said, 'Here, you need these.'

"The umpire immediately said, 'You're outta here!'

"Someone said, 'Who?'

"The umpire said, 'Uh, the pitcher.'

"Either he really could not see, or he had a complete loss of concentration. I did not want to get thrown out of the game, but I did not want Rex to be either. It did not matter, because the umpire would not change his mind, either about the base runner or the ejection.

"When I walked off the field, my father ran up to me and said, 'Did you cuss him?'

"That would really have gotten me in trouble. When I tried to explain what happened, he believed that crazy, if true, story. Then he went after the umpire.

"Over the years, Rex and I have brought up that story dozens of times.

"The story got a bit better after we had graduated from Lancaster, and I was playing basketball in an industrial league in town. Rex happened to be home at the time and showed up to referee. I went up to him and asked, 'Did you bring your glasses?'

"We never figured out what he was doing with glasses frames on a baseball field, but we did win the game.

Rex replies: Dick, I found those frames early in the season and waited patiently for the opportunity to present them to an umpire.

"Junior year at Lancaster we had a good team but lost before we got to Columbus for the semifinals. Senior year we had some good seniors, some good juniors joined us, and we had some luck. As we were getting ready for the semifinal game, the Pittsburgh Pirates, who had been considering drafting me, told me I was not tall enough. I said, 'I'm six feet tall, my record is six and zero, and I'm pitching in the state semifinals this week.' But they knew what they wanted, and I did not have it. The Mets took a look, but neither team drafted me. There went my boyhood dream of playing in the majors.

"But back to the semifinal. We were playing Cincinnati Western Hills. The quality of baseball in Cincinnati was as good as anywhere in the state. They were 21–3, and Pete Rose's brother played for them.

"We were in an old-fashioned pitchers' duel—scoreless until the fourth inning. One of our guys dropped a pop-up, and the final score was 4–0, bad guys. The next day they won the state championship, 8–6, over Youngstown Boardman.

"All the other stories about Rex are good though. After the season, he had a date with a girl named Kathy Morehead. A couple of buddies and I found out they were going to the drive-in, so we decided to stop by. We drove around the car, honked the horn, and generally harassed them until the owners asked us to leave.

"Funny thing is, it was the only date they ever had. Funnier thing is, I started dating Kathy. Her last name became Daubmire. We recently celebrated our fiftieth wedding anniversary.

"When Rex was inducted into the College Football Hall of Fame, Kathy and I went up to South Bend to see him. There was a parade, we yelled at him, and he was surprised to see us. The next day there was an autograph session. Kathy dropped me off, with some baseballs and a football for him to sign. When I got to the front of the line, he saw the football and said, 'Are you going to throw a knuckleball?' When Kathy came to pick me up, he looked at me and said, 'Where did you find that good-looking girl?'

"I apprenticed as a mold maker at Anchor Hocking right after high school and worked there for forty-five years. Except for two years in the Navy during Vietnam, I have lived here all my life.

"One thing that has not changed over the years is, when Rex is in town, he stops to say hello. We talk for a while, then he says, 'Time to go see Coach (England).'

"We call, Coach says, 'I've got beer,' and we are off.

"What was his best sport? I really do not know. He was so darn good at all of them.

"One thing I know is, he would not have been a pitcher.

"Our senior year a couple of good pitchers had graduated, and it seemed we needed some pitching depth. Rex had a strong arm as a catcher and at third, plus he was a quarterback. Maybe he could pitch. I suggested Coach England try him pitching batting practice. He thought about it, and one day he did.

"Rex hit one batter twice, threw the ball over the screen, and the experiment was over in a hurry. Rex told me, 'Now I have more respect for you pitchers.'

"One last story about Rex.

"The summer of 1962, I played for the Lancaster Elks, a Pony League team. Most of the best players in Fairfield County were on the team, and we went 29–0. For some reason Rex did not play on that team, but he joined us the next year. A good friend of mine had played third base for the previous team, but he quit the first day of practice. He saw Rex warming up and realized the position was taken. That is the kind of reputation Rex had in eighth grade!

"We won the first twenty-four games of that season, running through tournaments like a hot knife through butter. Fifty-three straight! I wish there had been a national tournament then."

★ ★ ★

Bill Grein was a year ahead of me at Lancaster. We were teammates on two basketball teams and two baseball teams. When he graduated in 1966, he went to Bowling Green on a baseball scholarship. His nickname was Grinder.

Bill provided extensive insight to the success of the 1966 basketball team, discussed in chapter 4. Here is what he said on other matters:

"After the season, there was a party in Lancaster to celebrate the fact that our basketball team had gone farther than any Golden Gale team in history. Rex's girlfriend asked me if I was going to the party. I said I did not have a date. She said, 'Why don't you take Karen Bayliss?'

"'She is going with a friend of mine,' I replied.

"'No, they just broke up.' So I asked Karen Bayliss.

"Then my parents wanted to go to the party, and they would be driving the family car. I had sat next to Karen Bayliss in class all year and wanted to ask her out the whole time. I certainly did not want our first date to be in my parents' car with my parents. I asked Rex if we could double-date, and he agreed.

"Karen and I had a nice time, and four years later she was Karen Grein.

"For me, that was the best assist of a tremendous basketball season.

"The spring of 1966, we had a great baseball team. One of our strengths was pitching. Paul Callahan was our righty starter, and I was the lefty. He pitched at Louisville; I pitched at Bowling Green. In one Pony League game, we had pitched a doubleheader. I started the first game and pitched a perfect game; he started the second and pitched a no-hitter. We did not do that in high school, but his earned run average was 0.69 senior year, and we both remember mine was somewhere below 1.00. We were strong everywhere else. Some of the guys who went to the state tournament in 1967 have told us that the 1966 team was Lancaster's best.

"We won the sectional tournament but lost 2-3 to Ironton in eight innings. That was the end of the tournament dream.

"I went to BG on a partial scholarship, expecting to become a coach. We had first division teams, and I did OK."

Rex: Actually, a check of the BG records shows that, as a junior, Bill led the team in innings pitched and WHIP, walks and hits per inning pitched. For some reason his senior year is not shown.

"The best thing about baseball was the stories it provided. How many baseball players have seen Bear Bryant in the stands while pitching? It was our spring trip through the South. The Alabama students were on break, and a man in a houndstooth hat really stood out. And how many have seen Bo Schembechler in a towel?

That was in the locker room, after BG lost at Michigan. And thrown a knuckleball to Rex Kern when he was catching in a Pony League game? He caught it. And seen one of the longest home runs hall of famer Mike Schmidt ever hit? I had a good view from the pitcher's mound. And been called Sandy Koufax? I was pitching for the Marines in Japan, where the fans were not particularly familiar with the Dodgers star pitcher. At least we were both left handed.

"But I have to tell you about Mike Baughman. He was a three-sport star in high school, then went to Indiana on a football scholarship. As a sophomore, he started in the 1968 Rose Bowl, then Rex and OSU went to the Rose Bowl the next year. Imagine—two starters out of five on our 1966 basketball team in the Rose Bowl in consecutive years!

"Final story about high school: During senior night, seniors traditionally sang, danced, and performed for their parents and the underclassmen. In 1966 several of the senior players—Paul Callahan, Terry Webb, Steve Macioci, Dan Williams, and I—went to Rising Park and captured a duck. While a group of senior girls were singing, Terry threw the duck onto the stage. The crowd laughed. The girls were embarrassed and ran off the stage. As the curtains closed, the duck's head stuck out to look at the crowd.

"We never could have trained that duck to perform so well.

"Unfortunately, no one from Aflac was filming the show. We might still be receiving residuals on that commercial!

"Yes, I did enlist as an officer in the Marines, and, no, I did not serve in Vietnam. I was in Beirut in 1983 and got to see Europe; Guantanamo Bay, Cuba; Norway; and the Far East.

"My last duty station, I was put in charge of Toys for Tots for the Marines. Toys for Tots is a Christmas charity supervised by Marines that collects toys, books, and other gifts for underprivileged children. Marines are prohibited from asking for money, so when I retired and became a civilian I became the vice president of the Marines' Toys for Tots Foundation and their fundraising arm. I never made the Lancaster High School Athletic Hall of Fame but did make the LHS Hall of Fame, largely based on the fact that we raised over $500 million in toys, $150 million in cash contributions, and $33 million books for boys and girls.

"Getting back to Rex, whatever the scale, he is at the top as a leader, competitor, and teammate. Fine human being, easy to like, calm under pressure, reliable, always does his best, no excuses when things went poorly, but still confident, generated confidence in his teammates, patient, never late to practice. Is that enough? I could go on."

*　*　*

Perry Blum is not an obvious choice for the list of Lancaster people who influenced me. At the same time, he is perfect for the job. Perry tells the following story:

"There were eight elementary schools in Lancaster, and each had a team in the fourth-grade basketball league. We all arrived at the same time, learned which game we were scheduled to play, then waited until it was our turn. Those who played the last game saw everyone in the league that day.

"Rex was a fourth-grade legend. He killed the other fourth-grade teams, except he did not kill North.

"I had a great coach at North and loved to play defense. He taught us, 'Do not watch his hands; watch his belly button. He can't go anywhere without it. And if you have to foul, make sure he understands he was fouled.' He also said, 'Watch where the refs are. They can't call what they can't see.'

I was not intimidated by Rex. I loved the challenge of playing the best, and I had the attitude, 'He is not going to beat me this possession.' There were times when he did beat me but always during the play, not because I was intimidated before the play.

"One game, in sixth grade, I held him to four points in the first three quarters. Early in the fourth, I fouled out. He scored twenty points in the fourth quarter, and they won by two. How many times did I actually foul him? About twenty-seven.

"After playing against him from fourth through ninth grades, I was looking forward to playing with him in high school. He would play varsity as a sophomore, and I might be on the reserves, but eventually we would play together. I was not much of a scorer, but I was a good passer and liked to set up my teammates. Plus, I knew every shot Rex had and where he liked to take each one.

"On the first day of practice in tenth grade, the varsity coach met me at the door and said, 'You don't need to stay. I don't like you, and you are not going to make the team.' I had never met him. To this day, I do not know what that was about. I left and never tried out for the team again. So I never got to be Rex's teammate. It is probably the biggest disappointment of my life.

"Rex and I could not have been more different in high school. He never smoked cigarettes; I started at fourteen. He held school offices; I hated school from the first day. He was a solid citizen; I was a rebel and a hell-raiser. I doubt he ever had a detention; senior year alone I had 155 detentions. (The way Perry described himself as a Lancaster student was reminiscent of Marlon Brando in the 1953 movie *The Wild One*. When the Brando character is asked what he is rebelling against, Brando replied, "Whaddaya got?" Told about the movie, Perry said, "That was me.")

"I was focused on getting a golf scholarship; he was playing other sports. We never had a disagreement—we just never spent time together.

"I got the golf scholarship, but I left college after one year and went into the military. I hated that, but it was probably the best thing for me. My wife and I were stationed at Eglin Air Force Base, Fort Walton Beach, Florida. Twice I got orders to go to Vietnam, but fortunately both times my wife was pregnant, and we stayed there. Growing up in a privileged white family in Lancaster, I had never seen Black people. There were many in the service, and it was surprisingly easy to get to know them. I made several Black friends who remain friends today. It was a good experience, but I was glad to be out after three years, ten months, eight days, and eight hours.

"After the Air Force, I got a job as a clerk at a bank in 1973. I spent my working life in banking and financial services, retired at fifty-eight, and now live in Florida. I have beaten cancer three times and am now clear. It is a day-to-day thing.

"I saw Rex at our tenth high school reunion. He was recovering from surgery and walking with a cane. It was good to see him, but everyone wanted to talk with him.

"At the fiftieth reunion, I remember someone saying, 'Did you know Rex is here?' I found him surrounded by classmates, as usual.

"When the crowd died down, I walked up and said, 'I'll still beat you in basketball any time.' He laughed. We hugged and had a good talk.

"He had never known that the coach did not want me on the team until that night. He said, 'You would not have started at first, but you would have as a senior, and we would have had a good team.'

"My girlfriend, who he knew from Lancaster, wanted to say hello, so we went back to see him later that night. Rex said, 'You were not the best person I played against, but you certainly were the dirtiest.' I took that as a compliment.

"Now we talk a few times a year.

"He was not only a leader for every team but he was a leader in the school. It is difficult to imagine someone so talented and accomplished being so kind and modest, but that is Rex Kern.

"When I was young, I imagined he hated me because I played so hard against him. Now I realize our friendship is based on mutual respect for competition and striving for excellence. It has probably always been, and I was too busy rebelling to notice."

Nicki Myers Baltz and I met at General Sherman Junior High in seventh grade and have been friends ever since. As a woman, she sees things differently than my male friends.

"Rex Kern was ornery as all get-out. He was very outgoing, fun, and friendly. He was always into something, stirring things up. Somehow he never seemed to get caught.

"Mom and Dad liked him, though that did not stop Dad from calling him 'that *unprintable* little redhead.' He always smiled when he said that though. Dad loved to watch Rex play sports.

"We were in choir and algebra together. The teacher liked us, which was the only way we got out of there.

"He dated a girl who lived near me. All the girls liked him. He had his harem. He may disagree, but that is the way it was. When he was a sophomore, he dated a cheerleader who was a senior.

"No, I was not in the harem. The closest thing to a date was going to a high school football game out of town with him, his parents, and Joe Edwards in junior high.

"When he got involved with the Fellowship of Christian Athletes, I admired that. He did mature; he's a nice man."

Later, Nicki researched her copies of the yearbook, *The Mirage*, and spotted me in pictures of the student council (three years), Spanish club (three years), Big Brothers, Key Club, school dance, chemistry class, and Buckeye Boys State (summer of 1966).

Mark Baltz, Lancaster Class of 1966, was the statistician for the 1966 state tournament basketball team, then married Nicki Myers. He is in Lancaster High School's Distinguished Hall of Fame.

"I was the first student trainer at the high school. While I was at Ohio University, I took a sports officiating class, reffed some intramural games, and got interested in doing that. During eighteen years at Anchor Hocking, I worked my way up to high school and college in Ohio. When I moved to Fort Wayne, with Anchor, I had to work my way up again. After leaving Anchor, I became a manufacturer's representative. As an independent rep, I had more time for officiating and eventually worked in the Mid-American Conference, the Big Ten, and the National Football League (NFL).

"Early in my Big Ten career, I remember a football game at Indiana. We were having a pregame meeting. There was a knock on the door, and basketball coach Bob Knight came in.

"The first thing he said was, 'I heard there were five blind men in here.' Everyone laughed. He said hello to the guys he knew and was introduced to the others, including me. Soon he went to the door, turned out the light, and said, 'Now you are in the dark.'

"I refereed in the NFL from 1989 to 2014. Rex was always quick to call when he saw me on television. During one eight-year period, I had the Thanksgiving Day game six times. When my wife was asked what our family did during the holidays, she began to reply, 'Most of the family got together and had our turkey, then we turned on the television and watched our turkey.'"

A proud member of the Lancaster Class of 1966, Mark says, "We always thought of it as the senior class plus Rex. He was a great athlete, personable, everybody liked him. Like Rex, I am thrilled to be from Lancaster in the sixties. Wouldn't want to have grown up anywhere else. Rex made his memories for himself. He is a great person; I am proud to be his friend."

Soon after we talked, Mark was inducted as president of the Indiana Basketball Hall of Fame. As a high school referee in the state for forty-three years, he expected "every deceased player and coach to be spinning in his grave."

* * *

Debbie Clark Reid was homecoming queen for the Class of 1967 and represents another welcome female voice among the many men.

"When I think of Rex, I laugh. He was always fun and often funny, friendly, a little shy, full of personality. I was smitten with him. We had some casual dates. They never turned out the way I wanted them to. But it was fun sitting on the porch talking to him.

"We were on the other side of the tracks, so we met in junior high. We went to different churches, but I remember the youth camp we both attended when he accepted Christ. I would describe him as humble and kind. With all the acclaim he has received, it is a real achievement to be humble.

"I enjoyed sports myself—basketball, softball, gymnastics, and especially volleyball, track, and tennis. Of course, back then girls' sports got no recognition at all. It was nice—six or seven years ago, the woman in charge of girls' sports at Lancaster gave us letters for our participation.

"I remember going up to Columbus to Riverside Hospital to see Rex with some girlfriends the summer he had his back surgery, between freshman and sophomore year in college. We went to cheer him up. There was a question if he would be able to play football again, but you could not tell it from him—he cheered us up!

"My husband and I are Browns Backers, and I asked Rex to sign a couple of his football jerseys for a scholarship auction we were having. He sent five, with his name and number.

"Once a friend, always a friend."

★ ★ ★

Tim Bailey went to North Elementary, so we met in junior high at General Sherman.

"In seventh grade, there was no football team at that time. I was second-string quarterback on the seventh and eighth team. In eighth grade, Rex showed up, and the QB position suddenly got very crowded. I was switched to fullback. The next year I played slotback and enjoyed catching the occasional pass. In high school, it was back to fullback. Coach Jones wanted his fullbacks to also play linebacker, so I started to work there as well.

"I did not play regularly as a sophomore. Before my junior year, some personal issues came up. I loved football but thought it would be best to give it up. My coaches spoke with me but did not change my mind. Then Rex and Joe Edwards came to my house. They said, 'We'd love to have you on the team, but we will respect any decision you make.' That night I wanted to play.

"I called Coach Jones, who said, 'We'd love to have you back, but the players have run their miles, so you would have to do that.'

"I said, 'Tell me where and when, and I will be there.'

"When I arrived to run the mile, there was Rex. I said, "What are you doing here?'

"'I came to set the pace for you,' he replied. 'It's hard to run by yourself, so stay with me, and you will make your time.'

"The required time was set by position. As a fullback, I had to run under 5:40 for the mile. With Rex's help, I ran 5:36.

(By now an accomplished, retired family man was speaking in a halting voice.)

"That meant the world to me.

"Between 1964 and 1966, we won three straight Central Ohio League championships. I am not sure we were as talented as seniors as the Lancaster teams before us, but we were very close as a team. A large part of that was due to Rex. He was one of the greatest athletes in Ohio high school history—up there with people like John Havlicek in three sports. But he was also a better person than he was an athlete. He treated every player the same. He was the same steady guy every day, and he loved his teammates. Plus, that smile just melted people. They gravitated to him.

"The middle and late 1960s were a confusing time for many people. We graduated about four hundred people in our class, but only thirteen seniors went out for football. Several guys who were good players in junior high were just not interested. Vietnam, civil rights, and other matters were more on their minds. But the kids we had were really dedicated. They had to be because depth was an issue at some positions.

"The COL was one of the best leagues in Ohio, with Chillicothe, Ironton, Lancaster, Marietta, Newark, and Zanesville. That year, Marietta was picked to win.

"Besides that, before the conference started, we lost to the top two teams in Ohio, Bishop Watterson and Upper Arlington, plus Portsmouth and Steubenville Central Catholic, which were very strong. We were 1–4 to start the season, but maybe that brutal nonconference schedule prepared us for the conference.

"We clinched the COL title with four straight victories. The coaches did an especially good job before we played Marietta, picking up some offensive tendencies and changing our defense to stop them. The score was 38–0. The Zanesville game was rugged. To win that game 12–7, we had to stop them three times inside our five-yard line.

"The last game, against Newark, was disappointing. Maybe we relaxed because the championship was decided, but your last game is a memory that never goes away. We had a terrible first half. We came back but fell short, losing 26–28.

"I loved that senior season, spending so much time with guys I cared about, playing a sport I love against the best teams in the state, and blocking opponents at 210–220 pounds while weighing 160 pounds myself. I played with a bruised kidney and expected to finish the season that way, but my cousin told my father. That cost me three games.

"The first game back I had a cut on my forehead. Rex saw it and said, 'Timmy, you are bleeding.' He and my grandmother were the only people who could get away with calling me Timmy.

"I said, 'I'm fine. Call the play.' I was not missing any more of the fun.

"Today I have two sports seasons: football and waiting for football."

* * *

Dr. John Holland played varsity baseball at Ohio University, graduated, and served as a student-teacher at Lancaster High School before he was hired to teach science and coach football and basketball at General Sherman Junior High School. After seven years, with a master's degree earned at Eastern Kentucky University, he decided to attend Indiana University and obtain a doctorate in exercise physiology. From there, Dr. Holland became chairman of the faculty senate at the University of Houston before moving to the National Defense University in Washington, DC, as founder and executive director of the Wellness Center. There he worked and socialized with many prominent figures, including President George H. W. Bush and his wife, Barbara.

In the fall of 2020, Dr. Holland looked back on his friendship with an athlete he coached and a fellow Ph.D., Dr. Rex Kern.

"While Rex had tremendous athletic ability as a youngster, what set him apart was the support system he had, beginning with his home life. His mother, father, and older brother, Keith, helped Rex learn values, priorities, a work ethic, and a belief system that helped Rex accomplish marvelous things in athletics yet remain modest and truly team oriented, inside and outside sports. When he completely dominated the Biddy Basketball League, he stayed the same person. When he made Prep All-America, it was the same thing. Third in Heisman Trophy voting as a junior and fifth as a senior? Same thing. Playing in the NFL? Same thing. Today it is still the same thing.

"There was a boy at Lancaster after Rex who could have been an Ohio State–caliber athlete, but he did not have that kind of support system. It is difficult to achieve much of lasting value in the world without help.

"I went up for an Ohio State practice when Rex was a freshman. He was their quarterback, leading them against the varsity. Jack Tatum played fullback for the freshmen, and he was incredible. When he went out, John Brockington went in, and he was remarkable. He went out, and Leo Hayden went in, clearly NFL talent. Those three played the same position for the freshmen, and Rex was their leader.

"After his freshman year at Ohio State, we worked together at Anchor Hocking, where we were told to 'give a good day's work for a good day's pay.' We were 'gophers'—go for this, go for that—often working at a blast furnace making glass. In the best of times, the work was hot, and 1968 was a hot summer. He went to work with the rest of us every day, though he had already made a name for himself on the Ohio State freshman team. His innate intelligence was clear one day when he looked up, wiped his forehead, smiled, and said, 'There has to be a better way to make a living.' Then he went right back to work. That tells you about his character and his resolve to persist during difficult times.

"Some other thoughts on Rex: He had big hands, which helped his ballhandling. I taught him the bootleg fake he used at Ohio State—it was successful in eighth grade and the Big Ten. Back in those days, not every game was on television. I remember listening to his game on the radio, and the announcer apologized to the audience. 'I'm sorry. I just can't see where the ball is.' Rex had this ability to play hard yet have another gear when the team really needed it. It was easy to see it coming at General Sherman because he had this little smile on his face. I remember watching a close game at Ohio Stadium and seeing that little smile. OK, there were ninety-some thousand fans, I was far away, he had a helmet on, and maybe I did not see it. But it was there.

"One Saturday night I was watching *The Woody Hayes Show* after a victory, and Woody said, 'If Rex can't do it, it can't be done.' I would second that.

"Having said all that, I would say that, at eighty-one, one of my greatest hopes is to sit down and talk with Rex Kern one more time."

★ ★ ★

Mike Baughman, the former Lancaster three-sport star, started the conversation by talking about his brother Larry, a fine Lancaster athlete.

"Larry called recently and mentioned a couple of things that may be of interest.

"He was first-team All-Ohio as a running back, and many schools wanted him for football. Woody Hayes told him they were bringing in Bob Ferguson to play fullback, and they wanted Charlie beside him in the backfield. Woody said, 'I'm going to see that you both make All-American.'

"Meanwhile, the Phillies wanted Larry, a catcher, to sign with them. They offered $100,000, plus college, plus advanced degrees. He eventually earned a Ph.D., and the Phillies paid for all three degrees.

"One of the reasons he signed with the Phillies was that the team called Woody Hayes and asked him to back off in recruiting Larry for the good of the family and because he would still have his education paid.

"Woody later recruited my brother Jeff, who went to Miami (Ohio) and played for Bo (Schembechler) and myself. He was oh for three in the Baughman house.

"I really only played one year of varsity football at Lancaster. I broke my arm as a junior and missed the whole year, after only playing one game as a sophomore.

"In 1965 we had a tremendous football team. We lost early to Upper Arlington and Bishop Watterson, and I think we could have won both games. We made mistakes in both games we did not make later in the year. I won some awards, including Ohio Lineman of the Year and All-American Top Ten, mostly because of my teammates and especially Rex Kern. If he was not our quarterback, I would not have been as effective at receiver.

"After my senior year, Coach Earl Jones asked me to stop in his office and said, 'Where do you want to go to college?' The way he said it sounded like I had my choice of anywhere. I just remember Alabama and most of the Big Ten.

"I chose Indiana—to play wide receiver and study psychology.

"Soon after I arrived, they told me I could start as a sophomore if I was willing to move to safety. I wanted to play, so I did, expecting to move back to receiver as a junior. That did not happen; I started at safety all three years. As they say in amateur sports, it's a business.

"But sophomore year was like a dream. Indiana went to the Rose Bowl for the only time in history! We started out unranked and ended up fourth in the country!

"Besides football, I started in baseball for three years. After playing left field at Lancaster, I moved to center field in college and liked that better. As a junior, I was unanimously selected as center fielder on the All-Big Ten team.

"I am glad to help Rex remember growing up in Lancaster because I agree that the city played a big part in the success we all had. There was a real emphasis on education, even though many of our parents had not gone to college. Well, Fritz Reed's father was a doctor, but he was the exception. I wish young people could grow up today like we did as kids in Lancaster.

"As seniors, Fritz and I decided we wanted to buy a *Playboy* magazine. I'm not sure the drugstores in Lancaster carried them then, but we heard the sporting goods store downtown, the Sporting News, had them. We had no trouble buying one, but when I got home about ten minutes later my father asked to see it! News sure does travel fast in a small town. Fritz had the magazine, but I did not try to deny the charge.

"Thinking of Fritz takes me back to senior year at LHS, 1966. Football was fun, but I wish we had playoffs then and a chance to prove how good we were at the end of the season. We did have that chance in basketball. We had a great ride but did not finish the deal. I will always remember the support we had. As for baseball, I think we ran out of gas after the long basketball season and the celebrations for that team. We had good baseball players and just missed the state tournament. If we had gotten there, who knows?

"One last story that might interest the players on the 1966 basketball team: At Indiana I met Joe Cooke, the star of our game with Toledo Libbey. He was not eligible to play in college as a freshman, so they played against local teams before varsity games. We played against each other several times and talked after the games. He had a fine college career and played in the NBA.

"He was a nice guy and came from a similar economic background. IU was a wake-up call for both of us.

"After college I wanted to try to work my way into the majors, but Indiana wanted to give me much more money to get my MBA. My athletic career was over."

Baughman's wife, Susie, passed away in 2001. They were married for thirty years and had three children.

* * *

Randy Groff grew up on the east side of Lancaster, and we did not really know each other until tenth grade, playing on the high school football team.

"Of course, most people in Lancaster knew of Rex, at least as an athlete, long before then. One of my proud memories from junior high is that our Thomas Ewing team beat the General Sherman team, quarterbacked by the future Buckeye, 8–6. Yes, I do have proof.

"Despite his athletic fame at an early age, Rex was an easy guy to like. We became friends quickly. In fact, he borrowed my 1962 Corvair to go on a date.

"Cars were made more simply than they are today, and I had a knack for fixing them. This came in handy when the Corvair broke down while Rex and his date were in it. Rex did not have his cell phone in the 1960s, but he called, and I went to pick them up.

"Turns out it was possible to fix a 1962 Corvair with duct tape and a donated bra strap. Moving on ...

"As much fun as the football was, my first memories go to bus rides to the away games, teasing each other and talking about girls.

"Earl Jones was our head coach in football. He also taught driver's ed. When I was in the class, he liked to stop at the Dairy Queen. If I had made a perfect tackle in the previous game, he bought me a milkshake. I played cornerback on defense, halfback on offense.

"Most of my athletic success came in wrestling. I won the COL and advanced in the sectional and district. Unfortunately, before the match to go to the state meet in Columbus, I got the flu. I had a 103-degree temperature and was seeing double. I lost by one point. Iowa offered me a scholarship to wrestle there, but I always wanted to go to Ohio State and did not have a passion to continue wrestling either.

"Terry Webb and I double-dated frequently in high school. When I was seventeen, Terry gave me his draft card to use as my first fake ID. The match was perfect, except for a *V* scar on the back of the left hand. I took out a knife, gave myself a *V*, and the ID worked every time, even when we were in the same establishment at the same time.

"At Ohio State, Rex asked me to walk on—that is, play football without a scholarship. He even introduced me to Woody Hayes. But at 150 pounds, my future did not seem to be in football. I did pay attention to their defensive backs, and the three Super Sophs, as Rex's class was known, had successful NFL careers. Not playing football any longer was one of my good decisions.

"Rex was in the South dorm. I was in East Baker, but they had a common dining room. It was good to see him from time to time.

"After freshman year I enlisted in the Marines in 1968 with a classmate, Tim Bailey. We expected to go through basic training together and serve together. After basic we never saw each other in the Marines.

"At the end of 1968, I was stationed at Camp Pendleton, in California, within two hours of the Rose Bowl. Sadly, I could not get liberty to go to the game.

"There were, however, compensations. We watched the game on television as Rex Kern led the Buckeyes to an upset victory over the University of Southern California (USC), 27–16. Many on the base were from Southern California and expected USC to win their second straight Rose Bowl behind O. J. Simpson. I was the only Buckeye in sight and took all the bets. There were a lot of disappointed (and broke) Californians on the base. Rex was MVP and found the future Mrs. Kern.

"It was a good day.

"This may surprise some classmates, but after the Marines I became a strong student and graduated from OU! The experience served me well."

(My friend and classmate Randy Groff wrote about his life at the request of his daughter for the sake of their family. Friends of Randy may be able to obtain his computer file titled "Common Life—Uncommon Luck" from him. It includes a detailed discussion of the Vietnam War and more experiences than you can imagine. Rex)

* * *

Paul Callahan, class of 1966, recalls, "Most people in school called me Sticks. Being six four, 165 pounds may have had something to do with that. Rex has always called me Chrome. Once he thought my haircut was too short. Eventually, all the barbers in town knew what a Coach Hill haircut was, and basketball players just asked for that.

"Bill Grein and I pitched for LHS and also pitched together in American Legion. In a doubleheader July Fourth weekend, 1965, between junior and senior year, he pitched a perfect game, and I followed it with a no-hitter. As a senior, I had an era of 0.69. That summer I was named All-American American Legion.

"After our trip to the state tournament senior year, the University of Louisville offered me a basketball scholarship. At first I did not realize a basketball scholarship covered everything, while most baseball offers are partial. I decided to try the highest level.

"Freshmen were not eligible, and sophomore and junior year I was behind Butch Beard, an all-time U of L great. When I saw the skill level of freshman Jim Price, like Butch, a future NBA first-round draft choice, I switched to baseball and had more success.

"Looking back, the Mid-American Conference or the Ohio Valley Conference might have been the best level for me for basketball, but it was fun to letter in two sports in college and to compete against some great athletes.

"I had a thirty-year career as a teacher, coach, and athletic director. I coached boys' and girls' basketball and boys' golf. During my eleven years as an athletic director, I was eventually named Athletic Director of the Year in Kentucky in 1999.

"The best part of my career was meeting and marrying my wife, Sandy. She was also a coach and athletic director. In fact, she has been inducted into three halls of fame. I am glad the days of our teams playing each other are over!

"Back to Rex Kern. He was the best competitor and the consummate teammate. As a leader, he did what the team needed to win. In basketball, for example, he could score twenty-two or two and be happy with a victory. He was the only junior in the starting lineup on the 1966 team, and I was the captain, but he was a coleader."

Rex replies: Chrome, that short haircut lasted at least a year. You earned that nickname! Thanks for helping with this.

Captain of the 1965–1966 state tournament basketball team, Paul contributed significantly to a later chapter discussing the season.

★ ★ ★

Baseball Coach Dick England and his wife bought a starter home in Lancaster in 1958 and still live in that house. Their cars now cost more than their house did.

"I came back from the service as assistant football and assistant baseball coach at Lancaster and served as head baseball coach from 1959 to 1969. We went to the state tournament three times: 1961, 1964, and 1967, the first three times a Lancaster baseball team had been to Columbus. They have been back three more times, without winning.

"In 1964 Keith Kern was a senior and played second base. When Keith graduated, a well-known athlete named Rex Kern, Keith's brother, was eligible as a sophomore. He was already playing varsity football and basketball. I thought he could play third base or shortstop for us, but we had returning starters at both positions. When the third baseman hurt his ankle, Rex moved there full time and stayed for three years.

"Early in the year, we were indoors, practicing situations. I explained our approach with runners on first and third—that the shortstop (Rex) would cover second, and the second baseman would charge the throw from the catcher. If the runner on third went home, the second baseman would cut off the throw and go home with it. If the runner stayed on third, the second baseman would let the ball go through for the play at second.

"I thought they understood and that everyone was ready, but when the ball went through to second, Rex's hands were at his side, and the ball hit him directly in the mouth. His head was bent over. Second base was covered with blood, and his two front teeth were missing. He put his thumb in his mouth and pushed them down from the roof of his mouth. The only thing he said was, "Let's do it again, Coach."

"Of course, I knew his parents because Keith had played for us. I called, told his mother what had happened to Rex, and advised her to take him to the dentist to have everything checked. The dentist said he could not believe it, but everything was fine.

"I did not want to have that happen again and called him 'Stupid Soph' for two years to remind him.

Rex: Coach, the second baseman blocked my vision! As for the teeth, that night I slept with my football mouthpiece in and kept it in except for school and practice for a while. I still have my two front teeth.

"That name was teasing. Rex was a natural on the diamond, just like he was on the gridiron and the court. Unlike most batters, he did not hit with his hands together. Like some of the old-timers— Ty Cobb, for example—his hands were separated on the bat. He was a coach on the field.

"My favorite story about him was in our game with Wooster in 1967, regional finals—winner went to the state tournament. In a scoreless game, he led off with a triple. As I noticed that the pitcher was not paying much attention to him, Rex crossed his arms. That was our signal for the steal. We had a left-handed batter at the plate, normally making it a bad time to steal because the catcher can easily see the runner coming home. But I thought, *If the redhead thinks he can do it, we're going to do it.* Rex broke for the plate, the catcher took a quick look at him, and the ball went to the backstop. We won the game 2–0!

"In Columbus, we were in a close game in the semifinals. Dick Daubmire was pitching well on a sunny day. One of our players forgot to take his sunglasses on the field, dropped a pop-up, and we lost, 0–4, to Cincinnati Western Hills, which won the state title.

"Some weeks later, Rex was selected to play in the All-Ohio game in Jets Stadium in Columbus. He played third base for us, center field in American Legion—he could play anywhere. That day he played first base.

"I went up with an old friend, Larry Thomas, a scout for the Boston Red Sox, and told him Rex was originally a catcher. Teams always need catchers, so that helped his draft status.

(A total of 974 players were drafted. Rex was taken 306 by the Kansas City A's. Thirty-four prospects taken after him played in the majors, including all-stars Dusty Baker, 242 home runs; Chris Chambliss, 185 home runs; and Steve Rogers, 158 wins.)

Rex interjects, "My father said at the time, 'Rex, you promised Fred Taylor and Woody Hayes that you were going to Ohio State. You need to be a man of your word,'" and that settled things.

As Coach England looked around his rec room, he pointed out, "That picture of me with Rex, Dick Daubmire, and Lenny Conrad," the one which says, "To Connie and the Coach, Keith and Rex." "The 1968 National Champion Ohio State team," which Rex brought us, and "The one of Rex with the Colts."

"Because of Rex, Connie and I went to California three times in five years. We went to the 1969 Rose Bowl, the 1971 Rose Bowl with Stanford, and to his wedding to Nancy in 1973.

"I left Lancaster for one year in 1970 to assist Bob Wren with his baseball team. We went to Omaha and finished fourth in the College World Series. Mike Schmidt was the star of that team and invited us to Cooperstown when he went into the Baseball Hall of Fame. Rex invited my son Jeff and I to his induction into the College Football Hall of Fame, which we enjoyed as well.

"I came back to Lancaster as athletic director after one year, no coaching, and stayed until I retired in 1989. I am eighty-eight, and Connie is eighty-two—happy in our starter home."

* * *

Paul Kendrick began, "It's funny the things you remember from childhood. I remember playing tag as a child, and I remember a group of us camping out at Mike Baughman's house during a torrential rainstorm. We tried so hard to be tough, but we were miserable and finally gave up and went inside.

"And I remember seeing a third grader play catcher with a fire and a passion far beyond fourth graders like myself. I was watching Rex Kern.

"Rex and I went to different junior highs, so we did not really know each other until he came to high school. He was second string quarterback, and I was a reserve receiver. I remember how much fun it was to hear the varsity coach, Earl Jones, yell at the first string when we scored against them.

"My older brothers had both been quarterbacks at Lancaster. One graduated in 1953, the other 1955. I was too young to know what was going on then, but I read their yearbooks and wanted to be just like them. I knew it would be difficult to beat out Rex my senior year, his junior, but that was the task.

"Before fall practice, Coach Jones came up to me and said, 'It's going to be hard to keep Rex out of the lineup, but we like you as a player and want you in the lineup too. We want you to play running back and use you to catch passes out of the backfield.' I realized the two end positions were already taken by future college players Mike Baughman and Fritz Reed.

"Looking back, I am glad I agreed to do what was best for our team, but I wish I had asked to be backup quarterback as well. Someone had to be that guy, and the quarterback position was always my dream.

"Turns out it did not matter. I tore a knee ligament in a preseason scrimmage at Athens and my leg was in a cast for six weeks. Then there was rehabilitation, then football was over, then getting into shape for basketball, then learning a new coach's system. I was not able to earn much playing time on a very good team.

"I remember being distracted from the task, thinking 'How can I make up for all this lost time?' My focus should have been on doing the best I could. That is really all you can ever do.

"For me, part of my high school education was that obstacles come into your life, and you must deal with them, sometimes set new goals. Senior year that meant being the best teammate in football and the best practice player in basketball I could be. They were two outstanding teams, with many great guys and lifelong friends.

"After LHS, I earned two engineering degrees, which helped me find work that was challenging and rewarding, in the Air Force and in private industry. More importantly, my wife of forty-eight years and I raised two wonderful children and enjoy spoiling our grandchildren.

"Rex, I was glad to participate in this project for your family. My suggestion for them is, 'Go after your goals, even if there is a player on your team as good as your grandfather was at football and basketball. You may beat him out. If not, you may develop skills that make you pretty darn good at other things, like raising a family and earning a living.'"

★ ★ ★

I called an audible for this last influencer. The original intention was to limit this section to friends and mentors from my childhood in Lancaster. I met Dave Cheney at the North-South football game, where we were teammates and roommates in the summer of 1967. It was after graduation but before enrollment at Ohio State. We became friends and teammates at Ohio State, roommates for two years, and national champions. Since he was a lineman sworn to protect his quarterbacks, and we have been almost lifelong friends, it seemed he could represent my transition from high school to college.

There is one thing to mention about Dave. Every quarterback knows he is going to receive suggestions from receivers who are open and running backs who think they can gain five yards any time. Sometimes a lineman will suggest a play to gain a much-needed first down.

Dave was different. He always suggested the same play for the same reason: "Rex, why don't you scramble around in the backfield for a while," he would say. "Try to give me a good angle for a crack back block on that guy over me. He's giving me a lot of trouble. Maybe I can get him out of the game."

My response was always the same: "If I do that, Woody will take me out of the game. If you miss the block, I will get hammered, and they may carry me out of the game."

Since he was an All-Big Ten tackle, not many players gave him problems. He usually wanted me to scramble just for fun—his fun.

Here's Dave.

"We were in Canton practicing for the game for two weeks. I remember thinking, *What's everyone talking about with this guy?* He was good, but everyone there was good. In practice, he was nothing special. Eleven of the fifty players were in Ohio State's Super Soph class, and some of the others could have been.

"When the game started, it took me half of a quarter to see what was special about Rex Kern! He had another gear in the game. The score was South 40–12, South, a record for the winning team in the twenty-two-year history of the game, and his running, passing, and leadership were responsible.

"Kern is everything they say he is and more," said South coach Lou Florio of Hamilton Garfield.

"We knew he could run the option but did not know he was that good," said North coach Bill Gutbrod of Cleveland St. Joseph.

"'King' Kern Leads South to Victory,' screamed one headline. 'Redhead Shows All-American Poise,' shouted another.

"We had fun as roommates those two weeks. He always had a

great smile. Frankly, it was an ornery smile. You never knew if he had just decided how to stir something up or was still working on it. He was always up to something; he generated fun.

"I don't think he ever touched alcohol. Most people equate fun with drinking. He had fun without it. I hope his grandchildren know that about him because they can do the same thing.

"By the way, did he tell you what happened after the North-South game? I went straight from Canton to Athens for an American Legion baseball tournament. Lima beat Lancaster, Rex's team. We knocked them out of the state tournament, then we won it!

"Despite that, we roomed together for two years at Ohio State. I can tell you from firsthand knowledge that his accuracy is underrated. No, not with a football, with water balloons! Freshman year we lived on the ninth floor, and he got our RA (resident advisor) right on the chest while he was sunbathing. Students learned to walk quickly on our side of the dorm.

"He was the best athlete I ever saw. He might not beat someone like Jan White in the hurdles but was very talented in many athletic endeavors.

"One more thought for Rex's grandchildren: I got a low grade on my SAT in English as a junior at Lima Senior High School. Senior year I walked into a class with the best English students in the school. There were twenty-three girls and seven boys! That seemed like a mistake, so I went to see the principal.

"'I put you in that class on purpose,' he told me. 'You are going to college on an athletic scholarship, and English is often used as a flunk-out course. Work hard for that teacher in that class, and you will be ready for college.'

"I may not have liked working so hard in that class, but I was ready for college. I got a B in freshman English at Ohio State.

"Sometimes people challenge you because they care about you. Respond by accepting the challenge and doing your best. Sometimes challenges stand in the way of reaching your goals. It may be an English paper or a mile run or getting a job or making a speech. Face your challenge, defeat it, and go about reaching your goals. Challenges are stepping-stones!"

Rex: What Dave did not mention is that the writing ability he developed because his principal challenged him served him well throughout college, where he made All-Big Ten Academic twice and All-Big Ten as a senior. It also helped him graduate from law school as well as throughout his legal career, which included presiding over hundreds of criminal and civil cases during six years as a judge of the Allen County Court of Common Pleas. He retired from the bench in 2018.

While "Spook" makes many good points, I have some different memories. While he wanted to leave that nickname in Columbus, our teammates agree with me that it is his forever. That's for asking for us to wait while you listened to a guy named Spook Beckman on the television and for almost getting us in trouble at the Rose Bowl.

Also, he hit the dorm advisor from the ninth floor. I was not in the room at the time. Just as I got out of the elevator, the RA walked in, soaking wet, in a suit. He accused me, but I had an alibi.

And Cheney forgot to mention the food fight at the dorm, which he started. Actually, I do not remember who started it, but I better accuse him before he blames me. We were identified as instigators and found guilty in dorm court, though Nick Roman and Bill Pollitt were likely suspects as well. Cheney and Bill were probably doing "legal research" to prepare for their careers. Wasn't our punishment taking out trash or something like that?

CHAPTER 3

FALLEN HEROES

"Preparing for the '69 Rose Bowl was a lot of pressure. The perfect break was playing with childhood friends, teasing them about running the wrong routes, them telling me the pass was not well thrown, everyone laughing."
Rex Kern

S hortly after deciding to write a book to honor the men and woman who helped me on my way, I realized too many of them had passed on. While it was important for the living to know how I felt about them, it was also important to remember those who could not read my thoughts. I refer to them as fallen heroes.

* * *

Reverend Larry Hard was the minister of the Sixth Avenue Methodist church.

When I was with him, I just felt I was in the presence of God. If there is a better compliment for a person, what would it be?

In person, one-on-one, or in small groups, he was humble, kind, and sensitive. In the pulpit, he was a strong and powerful presence.

When I made my decision to follow Christ, he was our minister. He became my guide. As he saw my growth and sincerity, he gave me the opportunity to be involved in speaking at services. At first I was hesitant, but I believed in him more than I believed in myself. *If he thinks I can do it, he is probably right*, I thought. Maybe he saw me getting out of line and smoothly guided me back, though I never realized he was doing it.

Outside of church, he loved to rehash the games.

When I learned that the Methodist Church had a philosophy of relocating ministers every few years, I was deeply disappointed. I had assumed he would be part of my life forever. I later discovered he had led the Methodist church in Edon before coming to Lancaster. He went to Lima and asked me to speak to his new congregation. He eventually moved to Westerville and Kettering before retiring.

He died April 11, 2014. His obituary read, "He was dearly loved as a father, brother, husband, minister, and friend. His loving spirit, warmth, and humor will be missed." One of the people he guided wrote, "What a gift to this world Larry was."

Amen.

★ ★ ★

Fritz Reed played football, basketball, and baseball. He was a member of the class of 1966, and we played two years together in all three sports.

In football, he was so good he was a cocaptain in the North-South All-Star game. He was overshadowed as an end because the Ohio Lineman of the Year, Mike Baughman, played at the other end spot. One game the defense dictated that we go to Fritz, and he delivered, something like six or eight catches. I was not surprised when Harvard moved him to tackle because he had quick feet and was very intelligent. The Ivy League did not have six five, 260-pound tackles like Dave Foley and Rufus Mayes at Ohio State. Actually, Mayes was a converted tight end himself. Today they all sound small.

On the basketball team, Fritz was an early substitute on the 1966 team that played in the state tournament. Both Paul Callahan and Bill Grein were a bit on the thin side. When Coach Hill wanted a more physical presence inside, or there was foul trouble, Fritz got the call and delivered.

Fritz was the catcher on the baseball team. When he was on the bases, he used an aggressive slide. He slid on his right hip like everyone else, but his left foot was straight up in the air. I was afraid the infielders on the other team would get hurt, so they must have been very conscious of the risk.

Fritz went to Harvard and played football. Like all freshmen at the time, he was ineligible. As a sophomore, he started at end, just as he did for three years at LHS.

As a junior, he was moved to tackle. According to the book *The Game: Harvard, Yale, and America in 1968*, by George Howe Colt, Reed was none too pleased by the move. "I thought tackles did nothing but grunt, and groan and just plow ahead," he told one reporter. On the way out to practice, he often said, "Well, I guess I'm down here with the farm animals again." But he excelled at the position of left tackle for two years.

Beside him, at left guard, was a kid named Jones from Texas, who was interested in acting. When Jones left after practice for rehearsal, Reed liked to shout, "Are you bolting so you can do that 'to-be-or-not-to-be-(stuff)?"

Tommy Lee Jones, described as "hulking" at 195 pounds, paid no attention and went on to a very successful career in television and movies. But first he was a guard for Harvard.

On November 23, 1968, when most of the country was focused on number two Ohio State versus number four Michigan for the Rose Bowl berth, the Ivy League was talking about Harvard playing Yale the same day. There was good reason.

Though both were unbeaten, Yale was heavily favored due to their two stars, quarterback Brian Dowling and running back Calvin Hill.

The day before the game, an article in the *Harvard Crimson* discussed how two players new to the position were playing well at tackle and might be essential to beating Yale in "the game."

"Switching Fritz (Reed) to tackle was probably the most significant move we made at the beginning of the year," said head coach John Yovicsin. "Fritz's play at tackle is one of the big reasons we are undefeated," the coach added.

"Fritz is quick enough to get everything done," said offensive line coach Jim Feula. "He can handle any man he faces, does a terrific job on downfield blocking, and has the knowledge and confidence to make the blocking calls."

The next day Yale was leading 29–13, when Reed's quickness played a significant role. With just a few minutes remaining, Fritz recovered a teammate's fumble and rambled for a twenty-six-yard gain to continue a drive.

After Harvard scored a touchdown, making the score 29–19, they went for the two-point conversion. If they made it, all they had to do in forty-two seconds was recover an onside kick, score a touchdown, and make the two-point conversion to tie the game. It was a longshot, but it was a shot.

A pass interference penalty moved the ball to the 1.5 yard line. Future lawyer Reed made a strong case for a run by Gus Crim, a Lancaster nemesis during his high school days at Upper Arlington. Fritz wanted the play run behind himself and Tommy Lee Jones. Reed, Jones, and Crim did their jobs. 29–21.

Miraculously, the game ended in a tie. For full details, read George Howe Colt's fine book, *The Game*.

The next edition of *The Harvard Crimson* carried the now famous headline "Harvard Beats Yale, 29–29."

Personally, I like the score 50–14, Ohio State, but the old Golden Gale Fritz Reed was a big part of a great game as well.

After graduating from Harvard, having made All-Ivy and All-East in football, and graduating from Ohio State Law School, Fritz became chief financial officer for Wendy's International. When he passed away too soon at fifty-nine, he was a business consultant for Development Specialist, Inc.

★　★　★

George Hickman was our Sunday school teacher at a very important time in my life, soon after I had accepted Christ.

★　★　★

Joe Edwards was a west sider I did not know well from elementary school, but we became close friends at General Sherman Junior High.

There was no seventh-grade football team. Seventh graders had to make the eighth-grade team. Joe went out for the team and sat on the bench, with most of the other seventh graders. I joined the Hocking Hornets in the peewee league and actually got to play.

We became friends on the seventh-grade basketball team, coached by Mr. John Holland. I remember a competition we had over several years to see who could jump higher. Who could touch the net? Who could touch higher on the net? Who could touch the rim? On snow days, I would call Joe and say, "I'll call Mr. Holland to see if he will open the gym. Can you come?" He'd come if he could.

In high school, Joe played football as a defensive end and backup tight end and ran track. He got caught in a numbers crunch at the varsity level of basketball. We only played one sport together, but we were inseparable the rest of the time, often double-dating.

Like his older brother, Johnny, Joe went to Ohio University. When I had time off at Ohio State, we would spend time together.

I remember as a sophomore being home for a short time and calling to ask if he could get a couple of guys to catch some passes for me. We had a Rose Bowl coming up, and I wanted to be sharp.

It was relaxing to play with childhood friends, teasing them about running the wrong routes, them telling me the pass was not well thrown, everyone laughing. Preparing for the Rose Bowl was a lot of work and pressure. This was the perfect break before returning to serious preparation.

After college I would see him when I returned home. Once Joe, his wife Karen, and some friends came to Baltimore for a Colts game and dinner at the Golden Arm restaurant, founded by legendary Colt Johnny Unitas and his Colt teammate Bobby Boyd.

In about 1994, Nancy and I moved back to Columbus, and I was listening to the morning news. There was a report that a young Lancaster policeman had been killed in a car chase. It was Joe's son Chad. I called immediately. It was a sad conversation. Like Joe, Chad was full of life.

Joe graduated from OU and had a successful career as a real estate appraiser and many nonprofessional interests. He loved the outdoors, horses, and was a private pilot. At sixty, he began to run in earnest. At sixty-five, he ran in the Boston Marathon. He loved people, and he loved God.

We spent time together just before he died on May 6, 2020. I miss my friend.

* * *

Earl Jones was my high school football coach and much more.

Coach Jones graduated from Granville High School in 1949, with eleven letters in football, basketball, and baseball, then attended Miami (Ohio) to play football for two College Football Hall of Fame coaches, Woody Hayes and Ara Parseghian. Coach and his wife of sixty-nine years, Barbara, moved to Lancaster, where Earl taught and served as assistant football coach. When he was elevated to head coach in 1964, the team tied for the Central Ohio League championship. The Gales won it outright in 1965 and again in 1966. In both 1964 and 1965, he was named COL Coach of the Year. Many other honors followed. He was the first coach inducted into the Lancaster High School Athletic Hall of Honor in 2019.

I remember him most for being genuinely interested in education. My parents taught me a great deal, but they were not academic people and did not emphasize education at home. I did not know how to study, and I especially dreaded standardized tests, like the SAT and the ACT, which always seemed to be held Saturday morning after a Friday-night football game!

Earl Jones and his assistant Jim Posey tutored me. When they took me on a trip to look at Eastern Kentucky as preparation for the recruiting process, they grilled me both ways on my classes. I may not have enjoyed it at the time, but I did realize—and always remembered—that they cared about me as a person and a quarterback.

Coach's son Eric Jones quoted his father as saying, "Rex could hide the ball like no one." That was a skill my junior high coach, John Holland, first taught me, and Coach Jones enhanced it during one-on-one practices in his backyard.

In the summer of 1965, I played American Legion baseball in the summer and missed several football workouts. When time permitted, I convinced our receivers—Mike Baughman, Fritz Reed, Joe Edwards, and others—to join me running routes at Rising Park. Coaches were not permitted to observe such workouts, but frequently Coach Jones would critique what we had done. We playfully referred to him as "Earl the Squirrel," implying he had disguised himself and climbed up a tree to watch.

In all seriousness, I owe Coach Earl Jones a debt of gratitude for two football careers.

First, for my college career, he developed me as a quarterback. I was able to start at Ohio State for Woody Hayes as a sophomore and be part of a national championship team. We won a Rose Bowl, two Big Ten championships, and twenty-seven of twenty-nine games in three years. That is more than anyone could ask.

Second, NFL scouts did not believe in me as a quarterback but drafted me as an athlete, someone who might be able to contribute at several positions. Fortunately, I also played safety on defense for Earl Jones. The fundamentals he taught me for that position enabled me to play cornerback for four more years, another football career, before the doctors ruled me ineligible to continue.

Thank you, Coach.

Earl Jones died on August 31, 2019, at the age of eighty-eight. He had lived in Lancaster since 1953. The Coach Earl and Barbara Jones Press Box was built at Fulton Field in 2020.

★ ★ ★

Jim Posey was my junior high physical education teacher as well as the offensive and defensive line coach for the high school varsity football team. He certainly looked like a football lineman—big but not fat.

I would do anything to impress Mr. Posey. He was the kind of teacher you could go to with a problem. Around him, I was always on my best behavior.

He suggested I run for student council president. That did not sound interesting, but he persisted. "It will be good exposure," he said.

"I couldn't do that," I replied.

"I'll help you write the speech," he countered.

Then it occurred to me! The girl who had just dumped me was running. I ran to beat her more than to be elected. It would be a "revenge" election. Not my finest hour, but my father always insisted on the whole truth.

A few days later, I was called in to see the principal, who said that a few of my west-side friends were going around telling students to vote for me, or they would get beaten up.

I was shocked. It was the first time I was accused of something I actually did not do. Yes, I won the election.

I was unable to locate Mr. Posey's obituary. I have no further details on his death but still wanted to include him in this chapter.

*   *   *

George Hill was our basketball coach, who gave a team with no returning starters from a mediocre 1965 campaign the gift of the wonderful 1966 basketball season. An entire chapter is devoted to that team and our coach.

*   *   *

Ed Klinker and I were in the same home room. He kept me up on the high school gossip; I told him what was going on with the sports teams. He was a fan, but not a player. He was probably my closest friend other than the athletes.

Before one game, he paid a price for being a fan. He was in the restroom, and some visiting students came in and said, "Are you a friend of Kern's?"

When he replied that he was, they hassled him, and I guess you would say assaulted him. Then they said, "Give him that from us."

I do wish they had delivered the message personally. My father's boxing lessons might have evened things up a bit.

By the end of our sophomore year, we were in driver's ed.

together, and he taught me a new word, *turfing*. Eventually, I had to ask what it meant. Eddie said he carried a blanket in the back seat of his Rambler just in case he had the opportunity to neck with his date. Eddie helped me expand my vocabulary. After high school he went to Capital University, outside Columbus. I went to visit him, told some students who I was and who I was looking for, and eventually found him. We enjoyed a few hours together. Later he told me that his stock went up because of me. Who knew Capital students would be interested in a freshman at Ohio State? I later learned how many people around Ohio care about the Buckeyes.

Years later, our son John-Ryan, who lives in Dublin, just north of Columbus, told me a man at church had introduced himself by saying he went to high school with me. When I heard the name, I immediately said, "That's Eddie Boy!" Many times, four Kerns, two Klinkers, and their pastor spent time together when we visited Columbus.

Boyd Edwin Klinker Jr. died of lung cancer and bone cancer on July 29, 2020, just after his seventy-first birthday.

★ ★ ★

Terry Webb made the Lancaster varsity basketball team his junior year, missed the first part of his senior year for a reason we can't remember, joined the team in midseason, and immediately improved our talent level as our primary ball handler and a regular scorer. He became more effective as Coach Hill showed us how to work together and was the only Gale to be named to the district, regional, and state finals teams. There will be more about him in the chapter on the 1966 basketball team. For now, let's just say that Lancaster does not beat Columbus Linden McKinley and Columbus East to go to the state tournament without him.

Terry was easy to like, but he was not easy to get to know. He did not seem comfortable talking about himself, his interests, or his family. My primary connection with him, other than basketball, was on snow days. When one of those came along, he liked to walk the short distance to our house and see if I wanted to play Monopoly. We battled like tycoons and wished for more snow days.

From Lancaster High School, Terry went into the Army. After about nine and a half months, he was sent to Vietnam as a member of the 173rd Engineering Company, 173rd Airborne Brigade, United States Army. Corporal Terry E. Webb was killed in action two and a half months later in Saigon, South Vietnam, at the age of twenty. Rick Torrence, Dave Thimmes, Earl Pierce, Frank Kluz, Randy Groff, and I were honored to serve as his pallbearers.

Terry Webb was a friend, a fine basketball player, and a true American hero.

CHAPTER 4

MY FAVORITE HIGH SCHOOL SEASON: JUNIOR YEAR BASKETBALL, 1966

"Two seconds remaining, score tied, Rex was fouled. I remember think-ing "I can't even feel my arms." But Rex had a confidence and faith in himself that average young players did not. We were glad he was there."
Bill Grein. LHS 57- Cols. Linden-McKinley 56, 1966 regional semi-final.

As mentioned in the Preface, with the aid of a video of the Columbus Linden-McKinley game, several conversations with then seniors Paul Callahan and Bill Grein, and articles in the *Lancaster Eagle-Gazette* and the *Columbus Dispatch*, Lee Caryer wrote this chapter. I agreed with his suggestion that it might be difficult for me to be objective.

"In November, one or two games over .500 would have been hopeful. Then they battled for the Central Ohio League title. As the tournament started, a couple of victories would have closed out a big year." Ron Johnson wrote those words in the *Lancaster-Eagle Gazette* as the 1966 Lancaster basketball team, with a 17–5 record and four tournament victories, prepared to face powerful Columbus Linden-McKinley in the regional semifinals at the Fairgrounds Coliseum in Columbus, Ohio.

How did a team that lost all five starters from a 10–9 team in 1965 get to the 1966 regional, much less win it, against two powerful teams from the Columbus City League? As the first Lancaster basketball team to play in the state tournament in its forty-four-year existence, were they lucky or good? If they were good, how good? What do we know about the players, on and off the court? Were they true student-athletes? Did five of the top six players really compete in three sports each?

It is time to ask the players and read some clippings to answer those questions.

"The team from the previous year, 1965, should have been the first to take Lancaster to the state basketball tournament," said Bill Grein, one of five players who contributed in every game in 1966. "They had size, major college recruits, everything you needed, but were just not coached to play together. The coach favored one player, which was part of the problem. Against a good opponent, with just a few seconds left, he called time-out and designed a scoring play. Each player was assigned a job on the floor, but no one was assigned to take the ball out. The referees called delay of game. Lancaster lost the ball and the game.

"Rex Kern was the only sophomore on the team," continued Grein. "He and I played half of the reserve game, then dressed varsity and were allowed to play as much as two quarters of the varsity game, if needed. Toward the end of the season, I was not playing at all. Since I was going to be a starting pitcher on the baseball team, I asked permission to leave the basketball team and start playing baseball. The coach said how much the team needed me, and I gladly agreed to stay on the basketball team for the rest of the tournament. The day of our first tournament game, the coach threw me off the team and told the other players how selfish I was—that I did not care about the team.

"You could say his people skills were lacking.

"That team lost its first tournament game, continuing a long-standing tradition at Lancaster," said Grein.

New Coach

The officials at Lancaster High School decided the team needed a new coach. They found a former Portsmouth High School three-sport athlete who was coaching in Alabama, with attractive credentials and a desire to return to Ohio.

George Hill, thirty-five, came to Lancaster with an established resume as a player and coach. He lettered in all three years as a basketball player at Auburn, leading the team in free-throw shooting in 1951, making sixty-one of seventy-six, .803. He graduated from Auburn in 1951 after being named honorable mention All-American by the *Sporting News*. Hill coached Pensacola Escambia to the Florida final four in 1961, 1962, and 1963, and Mobile Murphy to the Alabama final four in 1965. The selection committee had found an accomplished coach.

"He called a meeting the first week of school and said, 'If you don't play football, you are going out for cross country to get into shape,'" Grein recalled. "We tried to tell him we needed to work on our shooting, but he said, 'I can teach you to shoot in two weeks, but I want you to be in shape. You are known as the Lancaster

Golden Gales, but you are going to be known as the Lancaster Golden Gazelles!'"

"Paul 'Sticks' Callahan, six three and about one hundred sixty pounds; Terry Webb, our five seven guard; and I were starters that year after taking cross country very seriously, along with the others who did not play football. Our other two starters, Rex and Mike Baughman, played football with Fritz Reed, who was our sixth man in basketball.

"When the basketball season started, we were all in excellent shape. We won games early in the season with a full-court press, when other teams tired in the fourth quarter," concluded Grein.

"Coach Hill was committed to building a program," Captain Paul Callahan remembered. "He promoted the team and sold five hundred season tickets, not including students. He organized the pep club and took speaking engagements around town to create enthusiasm. Most important to me, he convinced the booster club to provide money for the Rebounder, which he had found valuable as a coach.

"It was a piece of equipment that required you to learn the proper technique for rebounding, meaning with two hands. It could also be used for tip drills, in situations when it was impossible to get two hands on the ball.

"Put it this way," Callahan said. "In 1965 I was a sub with small hands, never starting a game on a ten and nine team. In 1966 I set a school record for rebounding. What I know for certain is that when I became an assistant high school basketball coach I convinced the head coach that the team needed that piece of equipment. He got it and thanked me."

The Season Begins

The football players were not yet in basketball shape, and LH struggled with Riverview at home in the opening game, trailing 39-41 after three quarters. The final was 57–53, Gales. Team shooting was surprisingly good – 53 percent from the field and 79 percent at the line. Senior Dan Williams led the scoring with sixteen points.

"Coach asked me to jump center, then move outside with Rex," said Callahan. "I think what Coach Hill wanted was to get what he perceived as the best players on the floor. I had never played guard, though the experience helped when I went to Louisville and had to play there. I figured I was holding down the fort until Terry Webb was eligible. He was five seven and a natural point guard, but he was ineligible the first semester."

Two lopsided victories followed. Bill Grein's 24 points and nine rebounds led the team past Circleville, 87–50, and Mike Baughman led the scorers with 19 in an 87–46 win over Fairfield Union.

Visiting Miami Trace, a team with size and experience, shaped up as a challenge in the next game, and led by three at the half. The final sixteen minutes were much different, with the home team scoring forty-four, Trace twenty-seven. Grein had twenty points, and Kern sixteen. Paul Callahan seemed to have recovered from his bout with the flu, grabbing ten rebounds.

Chillicothe, "rated a strong favorite to battle for the COL title," by the *Eagle-Gazette*, came to town on December 10 and fell, 60–55. Grein led the scoring with twenty-one points and added seven rebounds in a good start to the conference season. Foul shooting was strong.

The next night, the Gales went to Portsmouth and fought through physical play and an abusive crowd to win, 81–68.

Ron Johnson, with the *Eagle Gazette*, reported, "Victory in such a well-executed fashion over the perennially tough Trojans also indicated Lancaster has finally shaken the doldrums, which the school has been mired in for over a decade—as far as the cage sport is concerned."

He later added, "Portsmouth came out in the second half (trailing 32–20) determined to either win or cripple ... Grein and Kern spent so much time at the line they wore a spot in the wood." Each player sank thirteen free throws. The team was thirty-nine of forty-six on free throws and shot fifty-seven percent from the field, showing poise and patience in running the offense. Callahan battled inside to add twenty-six points and eleven boards.

The Auburn Shuffle

About that offense: Coach Hill believed in the Auburn Shuffle, which he had played in college. "The kids don't know who is going to get that good percentage shot, and they work a little harder, running cuts, setting screens, and moving the ball to the open player," he said later in the season. "Coaches up this way haven't seen it much either," Hill added.

In a separate article the same week, Johnson wrote, "All of them (players on the team) have tremendous character ... and are just plain 'characters,' the kind you like to be around and know." He added the following qualities in explaining their success: "Faith in Coach George Hill, which is reciprocated ... good coaching, strong fan support ... athletic ability ... guts, pride, stamina, and confidence."

December 17, 1965, the Gales traveled to Ironton, looking for their seventh straight victory and their second COL. win. LHS had no problem with the Tigers, winning 79–58. Kern led the scoring with 26 points. Callahan pitched in with 17. It was the first time Lancaster had opened the season with seven straight victories since the 1926–1927 season, nearly forty years ago.

First loss

After Christmas, the trip to Athens was not as successful. Lancaster was tied with the home team, 40–40, after three quarters, but was outscored 15-25 in the last quarter. Rex Kern remembers the team having difficulty stopping Mike Wren, son of OU baseball coach Bob Wren, on defense, and the Gales struggled to score against the Athens zone on offense. At least it was not a conference game.

But the first game of the New Year was, and Lancaster lost a home game to Zanesville, January 7, 50–57. The team could not come back from a 10–21 first quarter. It is difficult to win with 50 points.

Powerful Newark visited next, and the Gales were ready for a challenge, shooting 56 percent from the field in a 59–54 victory. The scoring was spread among eight players; Kern led with 21.

The following night, January 15, Lancaster beat Circleville again, this time 90–63. LHS had beaten the Tigers eleven straight in the series. Everyone got to play, and ten Gales scored.

By now most of the easy games were over. In the future, the bench would get shorter, there would be less playing time for some players, and five-seven Terry Webb would be eligible. Webb would provide ballhandling, speed, and quickness, taking away playing time from early season contributors.

The way Steve Macioci, Warren Ticknor, Rick Torrence, Dan Williams, and Paul Kendrick responded to this lack of time on the court showed they were true champions.

"They never complained, practiced hard, and gave the starters good competition in scrimmages," remembers Captain Callahan. "I remember being happy that Coach Hill kept so many seniors. We only had two juniors: Rex and Warren Ticknor. Often a new coach will play young players just to give them experience for the future. Coach valued experience because he wanted to win right away, but he had to find young men with the kind of character to stay the course.

"I may not have noticed it much at the time, but when I went to the University of Louisville and found myself behind two NBA first-round draft choices, I learned how difficult the job of practicing is when you probably will not play. They were great teammates, and their many contributions were valued," said Callahan.

At Marietta, the Golden Gales outplayed their hosts in three quarters but lost the game in the third quarter, when they were outscored 7-19. With the final score, 64-71, LHS "won" the other quarters 57–52. Too bad that did not matter.

Having lost three of their last five games, it was difficult to be optimistic on the bus to Chillicothe, where Lancaster had lost sixteen straight. On January 28, that number became seventeen straight after a 47-50 loss. Terry Webb played his first game of the season, and contributed 11 points, but the scoring was a season low.

"It was at times like this," remembers Captain Callahan, "that assistant coach 'Corky' Sparks was especially valuable to the team. After a tough game or a demanding practice, he knew what to say to get you back up, excited about the future and not upset about the past."

The next night, Lancaster dominated visiting Portsmouth, 75–48. The offense was clicking, led by Grein's 26 points and Baughman's 16.

Poor shooting—38 percent from the field—and lethargic defense—Ironton made 16 of 24 field goals in the first half—caused LHS to look up to the visitors most of the game. The Gales grabbed the lead for the first time with 4:28 to go in the third quarter and finished strong to win, 72–59. Callahan led the rebounding effort with an impressive twenty off the boards. He seemed to have his eye on the school record.

Balanced scoring, 51 percent from the field, and stingy defense were the keys to avenging their only home loss with a victory at Zanesville, 57–50. Strong board work by Callahan, fourteen rebounds, and Baughman, ten, helped as well. It was the first time LHS had won three straight since the seventh game of the season.

But the streak ended at Newark, 59-60. An eight-point third

quarter and an offense shooting 41 percent were too much to overcome. Could the Gales start another streak?

Oh Yeah

In the final game of the regular season, Lancaster earned another revenge win, beating Marietta, 61–54. The shooting was far below par at 38 percent, but the Gales found a way. Grein (16) and Webb (15) led a balanced attack. LHS beat every COL opponent at least once for the first time since 1949—the last time the school went to the regionals.

Closing the book on the regular season, LHS was 13–5, 6–4 in the COL, good for third behind cochampions Zanesville and Newark. Kern led the balanced scoring with 14.6, followed by 14.4 from Grein, 11.7 from Webb, 11.1 for Baughman, and 10.3 from Callahan. Kern was believed to be the first LHS player to score in double figures every game.

Callahan set a school record with 203 rebounds, 11.3 per game. Grein was second, and Baughman was third.

Kern led in assists, steals, and free-throw shooting, with Grein second in all three. Grein led in field-goal shooting at 52.1, followed by Kern (49.2) and Baughman (47.2). The team shot 48 percent from the floor.

Tourney Time

The sectionals were next, at Paint Valley High School. Lancaster had not advanced through the sectionals since 1949.

Lancaster set a school scoring record, defeating 7–12 Hillsboro, 98–66. The next night, they became to first Lancaster team in ten years to defeat Chillicothe twice in one season, with a 76–66 win. Kern, 23 points, Callahan, 19, and Webb, 17, led the scoring. Captain Callahan accepted the trophy for winning the sectional. "I remember being stunned. I had never accepted a trophy for a team."

The district tournament was held in Athens, Ohio, in the Grover Center, a big step up from Paint Valley High School. Several of the Gales had played American Legion baseball at OU, but state tournament basketball in a college arena is a different story.

The first challenge was Portsmouth, facing them for the third time that season. An age-old adage in basketball has to do with how difficult it is to beat any team three times in one season. An adage in southern Ohio is, "When you get ready to play Portsmouth, buckle your chinstrap. It will be a physical game."

There were three keys to the 73–57 Lancaster victory: First, the referees called the fouls, and the Gales made their shots, 39 of 46. Second, with Callahan grabbing thirteen rebounds and every starter getting from seven to four more, LHS had a twenty-rebound advantage. Third, the press, led by Kern and Grein, took Portsmouth out of its offense and created some loose balls. Put them all together, and the result is a trip to the district finals.

Wellston was not often mentioned among the basketball powers in Ohio, but that year they were ranked number eight in Class AA, favored to win the game and advance to the regional.

"We did not think like that," recalled Paul Callahan. "We just knew we had another game and that Coach Hill was going to tell us how to win it."

Again, Hill did just that. Yet again, the players made the plan work.

The first quarter was back and forth, with the lead changing hands numerous times. Lancaster took over in the second quarter to take a 45–34 lead to the locker room. In the second half, the number eight team in the state could not challenge, because Baughman, Grein, and Callahan dominated the boards, 48–21, and Terry Webb dominated the scoring with 29 points, including

13 of 15 at the line. The 84–72 victory took the Gales to the regional tournament for the first time since 1949.

"This memory is much clearer," said Callahan about accepting the trophy. "I was accepting it for the team."

In the sectionals and district, over four games, the Gales had an incredible 195–95 margin over their opponents in rebounding, but after every step the competition became more challenging. Rebounds would be more difficult to recover.

In the sectional, Terry Webb made 28 of 32 free throws—87.5 percent.

It appeared that two outstanding Columbus City League powers would be ahead in the regional tournament. Could the dream continue? More and more Lancaster fans seemed to think so. The players wisely worked hard and listened to their coach.

"Our basketballs at LHS had narrow seams," Captain Callahan remembers. "Somehow Coach Hill had learned that wide-seamed balls were used in Columbus, and he had found a nearby school that used that type of ball. So, before the Linden-McKinley game, he took me out of school to get the wide-seamed basketballs he had arranged for us to use in practice. He was demanding of his players, but he demanded a great deal from himself as well."

Regional at the Fairgrounds

In the first game of the regional, March 16, 1966, Columbus Linden-McKinley was a major challenge. The Panthers were a tall, athletic team, with a 19–2 record and only one loss in the powerful Columbus City League—to champion Columbus East. The Panthers had advanced with a decisive 56–34 victory over Pleasant View and had five starters averaging in double figures.

LHS players with the ability to look into the future would have had more reason for concern. The following season, with most of its key players returning, Linden won the state title by demolishing Cleveland East Tech, 88–56, in the final game. Senior Skip Young would be named first-team All-Ohio and have a fine career at Florida State. Senior Jim Cleamons would sign with Ohio State, be named Big Ten MVP while leading the Bucks to the Big Ten title, then play nine seasons in the NBA. Head Coach Vince Chickerella would become coach at Capital University and be inducted into the Ohio Basketball Hall of Fame (2014), beside his former player, Cleamons (2008). Lancaster seemed overmatched.

The Golden Gales knew differently because they believed in Coach George Hill. They got into shape because he demanded it and saw the results. Each was capable of playing a full game while applying pressure defense. They were individually unselfish and open to his directions to become an unselfish team. They believed his offense, the Auburn Shuffle, would produce good shots when they were patient. Since the game after Terry Webb joined the team, they were 8–1, the only blemish being a one-point loss at COL champion Newark. Without Webb, they had lost at home to Zanesville, 50–57. With him, they reversed the score on the road. He made a difference.

Let the game begin!

In the first quarter, the Gales found that it would be difficult to score inside. Shots were blocked or altered, leading to fast breaks. Lancaster trailed, 12–18.

"We had never played all-Black teams until Linden," remembered senior forward Mike Baughman. "Then we played three in a row. I can't speak for the others, but I felt intimidated at the time."

Baughman made 56 percent of his shots over that three-game stretch. He may have felt intimidated, but did not play like it.

In the second quarter, Webb scored on four straight possessions: fast-break layup, long jumper from the right side, foul shot, and drive on the left side through traffic for a basket. That streak cut the deficit to four points, 22-26. When Linden went to 2-3 zone,

Lancaster did not react well. Webb shot an air ball and there were two turnovers. Fortunately, Linden did not capitalize. Patient offense led to a three-point basket by Kern. Just kidding—it was only worth two at that time. Linden made a layup, then Webb drilled a jumper almost as long as Kern's. Lancaster was down at the half by only two, 28-30.

Randy Groff remembered a play during the game in which "Terry Webb was tripped on a fast break, slid on his backside down the court while dribbling the ball, got up, and made a layup. The crowd was ecstatic, and the Fairgrounds Coliseum was shaking with excitement."

To begin the second half, Webb was fouled on a cut and converted the free throw. Then Linden got hot, and the Gales cooled off. Suddenly the score was 32-45, with 2:45 to play in the third. The situation looked gloomy. Kern missed a shot but got his own rebound and made two foul shots. With 1:54 to go in the quarter, Webb deflected a Linden pass. Kern dove into a pile with two Panthers, came out dribbling the ball down court and hit a pull-up from seventeen feet. The next possession, Rex hit another deep basket. In less than three minutes, Lancaster had cut the lead almost in half, 40-47.

Linden got the fourth quarter tip, missed a layup, then a rebound shot. Paul Callahan grabbed the second shot in traffic, fired a perfect outlet to Kern, who took one dribble, saw Baughman ahead, and threw a chest pass for a layup.

"I had been throwing post patterns to Mike all season in football, so it was second nature," Kern said, fifty-four years later. They never did it better on the gridiron.

With 1:58 to go in the game, the score was tied, 52–52. Linden beat the trap for a basket, then Cleamons made a steal, was fouled, and converted a one-and-one. The Gales were down, 52-56, with 0:40 to go. After a Webb turnover, the defense caused a jump ball and recovered the tip. Webb missed a runner, but Bill Grein rebounded and made a put-back, 54-56, 0:16 on the clock. "That was huge!" recalled Callahan. Pressure defense caused a turnover, and Linden switched to a zone. This time the Gales were ready. Webb was left open and swished his jumper from deep. After Kern drew a charging foul, Webb was cut off on a drive and found Kern, who drove and was fouled with 0:02 to play.

"I remember thinking, *I can't even feel my arms*," said Bill Grein. "But Rex had a confidence and faith in himself that the average young player did not. We were glad he was there."

As Gale historians know, Kern hit the winning free throw. He missed the second, Linden missed a heave, and the fans rushed the court to celebrate a 57–56 victory. Despite Paul Callahan's eight rebounds, Linden dominated the boards, 37–27. Free-throw shooting was almost even—10 for 10 by Linden, 9 of 12 for Lancaster. Field-goal shooting was even closer—24 of 54 for the winners, 23 of 54 for Linden. Five Golden Gales made one basket or more; every single basket was a game winner. Webb had 19 points, Kern 17—all but two in the second half—Baughman 13.

Three nights later, Lancaster faced Columbus East, undefeated in the Columbus City League, conqueror of Linden-McKinley and ranked number ten in the state. The East Tigers had advanced by crushing Cambridge, 64–44.

"Before we played East, every one of their players was dunking in the layup line," Bill Grein noted. "We actually stood and watched them. In the locker room, Coach Hill really chewed us out and got our minds on what we had to do. He said, 'They won the pregame, but we are going to win the basketball game.'"

Lancaster started fast and kept it up. In the first quarter, it was 19–11, then 39–31 at the half.

Though the Gales never trailed, the third quarter did get dicey. East scored 11 straight points, taking the score to 45–43. After Kern hit two foul shots—he finished 9 of 10 at the line—Lancaster moved to a 60–48 margin at 3:26. The coaches began to substitute so every player could participate.

After the game, Coach Hill said, "Our press worked well enough to get the ball back as often as we lost the ball to their press." Fortunately for both teams, turnovers were not kept.

Some statistics were surprising. Though fouls were very even— Lancaster had 20, East 19—free throws were lopsided. Lancaster was 25 of 32, while East was 13 of 23. Hill mentioned the team had three players over 80 percent and a team average of 70 percent going into the game.

More surprising was the 33–31 Lancaster edge in rebounding, a significant improvement from the Linden game. Callahan and Grein led the way with 8; Baughman had 7. Reed chipped in 4, and Kern had 3.

Besides free-throw shooting, Lancaster had a significant margin from the field. While Lancaster made almost 50 percent, with 19 of 40, East took 60 shots to make 19, 32 percent.

Offensively, Webb led all scorers with 18. Callahan and Kern added 17, Baughman had 9, and Grein contributed 6. Kern and Webb dominated their backcourt opponents, allowing only 4 points in total.

Captain Callahan accepted the trophy for winning the regional on behalf of the team and the school. "It was my best feeling in athletics to that point," he said.

The city of Lancaster was excited about being the first Fairfield County team to play in the state tournament. The fact that the other teams waiting for them—Dayton Chaminade (ranked number one in Ohio), Warren Harding (ranked sixth), and Toledo Libbey (ranked fifth)—were all 24–1 seemed irrelevant.

The *Eagle-Gazette* printed an editorial written by editor Perrin Hazelton titled "We're Proud of Our Gales," which said, in part, "Truly a notable achievement for a courageous and highly competitive crew of young athletes ... a momentous uplift for the school and the city these boys represent."

The enthusiasm felt great to the players, who remember that feeling today. There were signs in every shop and banners on every business supporting the team. With eight hundred Class AA schools in Ohio, the hometown team was in the top 0.50 percent! Unfortunately, there were only 1,250 tickets for each of the four schools.

After much deliberation, the Lancaster Board of Education established this priority for the scarce tickets: parents of varsity and reserve players; reserve players; all cheerleaders, though only six of the twelve varsity cheerleaders were allowed on the court to cheer; 125 for pep club members and season-ticket holders; 375 for students, distributed in a lottery; 520 for season-ticket holders; 40 for coaches and physical education instructors around the city; 2 each for office personnel; 60 for high school faculty and personnel, plus people who worked the gates for home games; 12 for news media; and board of education members, police and sheriffs, and the mayor.

With that, the tickets were gone. The only other way to be admitted to St. John Arena was to have a friend or relative in the allotment and convince that person not to go.

Semifinal opponent Toledo Libbey had beaten second-ranked and favored Lima Shawnee to advance. For the season, Libbey scored 74 points a game and allowed only 45. Lancaster would need a good game to beat them—maybe as good as the Linden game.

Not to Be

After a 4–4 start, Libbey was ahead the rest of the game. "At least nine times Lancaster lacked only a basket of catching up," wrote the *Columbus Dispatch* reporter. They were down 36-37 in the third quarter, and 42-44 in the fourth, when a 12–2 Libbey spurt sealed the game. The final score was 52-56.

Looking back, there were several key factors in the loss:

1. The best player in the game was Libbey's Joe Cooke, a second-team All-Ohio guard who scored 29 points on 12 of 22 shooting and grabbed eight rebounds. Cooke was no mirage. During three seasons at Indiana, he averaged 18 points a game and later played in the NBA.

2. "He was my man," Kern recalled. "I committed early fouls by trying too hard. Joe Cooke caused me to play the worst game of my high school career." Rex missed the entire third quarter and played only briefly in the fourth before fouling out. In close games, he tended to be at his best in the second half. "If I could go back in time, my mindset would be different. Cooke was too good for me to stop that night. I would have overplayed the passing lane and denied him the ball often, tried to contain him, make him uncomfortable by staying in front after he caught it. No reaching on the dribble—hands straight up on shots but no contact. Hopefully he would have scored a little less. I certainly could have stayed in the game, helped move the ball to the open man, helped on the press, and maybe made a few more points."

3. Lancaster's normally reliable foul shooting did not travel to St. John Arena. The Gales were 18 of 31 on the night. That is seven shots less than they made against East, in only one less attempt.

4. Field-goal shooting was only 17 of 48, 35 percent.

5. Part of the problem was shot selection. Some attempts were blocked, and others were rushed. Terry Webb had 18 points, but several of his shots were blocked. No other Gale had double figures, though Baughman, Callahan, and Kern were close in both points and rebounds. Coach Hill commented after the game that many long shots were taken. With no shot clock and no three-point line, that shows impatience.

6. Bill Grein was reported by the *Dispatch* to be "below par physically," with no explanation. Paul Callahan remembers having

"a bad fall at the beginning of the game, a slight concussion. After the fall, I do not remember the game."

7. Both Grein and Callahan mentioned being in awe of St. John Arena, though that is a challenge every high school player faces in the state tournament.

8. What about Perry Blum? Remember him talking about guarding Rex in fourth grade? Let's say the varsity coach before George Hill gives Blum a fair chance, and if there is an issue, requires him to do better, or he will be off the team. Maybe Blum responds to discipline and takes school, and life, more seriously because basketball means so much to him, or because he was loyal to his teammates. Others have responded to a second chance; Blum never had a first chance. Maybe Blum finds a role as a defensive stopper as a junior, with Webb or Kern getting a rest, or with Kern playing forward. Blum might have helped many times during the year, and he certainly would have helped against Joe Cooke and Libbey.

9. Last, but possibly most important of all, the press, which meant so much to the success of the team during the season, was hardly used. When Libbey lost a lead the next night, champion Dayton Chaminade's press received a good deal of credit for their comeback. Part of that was due to Kern being on the bench. He led the team in steals for the year.

So many things could have been different.

After the Dust Settled

The greatest achievement of the 1966 team was certainly a trip to Columbus for the state tournament, the first for the school in the forty-four-year history of the tournament.

When players throughout the Central Ohio League voted for their All-COL team, every regular starter on the Golden Gales was named on the team, a reflection of individual achievement as well as team cohesiveness based on individual sacrifice.

Rex Kern was named to the five-man first team, Paul Callahan and Mike Baughman to the five-man second team, and Bill Grein and Terry Webb to the seven-man third team. No other school had as many as four players selected. Chillicothe, Marietta, and Newark had three.

The players were not asked to vote for coach of the year. Since the Gales had no starters returning, and every player was greatly improved after a 10–9 season in 1965, Coach George Hill would seem to have received strong support for the honor. When the writers made their selection, however, Coach Don Stahl of Zanesville was named COY.

The writers chose Rex Kern, either first or second on the team in every statistical category except rebounding, for first-team All-COL, and Bill Grein, who had the same distinction and added a runner-up in rebounding, to the second team. Callahan and Baughman made the seven-man third team. Terry Webb was ruled ineligible since he only played five of ten league games. All five Gales were in the top seventeen COL scorers with ten-plus points per game.

Paul Callahan was named Coach and Athlete All-American for basketball, as Mike Baughman had been for football in the fall.

Coach George Hill deserved to be COL Coach of the Year in 1966. Captain Paul Callahan made that clear when he was asked to speak at Coach Hill's funeral less than two months prior to the fifty-year reunion of the 1966 basketball team:

"Fifty years ago, Coach Hill came into our lives," began Callahan. "Little did we know at the time how much of a difference he was going to make to nine seniors and two juniors. We just wish he had made his way to Lancaster sooner.

"Coach made us work harder than we had ever worked before.

We were frustrated at first, trying to learn his system, but we never complained—at least not to him. It did not take long for us to buy in to what he was teaching us—the Auburn Shuffle on offense and full-court pressure defense.

"The season had its ups and downs. We learned valuable lessons along the way.

"For example, after our first road win, some of the players were enjoying themselves, singing loudly and poking fun at our principal, Fred 'Moose' Lowry, on the bus going home. As we were turning on to the road to the high school, Coach told me to tell the players to put on their practice uniforms in the locker room and report to the gym. It was after midnight.

"Coach put us on the baseline and made us run suicide sprints. We ran and ran and ran, until a teammate asked me to ask Coach why we were running.

"When I mustered the courage to ask him, he said, 'Now do you know how to act on the bus?'

"Among our highlights were beating Portsmouth three times in a row; winning sectional, district, and regional titles; becoming the first Lancaster team to play in the state finals; coming from behind to defeat Linden-McKinley in the regional semifinal; and seeing the entire city of Lancaster get behind us during the tournament run.

"None of these things would have happened without Coach Hill.

"On a personal note, I coached boys' and girls' basketball for fifteen years before becoming an athletic director. My goal was to emulate George Hill in teaching my players to love and respect the game of basketball while helping them to become better people.

"At our team's fiftieth reunion, celebrating our trip to the final four, Coach Hill will be missed, but not forgotten. Everyone from that team knows he was the reason for our success.

"Meanwhile, George Hill has a team to coach. I am sure our teammates and team manager who have preceded him—Fritz,

Terry, Steve, Dan, Warren, and Brande—met him at the gates of Heaven and asked when practice starts.

"May God bless you, Coach."

In addition to the basketball ability of their players and guidance of their coach, the 1966 team had two very special qualities.

First, they were truly student-athletes. In college, Kern and Baughman each earned three degrees. Reed earned an undergraduate degree at Harvard and a law degree at Ohio State. Callahan and Paul Kendrick earned two degrees. Bill Grein, Rick Torrence, and most of the others earned college degrees. Asked about the academic achievements of the class, Callahan was quick to say, "Many of those guys were in National Honor Society. I remember being forty-first in the class, and quite a few were ahead of me, plus Warren Ticknor in the 1967 class."

During the tournament, Coach Hill had told reporters, "Nine of our twelve players are on honor role."

There is a carryover from academics to athletics, beginning with intelligence and including dedication and perseverance, which gives smart teams an edge in any game. The Gales had that edge.

Second, the young men were athletes as well as basketball players. Baughman and Kern were stars in football, baseball, and basketball. Reed was a star in football and baseball, and he was a valuable part of the basketball team. Callahan and Grein were both outstanding baseball pitchers, and like the other non-football players they ran cross-country before the basketball season to improve their endurance.

Basketball players with more athleticism and more intelligence start each basketball game with two distinct advantages over any opponent. The 1966 team had both advantages in many games. Ten years later, sports editor Ron Johnson of the *Lancaster Eagle-Gazette* remembered the team he had personally followed in 1966 in a column titled "Just 10 Years Ago."

Here is his understated summary of that team: "Many things

contributed to the year. The kids were class with a capital C, and while highly individualistic, they had an uncanny ability to play together. They had a good coach. You can't take away class."

This is my game winning shot to defeat
Columbus Linden-McKinley in the 1966
regional semi-finals, 57–56.

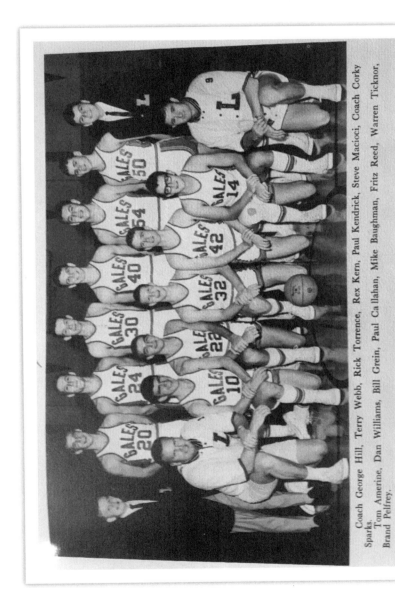

Coach George Hill, Terry Webb, Rick Torrence, Rex Kern, Paul Kendrick, Steve Macioci, Coach Corky Sparks.

Tom Amerine, Dan Williams, Bill Grein, Paul Callahan, Mike Baughman, Fritz Reed, Warren Ticknor, Brand Pelfrey.

I just wish we could also show the three trophies our 1966 Final Four basketball team won.

Head Basketball Coach George Hill

Assistant Coach Corky Sparks

CHAPTER 5

EIGHT MORE HIGH SCHOOL SEASONS

"My teammates and I have always remembered how strong that (1965 football) team was and would have loved to have been in the playoffs together."
Rex Kern

While the 1966 basketball season stands out in terms of team achievement and fan support, I have special memories from every varsity season at Lancaster High School. Here they are in order:

Sophomore football, 1964: I played two quarters in the reserve game and as much as two quarters in the varsity game all season. I earned a varsity letter by playing on special teams—punt and punt return, kickoff and kickoff return teams—plus very limited action as a quarterback. There were a few plays at defensive end that require a story.

In the middle of the season, we were allowing sweeps around one end. A senior, "Jump" Reid, was not playing well. His job as defensive end was to crash across the line, then hold his ground and force the runner inside. Finally, one of the coaches yelled, "We need somebody who is going to hit somebody."

I was one of those players who did not sit during the game when I was not playing. I hung around the coaches so they would notice me and send me in. I was used to being on the field. They wanted a volunteer, so I said, "I'll do it." I grabbed my helmet, the coach nodded, and I ran on the field. I played the rest of the game.

Afterward, I noticed that "Jump" was not too happy with me. As time passed, it became clear that none of the seniors liked me showing up their friend. "Jump" played the rest of the season, but the unwelcome sign popped up from time to time. It was uncomfortable. I did not mind when the last game of the season was at hand. I was ready for basketball.

Lancaster had a tradition of "senior tackle," similar to what Ohio State did. The difference was, instead of seniors hitting a tackling dummy, they chose another player—called a "specimen"—to hit. I heard "Kern" and "specimen" in the same sentence an unusual number of times that day.

So did our assistant coach, Jim Posey. Before the "senior tackle" practice, he stopped at my locker with some extra pads. I had pads underneath my uniform in places I had never worn pads before and double pads elsewhere.

That day about half the senior class got three to five yards away, took a running start, and speared me right in the chest. I never played another down at defensive end, and I never forgot Coach Posey for looking out for me.

The team finished 7–3, tying for the COL title with Newark at 4–1. We beat Newark 32–6, but we lost to Zanesville 16–20. It had been seven years since Lancaster's last Central Ohio League championship. The other two losses came in decisive fashion to Ohio powers Upper Arlington, 7-24, and Bishop Watterson, 8-38.

The Mirage listed the following players as first- or second-team All-COL: Gregg Brown, Mike Christian, Dick Dunkle, John Lynd, Larry McClurg, Jim Notestine, Marcel Page, Fritz Reed, Dave "Jump" Reid, Tom Reid, Don Seifert, Tim Speaks, and Jeff Upp.

Sophomore basketball, 1965: With Bill Grein, I played two quarters of the reserve game and up to two quarters of the varsity game. My role was primarily to keep the bench involved in the game. As Bill said, that team should have been better than 10–9.

Sophomore baseball, 1965: I had been practicing at shortstop and third base, but there were returning senior starters at both positions. I had stopped catching, which did not matter because Dick Dunkle was established there. I had played outfield in the summers but had not practiced there for the high school team. Maybe I would be a utility player?

I was too young to drive, and I remember Mom dropped me off for the first game. Coach England came about one hundred yards to meet me and said, "You better have been in bed by eleven last night. You are starting at third base." Our returning starter, senior Bob Heiskell, a starter on the basketball team as well, had been injured and never returned to the team. I started every game at third.

The highlight of the season was catcher Dick Dunkle being named All-Ohio and playing in the North-South All-Star game that summer. Our record was 13–4, including tournament play. We lost the first game of the sectional.

Junior football, 1965: The 1965 Lancaster football team was led by a strong senior class. I was a junior quarterback making his first varsity start. Powerful Upper Arlington came to Lancaster for the first game of the season.

Maybe I should have been nervous, but I was too busy concentrating on following the plan the coaches had established, executing one play at a time, and winning the game. We played a good game against a team that went unbeaten and ranked fifth in the state, but it was not quite good enough.

The Golden Gales actually led at the half, 14–7, but the visitors had two touchdowns in the second half while we could only manage a Fritz Reed field goal. Final score: 17-20. Some of the players remember losing on a late field goal, but the box score in *The Columbus Dispatch* shows differently.

Don Seifert and Jim Notestine scored touchdowns, and Reed added two extra points. It was just not enough, as Upper Arlington had another undefeated season.

Visiting Linden McKinley provided a breather for the Gales as Fritz scored three times, and Seifert and Tim Bailey added touchdowns in a 34–0 game. Powerful Columbus Bishop Watterson, which beat Columbus North, 52–9, was next.

Although the first quarter was tied at zero and the half was tied, 6–6, home field was not enough of an advantage as Lancaster failed to score in the second half. Watterson won, 6-22. The Gales were 1–2 on the season, but on their way to an outright COL title.

We rolled over Portsmouth, Steubenville Central Catholic, Chillicothe, Zanesville, and Ironton by at least two touchdowns before hosting Newark. This time home field may have been the difference, but two touchdowns and two two-point conversions did not hurt. Kern's five-yard run and thirty-eight-yard pass to Mike Baughman put six on the board; runs by Seifert and Notestine provided four more. Newark had two touchdowns, plus a one and a two-point conversion. Lancaster 16–15.

When Marietta fell 8–0, the Golden Gales had recorded an 8–2 season record, an undefeated COL championship, and set four school records: yards passing, 1084; total yards, 3150; passing percentage, 55 percent; and touchdown passes, 12.

With a record like that, individual honors were not far behind.

Mike Baughman led the way with Royal Crown Cola—Coach

and Athlete Magazine Prep All-American, Top Ten Scholastic, Ohio Lineman of the Year, first-team All-Ohio and All-COL, while setting school receiving records.

Don Seifert, Bob Danison, Jim Notestine, Marcel Page, and Don Johnson joined Baughman on the All-COL team. Page, Danison, and Fritz Reed made honorable mention All-Ohio. Rex Kern, Larry McClurg, and Larry Smith made second-team All-COL.

In the final statewide polls, Upper Arlington was fifth, Watterson seventh, and Lancaster tied with Athens for sixteenth in UPI. AP had Watterson fourth, Upper Arlington sixth, and Lancaster thirteenth. My teammates and I have always remembered how strong that team was and would have loved to have been in the playoffs together, but there were none then.

Junior baseball, 1966: The key to our team was our pitching staff, led by two starters for the basketball team, Bill Grein and Paul Callahan. In an early season doubleheader, they each started a game with Athens and did not allow a run. In the regular season, twelve of the sixteen opponents scored two runs or less. The opposition did not score more than four runs in one game all year.

We started the season with eight straight wins, then lost a one-run game to Newark and a 0-2 shutout to Upper Arlington. We beat UA in the second game of a doubleheader, then won three more before losing to Bishop Hartley, 1-2. We lost the first game of the COL tournament to Ironton, 2-4, won the sectional in two games, then lost the district semifinal. Ironton beat us again—this time 3-4 in eight innings. When we scored runs, we won. In our five losses, we only scored eight runs. Our record was 13–3 regular season—15–5 overall.

Senior football, 1966: The previous senior class, which meant so much to so many LHS sports teams, was gone. The 1966 football season began slowly. Lesser teams might have given up on the season, but not this group.

In the first game of the season, Upper Arlington beat us soundly,

15-42. At the weekly meeting of the Kiwanis Club, Coach Jones announced I was back playing safety—the original plan was for me to play only quarterback—and would not be coming off the field. I was happy to hear the news.

We beat Columbus Marion-Franklin, then Bishop Watterson beat us, 20-38.

We played Bishop Watterson—unbeaten in 1965 and this year to date—tougher than they expected. We trailed only 14-18 at the half, but they widened that lead in the second half.

I did not know it at the time, but that game was very important to my future. The following Monday, Bishop Watterson's coach, Dick Walker, called Ohio State Coach Woody Hayes to ask if the Buckeyes were recruiting me. Told that they were interested but had not decided, Walker extolled my performance from Friday night. Research showed I had scored two touchdowns on runs of nineteen and twenty yards and ran for the two-point conversion. Jeff Grunditisch scored the other TD on a one-yard plunge. A short time later, Woody Hayes needed a haircut. He drove down US-33 to my father's barbershop to get one. Two years later, when Lou Holtz left Ohio State for the head-coaching position at William and Mary, Dick Walker joined the Ohio State coaching staff as defensive backs coach.

Before returning to the 1967 season, there was one more thing about that game that might interest Buckeye fans. While they probably know that Brian Donovan of Watterson was a member of the Super Sophs at OSU, so was his teammate Tim Wagner.

Though small, at five nine, Timmy was an exceptionally tough football player, fast and quick, but Wagner blew out his knee very early in freshman practice and never recovered. Sure, his classmates included John Brockington, Leo Hayden, and Larry Zelina. After knee surgery, Timmy was tried at defense back and returning kicks, but in those days players were not recovering from knee surgery. Had he been healthy, somehow, some way, Tim Wagner would have contributed to our team on the field. He was that good.

After two more losses, our record was 1–4. Rather than giving up, we began COL play aiming for the conference title, and we achieved it. After four straight COL victories, we were two points behind Newark with a chance to be unbeaten in the COL. Coach Jones called for a long pass to our fastest receiver. I threw the ball as far as I could, and the ball went right through his hands. Still, a conference title was a fine achievement for the team the school yearbook, *The Mirage*, named "The Team of Dedication."

The Class of 1967 had been a part of teams that ended a seven-year drought of COL titles, then strung together three straight COL conference championships.

Coach Earl Jones earned Coach of the Year in the COL. Reed Riegel at guard, Kelly Milliser at offensive tackle, Bob Wolfinger at defensive end, Dan McCann at safety, and Tim Bailey at linebacker were very deserving of first-team All-COL honors. I would add that Tim was an outstanding blocker at fullback, both on running plays and passing. Those five players and the rest of our teammates helped me be named first-team All-Ohio at safety (AP) and quarterback (UPI) and All-COL at both.

Some other interesting notes about the season are that future Buckeye Super Sophs Leo Hayden, Larry Zelina, Brian Donovan, and Doug Adams were also on the UPI All-Ohio first string, and all had outstanding careers at Ohio State.

Also, Upper Arlington and Columbus Bishop Watterson, which beat Lancaster every year I played varsity and accounted for six of our ten losses in 1964, 1965, and 1966, both had excellent years again. They were both undefeated in 1964 and 1965, but not in 1966. Arlington beat No. 1 ranked Massillon October 21 before 15,610 fans and eventually earned the rank of number one, until Bishop Watterson beat them 32–0 three weeks later.

Additionally, when I was named Central Ohio Back of the Year, it was the first time a Lancaster player had received that honor in nine years, when Larry Baughman, Mike's brother, was selected in 1957.

Our success that season was special to me because of the outstanding talent we lost from the previous year, our challenging schedule, and the small number of seniors on the team. Those thirteen seniors provided the leadership, determination, commitment, and work ethic to overcome a 1–4 start to win the Central Ohio League outright.

Finally, there is a story about the team film sessions at the home of Earl and Barbara Jones and their four daughters: Dianne, Sharon, Linda, and Tracey. The sessions were held on Sunday nights in the family basement. At first the girls were a little rowdy, interrupting what the coach was telling us. That did not last long.

"In 1964, Dad's first season as head coach, I was in seventh grade," Dianne recalled. "Sharon was in fifth, Linda was in third, and Tracey was about four years old. To say we were excited to have high school football players in our house would be a huge understatement.

"Mom and Dad quickly established some boundaries. Every week we chose which player's lap we were going to sit on. The order of selection changed every week. No one ever forgot whose turn it was. We were allowed to come down the steps and say hello to everyone, then take our seat or lap. Sometimes we helped Mom pass out the sandwiches she had made. If we made any noise, we were sent upstairs, not to return that evening. Such a punishment would have been worse than any spanking or grounding!

"I must say that Tracey, the youngest, was a prima donna. When it was her turn, she would say, 'Maybe I should choose him, or maybe him. I just can't decide.' She took longer than the rest of us; we were planning our choice all week.

"We went to all the games, home and away. The players and their girlfriends were our babysitters. Oh, did the girls in my class envy me!

"Raising four daughters, our parents looked for ways to bring boys around in a controlled environment," Dianne continued.

"The players were very well mannered, and so were the young men from the Boys' Industrial School nearby, when Dad brought one of them to dinner.

"As the oldest girl, when Dad took one of his players on a recruiting trip to Ohio State or somewhere close, I got to go along. Dad wanted me thinking about the right college, and that was great experience," she concluded.

Rex: It was fun to hear Dianne remember our film sessions from the point of view of the Jones girls, except for one fact: I thought Tracey and I were sort of going together my senior year, and all the while she was really playing the field. Outsmarted—and by a girl who was then six years old!

Senior basketball, 1967: With only one starter and two lettermen back from the state tournament team, not much was expected of us. Actually, we had a better regular season than the 1966 team, losing only four games.

We lost two of the first three games, including a bad loss to Newark at home, then won seven in a row. After a loss to Worthington and another bad one to Newark, we won six straight to finish regular season 14–4.

The second Newark loss, 57-76, was before a standing room–only crowd in Lancaster, estimated at thirty-two hundred people and the biggest in school history. My mother's scrapbook has a picture of Ohio State coach Fred Taylor at the game. He may not have thought the trip was worth it, as I had two baskets and eight foul shots for twelve points. The article stated: "The Cats bottled up Rex Kern with as many men as they could spare." We finished second to Newark in the league.

We won the first sectional game against Greenfield McClain, then lost the second one by four points to a team we had beaten 67–56 in December, Miami Trace. The word "disappointed" does not begin to cover my feeling after that game. It seemed like there was a mistake; that the basketball season was over too soon. I remember twiddling my thumbs at home the day before baseball practice started.

George Hill was named Co-Coach of the Year in the COL. He deserved to be *the* COY in 1966 and 1967. Frank Kluz was our second-leading scorer and was named second-team All-COL. Earl Pierce and Greg Montague earned honorable mention. I was voted first-team All-Ohio.

It was reported that I was the first player in COL history to be MVP in football and basketball in the same year. I also received the honor of being named Coach and Athlete All-American in both sports and led the COL in scoring in basketball.

My single game high of forty-four points at Ironton set a school record and a COL record for teams still in the league. I never placed special importance on points, other than doing what the team needed to win, but I was pleased with my shooting that night. My seventeen baskets came on twenty-two attempts, and I was ten of twelve at the foul line. To give you an idea of how much I was "feeling it," on one fast break I dribbled twice past half court, stopped, and put it in. Since there was no one ahead of me, I might have been benched if I missed because a layup was wide open.

On the way to the team bus, Coach Hill shouted out, "Hey, Kernsie, do we need to ice down your arm on the way home?" It seemed a good time to just laugh.

Choosing a Scholarship

During the basketball season, I took some time to consider scholarship offers for the future. I did not miss a game or a practice—that would not have been fair to my Lancaster teammates—but an important decision had to be made.

In high school, I had the opportunity to play for three coaches who loved to compete and who genuinely cared about their players: Earl Jones in football, George Hill in basketball, and Dick

England in baseball. When it came time to decide on a college, finding a coach of that caliber was as important as deciding on the school or even the sport.

I visited Miami (Ohio) for football and liked the school and their coach, Bo Schembechler, but I thought he might be leaving for a bigger school. I went to visit Auburn for basketball, but only because George Hill played there and asked me to take a look. The campus was nice, but I had a very negative reaction to the racial slurs their fans shouted at opposing Black players. UCLA and North Carolina contacted me for basketball, but I liked the idea of a school close to home.

The most interesting offer came from Ohio University, about an hour south of my home. At a dinner with football coach Bill Hess, basketball coach Jim Snyder, and baseball coach Bob Wren, they explained I could have an athletic scholarship and choose which sport, or sports, I wanted to play, if any. They just wanted me to be a Bobcat. Of course, they knew me well enough to know I would play at least one sport. I felt very comfortable with each coach, but the ability to choose which sport(s) was a little confusing.

Through it all, my first love was basketball at Ohio State, starting with the 1960 Lucas-Havlicek-Nowell-Siegfried-Roberts team, then on to Gary Bradds and Dick Ricketts. Plus, Fred Taylor had been the first coach to recruit me. He had been to several of our games, and I had been on his television show as player of the week a few times. He had a simple approach to recruiting: "If you come to Ohio State, you will get a good education, and we will compete for the Big Ten championship." If that was good enough for my heroes, it was good enough for me.

Woody had not been interested until the fall of my senior year, when Bishop Watterson coach Dick Walker had recommended me to him after they played Lancaster, and we gave them a battle. Still, his interest seemed to be growing, and my favorite position in any sport was quarterback. There were so many challenges, from play calling to leading ten teammates to passing to running. If I could be good enough to play that position—and play basketball too—at Ohio State, that would be perfect.

I had no idea if it was possible.

During our basketball season senior year, Coach Hill asked where I wanted to go to college. I said Ohio State, but I do not know if they—Fred Taylor and Woody—would let me play both sports. George asked if that was the only reason I had not committed. I said yes! Shortly thereafter, he called Fred and relayed that message. The same night, both Ohio State coaches called to say it was OK! We arranged to make the announcement at halftime of an OSU basketball game with Jimmy Crum, WLW-C sportscaster who announced the Buckeye basketball games.

At the time, freshmen were not eligible to play intercollegiate college sports. The thinking was they needed the time to adjust to college academics. It was a good rule in general, and it gave me a chance to play both sports, with the blessing of Woody and Fred.

Thinking about it today, I believe Fred knew how much I loved his program at Ohio State. He could have taken a hard line and not given me a choice.

I owe Fred a debt of gratitude for giving me a choice when he might have been able to guarantee that I played basketball for him. At Ohio State, I would find other examples of him having the best interests of his student-athletes at heart, and I eventually discovered that 97 of his 102 lettermen earned OSU degrees.

Senior baseball, 1967: This was another team for which I had a special feeling. Again, we lost several good players from the class of 1966, but this time we overcame the losses and made it to the state tournament.

Dick Daubmire and Howard Bozman were our pitching aces and absolutely came through, each posting a mark of 8–1. Rod Miller's 3–1 record made the team 19–3. They contributed a total of six shutouts, five one-run games, and only allowed more than four runs twice. Fine pitching carried us through many close games, but the offense did contribute eight runs in each of three sectional games.

Daubmire, our .369-hitting right fielder Dave Camp, and I made the all-district team. My .463 batting average was a big reason I was selected to the All-Ohio first team.

At the time, there was an article stating it was the first time anyone had made All-Ohio in three sports since John Havlicek in 1958. Of course, I was a huge fan of his when the Ohio State basketball team won the NCAA title in 1960 and finished second the next two years. He went to the Boston Celtics and seemed to keep improving in the NBA. He had also started at first base for the Buckeyes. When he graduated, he tried out for the Cleveland Browns as a receiver, not having played that position since he was a junior in high school. He was the last player cut when the Browns kept their first-round draft choice—and future All-Pro—receiver Gary Collins, who was also a punter. But for years the Browns kept asking Havlicek to try out again, even when he was starting in the NBA All-Star game!

The next year, my future Buckeye and Baltimore Colt teammate Stan White joined the group of three-time All-Ohioans. He made first-team All-Ohio twice in football, once in basketball and once in baseball, batting .467 while playing catcher. Stan had a fine eleven-year NFL career with the Colts and the Detroit Lions as a linebacker.

But, back to our 1967 baseball team: Seven straight wins in the tournament got us to the state semifinals, where our bats went silent in a 0-4 loss to Cincinnati Western Hills, the eventual champions. My infield single was our only hit against the opposing pitcher, who was at his best that day. We did claim sectional, district, and regional titles—the regional title being Coach England's third at Lancaster. On a personal note, since my brother Keith's team won their regional in 1964, I was especially happy to match that.

Lancaster sports brought so many great people into my life.

Final home game of my Lancaster
High School basketball career.

THE OHIO STATE UNIVERSITY

AREA OF STUDENT RELATIONS
INTERCOLLEGIATE ATHLETICS
ST. JOHN ARENA
410 WEST WOODRUFF
COLUMBUS, OHIO 43210

January 9, 1967

Mr. Rex Kern
620 Garfield Avenue
Lancaster, Ohio

Dear Rex:

I see by the paper what you all did to my alma mater
again last week! You know all of us here are hoping
that Lancaster will be back in the Arena in March.

I'm looking forward to seeing you in the dressing room
following the Indiana University game and I still don't
know why the policeman didn't let you in after the Texas
Christian game.

Good luck and I hope you remember what we said about
the "roundball scholarship".

Please give our regards to your folks.

Sincerely yours,

Fred

Fred R. Taylor
Head Basketball Coach

Imagine a bubble coming from the catcher's mouth
with the words, "Picked the wrong time to call a curve."

Officially a Buckeye, intending to play
for two Hall of Fame coaches, Woody
on the left, Fred Taylor on the right.

CHAPTER 6

FAITH, MY PATH

*"Be strong and courageous. Do not be frightened and do not be
dismayed, for the Lord your God is with you wherever you go."*
Joshua 1:9

The reason for this book is to pass on to family members and
friends some of the important lessons of my life.

We all travel different paths. Even if the path seems to be the
same, we may interpret what happened differently. It is not my
intention to say, "This is the way." Rather, "This was my way, as I
understand it. If there is something I experienced that applies to
you, I am glad to be helpful."

My journey in faith began in my father's barbershop.

My father cut hair for a wide variety of people on the west side
of Lancaster. Many were blue collar, some Anchor Hocking execu-
tives, ministers, and shopkeepers. This allowed him to know what
was happening around town before most of the residents. One day,

when I was in sixth grade, Charlie Morris, the principal at West Elementary, stopped by in the late morning to get his hair cut.

"Rex got into a little trouble today," he said. "I'm going to have to spank him."

"No problem," Dad replied.

Later that day, Dad showed up at home for lunch. I was surprised to see him because he almost always worked through lunch. I would grab a sandwich, which Mom had fixed, and run back to school to play before classes began again.

"Rex, are you carrying a handkerchief?" he said.

I checked and told him I did not have one.

"It is always good to carry a handkerchief in your back pocket," Dad said. "You never know when you will need it." And he insisted that I go upstairs and get a handkerchief.

It seemed a little strange, but I was in a hurry to get back to school to see what kind of game was going on. I finished my sandwich, ran upstairs for a handkerchief, and ran back to school. Hopefully I thanked Mom for the sandwich.

That afternoon, Principal Morris sent someone to our room who said, "Rex Kern is to report to the principal's office. I did, got about twelve whacks, and was glad I had that handkerchief in my pocket. The lesson I learned was that someone who loved me might not interfere in my life but would help out when he could.

Others have mentioned seeing the four Kerns march to the Sixth Avenue Methodist church, just down the street, every Sunday. Reverend Larry Hard was a wonderful pastor, the best preacher, and the best man. Even in church, I got into things—sometimes good, sometimes not so much.

The summer between ninth grade and tenth grade, the boys were talking about a church camp that was coming up at the Lancaster Campground. There would be good food, sports, speakers, devotions, games; some of my friends had enjoyed it the previous year. They wanted me to go, and it sounded good.

Of course, I was playing American Legion baseball that summer, as always, but it seemed like I could combine the two.

At the camp one night, we saw a film about the apostle Paul's conversion to Christianity. It made me think about the time five years earlier, when we were all worried Keith would die. We had prayed that Keith would be healed, and he was. That experience and the camp environment of prayer made me think someone was listening.

As the film came to an end I wondered, "Do I make a decision to follow Jesus the way the apostle Paul did?"

Over the next few days, I thought about that. One thing on my mind was, *What do I have to offer*? The answer seemed to be athletic talents, but I was not certain what that meant, or what else there might be. Somehow I was comfortable with what I did not know, because I knew what I did know. I asked the Lord into my life.

The process of change

Going into my sophomore year, I went to church more often and did it with a purpose—to learn and to grow. I read the Bible more often and more seriously. Larry Hard asked me to speak from the pulpit, initially as a sophomore and later as a junior and senior. I was involved in the Methodist Youth Fellowship (MYF) at church and on the district level. I would pray not to win, but for God to receive the glory.

The first characteristic I noticed The Lord changing in my life was my temper. Losing it had become a bad habit, but that habit began to soften and be less frequent.

It is important for me to say, and readers to understand, that the habit of controlling my temper did not change completely overnight. Just as improvement in math, writing and sports require time, my temper did not magically disappear.

For example, my senior year we were playing Zanesville in basketball, and I was called for a foul. At the time, the person called for the foul had to raise his hand for the official scorer to see. I raised both hands, then defiantly pulled them down. I wanted everyone to know that I disagreed with the call.

Well, the referee disagreed with my disagreement and called a technical foul.

Another opinion had more impact.

My parents came to the game, which they did as often as possible. Afterward, my father was quite upset.

"If you ever act like that again, do not come home, because you are not welcome," he said.

The very next night against Worthington, I guarded their center on defense. He went up for a layup, and I got my hand on top of the ball before he could release it. Some blocks are deflections, some are stuffs—this was a stuff. Because he was off balance, it may have looked like I threw him to the ground. I did not; I just had leverage.

The referee called a technical foul for what he thought was a vicious play. I remembered my father's words and did not say anything to the referee. When I sat down next to him on the bench, my coach, George Hill, said, "Kernsie, you've had quite a weekend."

But I also remembered what Dad said about technical fouls. What was going to happen when I went home? How serious was he about what he said? Would I have a place to live? I delayed going home by driving around the neighborhood. Finally, I faced the music.

The first thing Dad said was, "That was not your fault. It was not vicious, and the ref got the call wrong. You have nothing to worry about." I later found out our principal, Mr. Lowry, waited for the official outside the locker room to disagree with the call.

I tell that story for two reasons. One, I still had a temper, but I was doing better in controlling it through the grace of God. Two, some things which we waste time worrying about never happen. It is best to face problems head-on because some were never issues; others will be solved more quickly.

That is enough about my temper—back to my faith.

After the 1969 Rose Bowl victory, my teammates Mark Steir, John Mulhbach, and I went to a Fellowship of Christian Athletes convention in Dallas. It was the first I had heard of FCA. There I met people like Tom Landry, famous coach of the Dallas Cowboys, and Bart Starr, the great Green Bay Packers quarterback. That experience catapulted me into speaking to different church audiences.

Nancy and I went to churches in Ohio, Indiana, and West Virginia. We would have gone to that state up north, but they never asked! She helped me with the driving. Those were our date nights. One quarter I had about fifty speeches in ninety days while carrying twenty-seven credit hours. My grades were good that quarter, with a little help from above.

My senior year in college, someone came to our psychology class. The teacher said, "Is Rex Kern in class?" I put my hand up. He said, "See me after class." When he gave me the note, which said, "Call the president," I assumed it was to call Ohio State president Novice Fawcett.

It was not the normal seven-digit number, but I called anyway.

"This is the White House."

"I'm sorry. I must have the wrong number," I said.

"What is your name, please?"

When I told her, she said President Nixon had invited me to be part of an FCA church service to be held at the White House. Former Yankee second baseman Bobby Richardson was the main speaker. I was to read the scripture verses. My parents and Nancy were also invited. We were picked up in a White House limo and taken to President Nixon's personal secretary, who said, "President Nixon wants to meet with you in his private quarters, the Yellow Room.

"You may know your coach, Woody Hayes, and I are dear friends," said President Nixon. "When we are together, I want to talk football and he wants to talk politics. As you can imagine, we talk politics."

That experience at the White House led to opportunities to share my faith around the country, which brought me into contact with many amazing people, some famous, some not.

While sharing my faith in public, I continued to do my best to live my faith out in my daily life, on and off the field.

The NFL

After a certain degree of fame in college football, I faced skepticism from the NFL. Despite three years as a college quarterback, I was considered too small to play that position professionally. The talk I kept hearing was that I would be drafted as an athlete and probably be tried at safety, wide receiver, or running back.

Before the draft, I was asked to play in two all-star games, which were designed to give pro scouts a look at their prospective future players.

First was the Hula Bowl in Hawaii. Jim Plunkett, who won the Heisman Trophy; Joe Theismann, who was second in the voting; and I were going to rotate at quarterback. Plunkett was six three and 220 pounds, exactly what the NFL scouts wanted, and was the first player selected in the draft. Theismann and I were exactly the same size. He was taken in the fourth round, the 99th pick, as a quarterback. After starring in the Canadian Football League for three years, he was traded to the Washington Redskins for a first-round pick, played for them for twelve years, and was named NFL MVP in 1983. I was drafted in the tenth round, 260th overall, by the Baltimore Colts.

During practice we all worked at quarterback. Just a few days before the game, Penn State coach Joe Paterno came up to me and said, "Rex, we are down to four defensive backs. If something happens to one of them, would you mind playing there?

I wished I had been able to practice longer and work at both positions but said I would be glad to shift if necessary.

Plunkett started the game, played a series or two and came out. I am not certain when I went in, but I am certain of two things: one, we drove down the field and I threw a touchdown pass to Gordon Bowdell, receiver from Michigan State, and two, when the defense went in after that, one of our defensive backs was hurt on the first play. The last pass I threw was a touchdown, and I made two interceptions at safety in the game. I was hoping someone noticed something.

Then it was on to the All-American Game in Lubbock, Texas. My coach was Charlie McClendon of LSU, whose quarterback, Buddy Lee, was also on the team. Coach McClendon asked if I minded playing defense. I agreed. Buddy was the seventh round choice of the Chicago Bears, roomed with my "Super Soph" buddy Ron Maciejowski in camp, but did not play in the NFL.

This time I was able to practice at safety, and it looked like I was going to be able to play the whole game. But our middle linebacker, who had been a middle guard in college, was not certain of the coverage we were using and speared me, breaking two ribs. It was my old Super Soph buddy Jim Stillwagon. I was having trouble breathing and he said, "You're in my way. You're not supposed to be here."

"No, you're in my way," I replied, and was taken to the hospital.

1971 NFL Draft

The 1971 Draft was held January 28–29, in the Belmont Plaza Hotel in New York City. Unlike today, it was not televised. No flashy suits, no high draft choices, no families and girlfriends, no fans cheering and booing, no "draft experts" evaluating the choices.

Times were different.

I remember sitting by the phone with Nancy in our apartment, waiting to hear which team had taken me in the NFL Draft and listening to reports on the radio. It was the first time the top three choices were quarterbacks—Jim Plunkett of Stanford, Archie Manning of Mississippi, and Dan Pastorini of Santa Clara. All had NFL fine careers, as did Archie's sons, Peyton and Eli.

John Brockington and Leo Hayden came by early the first day. They were excited to be taken in the first round, and rightfully so. I was excited for them, and a bit sad for myself. Jack Tatum and Tim Anderson were also first round choices. In all, thirteen Buckeyes would be selected.

The second day of the Draft, I had not been chosen but was on the way to an Easter Seals event with the OSU wrestling coach Casey Fredericks, who had asked me to be the honorary chairman. We were in the car when I learned I had been drafted in the tenth round by the Colts. That was a relief. The end result of the day was an Easter Seals poster of twin boys sitting on my lap. They had been born without legs, yet were sporting big smiles. That day is now a treasured memory and includes the message, "Relax, and remember who is in charge."

I graduated spring quarter with a BS, having taken my first master's level class.

Colts camp began in July. My ribs were not yet healed.

Fortunately, Tom Matte was the starting running back with the Colts. A Buckeye at Ohio State, he took me under his wing, teaching me to be a professional athlete. His strongest advice was, "Learn every conceivable position. You are like me, versatile, athletic, and smart. Learn safety and cornerback; that gives you four chances to see the field. Volunteer for special teams. Maybe you can be a possession receiver in a pinch. I played quarterback at Ohio State and with the Colts in emergencies—be ready if that opportunity comes up. Make yourself valuable."

Matte was going into the ninth year of a twelve-year career. His advice had worked for him. Why couldn't it work for me?

Another former Buckeye star, tackle Bob Vogel, had some good advice for me as well.

Bob had been an OSU captain and an All-American in 1962, then the number five selection in the NFL Draft, then selected to the Pro Bowl five times. Now he was coming to the end of his ten-year career with Baltimore, when he started all 140 games.

He asked what I wanted to do after football.

"I'd like to work toward becoming the Athletic Director at Ohio State," I said. Bob suggested I might want to contact the appropriate people at OSU to inform them of my interest. That led to a nonpaying internship in the athletic department. I also continued to think about what steps to take in order to reach my goal.

Tom and Bob served as perfect mentors for me—Tom was helping me get started in the league, and Bob was getting me prepared for the inevitable ending of my athletic career. Ironically, they were Buckeye teammates in 1960.

I was pleased when head coach Don McCafferty informed me that I had made the powerful Colts team, which had won the Super Bowl just a few months prior. Don had played for Paul Brown at Ohio State. In 1971 I was the fifth defensive back for all four starters and fielded short punts as the up man, because I had good hands and was an elusive runner. After ten games, I got my first start at corner and started the final six games, four regular season and both playoffs. We finished 10–4, beat the Browns in the AFC semifinals, but lost to the Miami Dolphins for the AFC championship.

Defense was the heart of the team, with first-team All-Pros Bubba Smith at end, Ted "Stork" Hendricks at linebacker, and Rick Volk at free safety. Mike Curtis, Freddie Miller, and Jerry Logan had made All-Pro multiple times themselves. Solid pros like Ray May, Charlie Stukes, Billy Newsome, Jim Duncan, and Roy Hilton rounded out an outstanding unit.

The Minnesota Vikings ranked first in points allowed, 139 to our 140. But we allowed only 2,852 yards to their 3,406, and 166 first downs to their 194. It was the perfect way for a rookie defender to break into the NFL, especially one playing cornerback, a position he had never played.

After the season, I continued to work toward my master's at Ohio State full time for two quarters. In June 1973, I graduated with my MA.

In my second year with the Colts, 1972, I only played five games, starting three at corner. That year I became the holder for extra points and field goals but got hurt during the fifth game. We were 5–9.

That was an important year for another reason. My Buckeye teammate Stan White joined us, and we were roommates. I had a chance to mentor him, as Buckeyes Bob Vogel and Tom Matte had mentored me. He mentioned me in a book titled *What It Means to be a Buckeye* for changing his life and his purpose in life by introducing him to my strength, Jesus Christ.

Stan was a seventeenth-round draft pick by the Colts, the 438th selection, but had an outstanding eleven-year NFL career. He also played two years in the USFL. He earned his law degree in only four years while playing for the Colts, and his son, Stan Jr., became a Buckeye player too.

After the 1972 season ended, I was asked by the United States Chaplaincy to visit five military posts in Germany with Don Shinnick, a former Colts linebacker from UCLA who was an NFL assistant for four teams. The trip took place in February 1973. Nancy and I had been married the month before, but she was not included in the invitation.

Don and I enjoyed sharing football stories with the men, who deeply appreciated reminders of home. I did not know it, but my Lancaster buddy Greg Woltz was stationed in Germany at the time. It would have been great to have run into him!

In 1973 I played in all fourteen games, starting eight at corner, and had my only two career interceptions. The Colts were 4–10. Linebacker and player-rep. Ray May refused to play for the new Colt ownership and was traded to Denver early in the 1973 season. I had accepted the position of alternate player-rep—in hopes of gaining administrative experience—and became the Colt's player-representative.

In January 1974, there was an announcement in the *Columbus Dispatch* that I would be working as a "sort of an intern in athletic administration," in the words of J. Edgar Weaver, the OSU athletic director.

In 1974 I was honored to be one of three finalists nominated for the Byron R. White Humanitarian Award, referred to as "the most prestigious honor presented by the National Football League Players Association." It recognized service to team, city, and country in the spirit of "Whizzer" White, former college and professional player then serving on the US Supreme Court. Floyd Little, outstanding running back of the Denver Broncos, was the winner.

On July 1 of the same year, the representatives of each team voted to strike because the players wanted to be able to switch teams when their contracts expired. They wanted free agency, the Rozelle Rule.

As player-rep, I saw my primary responsibility to be team unity. I expected the season to go on and wanted us to be united as a team. There were enough distractions in a season without reliving the strike and criticizing each other for positions we had taken. When the union voted to strike, that meant explaining to everyone why we should strike, together. Only two players decided not to strike, Mike Curtis and Stan White. The strike was effective July 1, 1974.

Soon after the strike began, General Manager Joe Thomas called me at something like 1:30 in the morning. At least he got straight to the point.

"Rex," he said, "I want you to know that if we can find players who are half as good as our current starters who strike, those starters will be cut."

"Joe, you can't do that," I replied. "Our labor agreement forbids it."

"Watch me," he said, and hung up.

When the strike was settled, Joe Thomas called me again, with an unusual request.

"Rex, would you do me a favor? We have an exhibition game out of town this weekend; could you not report until Monday?" he said.

I was surprised at first, then realized this was about money. There would be travel expenses for all the returning players—air fare, food, hotel rooms—if the veterans reported. In the spirit of good faith and reconciliation, I said, "Joe, if that helps you, we will agree to that."

When we returned, my background had been that "the best player plays, regardless," so I was looking forward to training camp. Practice was going so well that Howard Schnellenberger, by now my third head coach with the Colts, told me I was having the best practices of any defensive back on the squad. Since two safeties and two cornerbacks started, I expected to be named a starter soon.

The next day, I tore the plantaris muscle of the left calf and was placed on the Injured Reserve.

Almost immediately, Howard called me into his office. I was naïve enough to anticipate some words of encouragement and a "Get back soon."

"You are on IR now, but the day you come off we are placing you on waivers," he began. "You will report for therapy but have no contact with the team, at practice or be allowed in meetings. When that happens, we know you will not make any waves."

I was shocked. Finally, I asked, "Who is running this team: You or Joe Thomas?

"End of conversation," he replied.

"You told me I was playing the best of any defensive backs on the team," I said.

"We are done here," he concluded.

I turned in my playbook, then had to show up every day for therapy but not attend meetings or practice until I was cleared to play, at which time I was cut. Yes, that was more than a little awkward. It was especially disappointing that I was not allowed to say goodbye to my teammates.

There were twenty-four teams in the league at that time, and every player-rep was traded or cut. **QUITE A COINCIDENCE!!!**

Speaking of coincidence, if not as loudly, Howard was fired after beginning the season 0–3. Soon after the announcement I saw him at the grocery store. Not knowing what to say, and not wanting to say what I wanted to say, I chose to avoid him. Proving God has a sense of humor, we ended up in the same checkout line.

"Well, Rex, looks like he got both of us," he said. Howard was referring not only to me being cut but also to the fact that owner Robert Irsay had replaced him with Joe Thomas as head coach. Thomas had a 2–9 record before being replaced at the end of the season by Ted Marchibroda, who held the job for five years.

As soon as I came off the Injured Reserve List, Joe Thomas called to say, "You're cut, and free to go."

That night during dinner the phone rang, "Rex, this is Lou Saban, head coach of the Buffalo Bills," the voice said. "Would you like to play in Buffalo?"

I wanted to play but had heard stories about teams bringing in players and cutting them immediately.

"Coach, I do not want to go up there, run a forty-yard dash, and be told I am not fast enough before I get to play."

"What else are you going to do?" Saban replied.

"I'll go back to Ohio State and finish my Ph.D. in athletic administration," I said.

"You play in our conference," Saban said. "I know what you can do. Let me put it this way: if you come up here, you are starting on special teams this Sunday."

"I'll be there tonight," I replied.

In a blink of an eye, I went from a team with a record of 1–7, to an ex-NFL player, to a starter on a 7–1 team. It was confirmation of the expression, "The Lord works in mysterious ways, His wonders to perform!"

I was unable to get a flight from Baltimore, so Nancy had to drive me to Washington, DC. Neither of us had traveled to that airport, and this was before GPS trackers, Google Maps, and cell phones. After we found the airport, she had to get home by herself. At the apartment, her problems really began. She had to pack everything in boxes and suit cases, rent a U-Haul trailer, subrent our Baltimore apartment, and drive through the Pocono Mountains in late-October to my parents' home in Lancaster. In addition to driving a U-Haul for the first time, she was dealing with shooting pains in her abdominal region which would require surgery at Riverside Hospital in Columbus in a matter of weeks.

In 1974, this was the reality of the glamorous life of the wife of an NFL player.

When I arrived at the Buffalo airport, someone from the Bills front office picked me up. Almost immediately he said, "This has never happened before, but Coach Saban will be meeting you at the hotel."

He said hotel; I remember it as a **TRUCK STOP!** It would be my home for the remainder of the season. Nancy visited once. To sit on the couch together required phone books, bathroom towels, and old sweatshirts to reinforce the cushions. In addition to her physical pain, it was not a second honeymoon.

When I arrived, Coach Saban was waiting. After "Hello, Rex," he said, "What's going on there?" He meant in the Baltimore front office with regard to the moves they were making. I was happy to tell him what I could.

In 1974 the Bills were 9–5, same as the previous year. The star of the team was O. J. Simpson, star of the University of Southern California team the Buckeyes beat in the Rose Bowl. When people asked me what he was like, my response was always, "Great guy in the locker room, great guy outside it, great player." That was what I saw in 1974.

Dave Foley was another familiar face with the Bills. He was then the left tackle for "The Electric Company," which turned on "The Juice" in the Bills' running game. Dave had come into my life at Ohio State when he and fellow senior Rufus Mayes were All-American tackles who made life easy for the Super Sophs. Their reward, in addition to a national championship, was both being named All-American in 1968 and both being first round NFL draft choices.

Even today Dave is remembered fondly among his teammates for his support at the Illinois game that year. I was "knocked into next month," in the words of trainer Mike Bordner, on a rainy, windy day in Champaign and Ron Maciejowski came into the game. Foley greeted "Mace" with the motivational words, "You better not throw an *unprintable* interception."

Suitably inspired, Mace threw two passes, completed both for fifty-four yards, ran three times for twelve yards, and led us down the field for a 31–24 victory. The next week, he did roughly the same thing to defeat Michigan State in the Horseshoe, 25–20.

I could talk about Mace for days, but back to the 1974 season with Buffalo.

I played eight games at corner and safety but never started during the season. My sense was that the Bills were looking toward the playoffs when they acquired me because the playoffs were played at warp speed, much faster than regular season. I had played in two playoff games with the Colts, had that type of experience, knew my assignments, and was not as likely to feel pressure as a younger player.

As our first-round playoff game with the eventual Super Bowl–

champion Pittsburgh Steelers approached, I did not know how much I would play. My back likely needed surgery and I was having a problem with my hamstring. My body was wearing out. It seemed 1974 might be my last year if I did not have surgery.

Thursday night before the game I found out I was starting at safety!

I loved to play, to compete, and to go against the best, which the Steelers represented. I had always believed safety was the best position for me at the NFL level, and welcomed the chance to show that. I decided to put everything I had into every play, because this might be my last opportunity to do that on a football field.

Because we lost the game, 14–32, the ending was extremely disappointing. But I knew I had played well. At least to myself, I proved I was a solid NFL safety, when healthy. If I failed the upcoming physical, I would leave with a good memory of my last game. I just did not know my football future, if any.

Several months later, I learned Steelers running back Rocky Bleier was writing a book titled *Fighting Back* about his life and his career. When it was released in 1975, a friend read it and sent me a copy of page 186. The page was devoted to my play in that game:

> The best player on the field was a Buffalo defender, Rex Kern. He's the former Ohio State quarterback who now plays safety. He's a lot like me—too small and too slow. Sure, he led the Bills this day with thirteen tackles and recovered one fumble. Most of his stops, in fact, saved touchdowns. They were made on Franco (Harris) or me in the open field, after we'd popped for eight to ten yards and gathered a full head of steam. Poor little Rex was having his body kicked all over the place. But he hung tough.
>
> In the second half, he dislocated his finger on a play near our bench. In agony, he jumped up squealing, with his finger bent back at a grotesque angle. Any football player

recognizes that injury immediately. One of our guys grabbed his hand and jerked the finger back in place. Rex thanked him, went right back to his huddle, and never said another word. The guys on his team never even knew it.

Then Rocky mentioned the referee throwing a flag, weighted with metal so it would fly to the correct spot, and hitting me in the ankle. Bleier did not quote what I said accurately, but I did voice my frustration at being hit.

Everyone wants to be Super Bowl MVP on the winning team, but few even win their last game. My NFL career did not go as I had hoped, and certainly did not match my years at Lancaster and Ohio State. But I did play on two teams which made the playoffs. And the average career in the NFL is 3.3 years, so my four years was above average. When I got a chance to play my best position at safety, I had done very well. In my mind, I had done everything I could and took great satisfaction in that.

I did have back surgery January 1975, recovered well, and felt I was in great shape, much better than when I played against the Steelers. I reported to Buffalo for my physical, with Nancy staying in California with her parents, pregnant with our first child. Training camp was at the University of Niagara. I had a room by myself, and I remember distinctly being on my knees praying next to my bed, asking for God's guidance and direction for the upcoming season.

During my sleep that night, God revealed I would not pass my physical, and I would receive a clear indication why.

I did fail the physical and could not play for the Bills. Team doctors explained that if I took a hit in the lower lumber region of my back I could end up in a wheelchair for life. I could not ask for a clearer indication. The decision to retire was obvious. It felt good to have perfect peace about the end of my career.

After the NFL

I had been preparing during each off-season for my next goal in life after football—to eventually become the athletic director at the Ohio State University. I was ready to pursue that goal full time.

One path was to start at the bottom at Ohio State and work my way up. The other was to move from job to job, fill in my resume, then go back to the university.

There seemed to be several risks to moving from job to job. What if my family was settled somewhere else, and the time came to return to OSU? The kids would have to be taken out of school. At the time we did not have any, but we knew we wanted to have them. Nancy might have to leave a job she liked or a neighborhood she loved. I might take a job at another school and get involved in some problems which I did not cause but which reflected poorly on me as an OSU candidate. Since I knew I wanted to be at Ohio State; I knew any job there would bring me into contact with former players, coaches, and other mentors I already knew and cared about; starting at the bottom at Ohio State and working my way up made the most sense.

Not as I planned

After failing the physical, I made three calls. The first was to Nancy, the second to Mom and Dad, and the third to Ed Weaver. I was ready to start at the bottom and begin working my way up at Ohio State.

After explaining the situation to Weaver, I said, "Do you have a job for me?"

Weaver replied, "No, I do not."

I was stunned. The conversation was over.

In the off-season, I was involved in all sports on all levels, participating on committees and working on independent studies. I was learning about budgets, women's sports, building maintenance, and everything involved with a giant athletic program. I had been learning and contributing, but now I could not be hired for an entry-level position!

When I hung up the phone, I felt my world falling apart. My only source of income was occasional speeches for FCA and the Ohio Contractors Association, which ranged from free to about $100. Nancy was pregnant with John-Ryan, our first child. My vocational future seemed to be over before it had truly begun. But there was no time to feel sorry for myself, because I needed a job.

One of the most delightful conversations I had with anyone about my vocational future was with newly reelected Ohio governor James A. Rhodes.

After reviewing my situation, Governor Rhodes suggested I meet with the Republican Party chairman in order to plan to be elected state representative, earn a law degree, and eventually run for lieutenant governor.

I did meet with the party chairman, whose first question was, "Do you still get mail in Lancaster?"

He was excited when I said, "Yes, infrequently," because that allowed me to run against Don Maddox, a Democrat, and pick up a seat for the GOP. He brushed off my desire for our family to continue to live in Arlington, saying that would not be a problem.

I felt like I was cutting corners before even running for office. It seemed there would be more corners to cut in the future, and I did not like that feeling. Nancy and I discussed the matter briefly, though not seriously.

Ron Maciejowski was one of several former Buckeyes successfully working for Worthington Industries, and Mace arranged for us to meet with Billy Joe Armstrong, also a former Buckeye and the president of Worthington Industries. After a short while, Billy Joe said, "Rex, we would be happy to have you join us," but I knew I still wanted to pursue something at Ohio State. I thanked him and told him what was in my heart.

Dick Crawford was a dear Christian friend, sixteen years older than myself, who was in state government and an "honorary Phi Delt;" we actually had a ceremony to bestow that honor on him. One of his contributions was to help the Brothers find jobs while they were in school. As we worked together with the Fellowship of Christian Athletes, Adult Chapter, he had suggested I call a man named Jack Havens, who Dick had once described as a "young John Galbreath."

I did not know Jack, and therefore I did not understand how influential he was among the power brokers in Columbus. I met with Jack, explained my situation, and enjoyed the conversation.

"Let me make some calls, and I will get back to you," he said.

When I met with him again, he said, "You have an appointment to see Saul Segal." Segal was in charge of the development department at Ohio State. "He wants to meet you. After that, come and see me."

When I returned to see Jack, he extended his hand, but rather than saying, "Hello," he said, "Congratulations."

There Is a Job at Ohio State

I had a job at Ohio State, half paid by the development department, half by the athletic department. I would be housed in development but spend most of the time working with athletics. I would be able to continue working on my Ph.D. It was perfect.

One longitudinal study I made in 1975 was of the graduation rate of football players. The data showed that in Woody's first twenty-five years, 87 percent of the lettermen had graduated. Beyond that, more than one-third of the 87 percent had earned advanced degrees.

I was impressed and could not wait to congratulate him. His reaction surprised me.

"Hmm," he said. "I thought it would be better than that. I have some work to do."

When I left Coach, my first action was to call Jeff Kaplan, known as the brain coach for the team, to tell him he would be in trouble tonight. Sure enough, they went to work on the problem I saw as a success, and sure enough, improvements were made.

While working and learning at my job, my friendship with the Havens family was growing. Actually, it was our friendship because Nancy had become very much involved as well. An additional benefit was that I was learning from Jack too.

One day—it must have been in the spring of 1976—I was getting ready to sit for the general examination for my Ph.D. Jack called and said, "Rex, what do you think of Nautilus?"

I knew Buffalo had purchased the equipment when I was there. Of course, Woody had it because Michigan did. The Bengals had it, and others probably did too. I saw benefits when I worked out with it.

"It's a gold mine," I said.

My mind went back to a very brief conversation I had overheard passing by Ed Weaver's office, when Woody was in there.

"I ordered Nautilus equipment. Michigan has them, and I need them," shouted Woody.

Weaver began to ask questions about their use, comparable products, cost—completely reasonable questions a supervisor might ask. Woody was having none of it.

"I've already ordered the machines," he said, "I'm just telling you to pay for them."

Not that there were any questions about who was running things; this was just further confirmation.

Back to the phone call.

Jack Havens and other members of their family, with his daughter, Ellen, as majority stockholder, had purchased the California franchise from Arthur Jones, the inventor of Nautilus machines and the founder of Nautilus, Inc. Jones had been using Dick

Butkus, the retired Chicago Bears perennial All-Pro linebacker, to promote the equipment and suggested Butkus, who lived in California, as a possibility to run it for Jack.

"Thank you very much, but I have someone in mind," Jack had replied.

"Rex," he said, "If you want it, the job is yours. What do you think?"

I knew it was a great opportunity and a tremendous compliment. Did it change my Ohio State dream, which was more real than ever before? I did not know.

"I understand," Jack said. "Let me know what you decide."

By now I knew not to ask Ed Weaver about my future at Ohio State, so I decided to see Hugh Hindman, then associate athletic director.

"Hugh, you are certainly in line to succeed Ed Weaver as athletic director. After you would be Jim Jones, then Dick Delaney. I understand and accept that. My question is, is there a place for me at the end of that line?"

"No," he said. No explanation or qualification—just no.

The next morning it all hit me. I was in the shower, my energy drained from my body, and I slowly slumped to the floor. I broke into tears and thought, *I've got the credentials, the desire, past contributions, and they will not let me get in the back of the line.*

At least it was not like the first time I was rejected by my university. I had a great opportunity ahead of me and was thankful for that. I also had a responsibility—to tell Woody.

When I went to his office, I went straight to the point.

"Coach, I'm leaving the university and going into private business with Jack Havens and his daughter, Ellen."

"Why would you do that?" he asked. "You are the best we have in that department. Why would you leave?"

I had never told him about the initial experience with Ed Weaver, so I started there. Then I explained what had happened with Hugh Hindman.

Woody slammed his fist so hard on the table he almost broke it, launched into a list of words Sunday school teachers do not use, and concluded with, "Those guys are jealous of you." Then he said, "You keep your nose clean and do a great job for Jack! And be ready to come back here when OSU calls!"

So, in 1976, Nancy, myself, and nine-month-old John-Ryan moved to Ventura, California, to sell Nautilus equipment. My starting salary was $17,000—same as I was making at Ohio State when I left and the same I made as an NFL rookie. Anything more would depend on merit raises based on performance and stock investment, determined by increases in market value. I was officially a businessman and an entrepreneur.

While proofing this chapter, I noticed the number seventeen was good luck for us, tied into my starting salary in the NFL, my job at Ohio State, and with Nautilus. It was also John Havlicek's number with the Celtics. My Dad once said, "If you could pattern your life after an athlete, it would be John Havlicek." Dad was right. Thirty years after they met, Gary Gearhart, John's teammate at Ohio State, called him, "The most outstanding moral man I have ever known."

Of course, we know that inflation causes the value of dollars to decline over time. In 1971, my starting salary with the Colts would be worth $113,050 today, far below the NFL minimum of $660,000 in 2021. My 1976 salary at Nautilus would be worth $80,410.

Not much later, I was conducting a demonstration of some of the equipment at a convention of athletic trainers, and one of the Bills' trainers stopped. It was nice to say hello, and it was surprising when he said, "Lou Saban was trying to reach you midway through the season. He hoped you would be healthy. He thought you could help us at the end of the season, and everyone wants as much retirement credit as possible. Then (owner) Ralph Wilson got involved in making moves, and things never really developed."

Wow! Thinking back to that time, it would have been a difficult decision, but since we were still on the ground floor of establishing our California Nautilus franchise, it would not have been right to leave.

I was touched to learn the Bills had been interested, but things absolutely worked out for the best.

OSU Needs an AD

When Hugh Hindman retired in 1984, Jack Havens said, "If you want the AD's job now, we will help get it for you. But we still have things we'd like to accomplish on the West Coast."

Then Dan Heinlein, director of alumni relations, told me that he thought Ohio State wanted someone who had already been an athletic director at a major university. Having worked with Dan while sitting on the alumni association board of directors and feeling he was a confidant of mine, I asked Madison Scott, chairman of the search committee, to withdraw my name.

Rick Bay, an athlete and graduate of that school up north, got the job in May 1984. In his biography, *From the Buckeyes to the Bronx*, he acknowledged the efforts of "my friend Dan Heinlein" in helping him get the Ohio State job. At the time, Rick was in his third year at the University of Oregon. Here I thought Dan was my friend, but he was taking me out of contention so Rick Bay would get the job.

I had very little contact with the athletic department while Rick was there; however, when he resigned rather than fire football coach Earle Bruce after a 6–4–1 season and a career record of 81–26–1 (.755), I admired the stand he took.

Shortly after this, Jack began to discuss forming a bank charter in California. He also showed great confidence in me when he casually mentioned, "Hey, Rex, I think the banks of the future are going to be allowed to market brokerage products. Why don't you study for that test and get your license? It may be helpful for you."

I discovered "that test" is known as the Series 7 - General Securities Representative Exam. It was considered the most difficult of all securities licensing exams. It lasted three hours and forty-five minutes and had a pass rate of 65 percent. It was required to market stocks, corporate and municipal bonds, and mutual funds. Most people who took the test had one or two degrees in business, had been hired by brokerage firms, and had studied at work until they passed the test.

Jack said, "Get your license," like I might say, "Pick up a magazine at the store." It was not easy, but like the brokers who did not want to lose a job, I did not want to disappoint him. I was happy and relieved to pass it the first time.

While we did not pursue the bank charter, the investment knowledge I gained has been valuable to me for decades.

OSU Needs an AD, Again

Jim Jones was "next in line" for the job in 1987. Did that mean I could get it? In my heart, I wanted it, but my mind knew the timing was not right. My doctors were telling me yet another back operation was in my near future. It was a demanding job, and I had to be healthy to do it right.

When I called Woody to tell him I was not going to pursue the job, he said, "I've been waiting to hear from you." I had been laying low, due to the pain, which required upcoming operations.

"Are you sure?" he said. "I think you should get back here so our doctors could fix you up. If you are not going to be a candidate, I need to throw my support to Jim Jones and help him get the job."

What I did *not* say was, "Woody, when you had your gallbladder out a couple of years ago, those doctors left a sponge in you." I did think it. Jim Jones got the job.

Sometime later, my old Colts mentor, Tom Matte, knowing I had my Ph.D. in athletic administration, called to tell me Cornell was looking for an athletic director. He wanted us to be a package deal, though he did not explain how the package would be arranged.

Sports without a win-or-else mentality, without extreme recruiting issues, and without marginal students not interested in a degree did have an appeal. When a friend of Matte's called, I expressed my hesitancy based on back issues at the time. When he asked permission to float my credentials, I agreed.

This was on a Friday. About two hours later, he called back and asked me to fly in for the weekend to be interviewed.

I thought of a saying my father had frequently used. He may have heard Reverend Norman Vincent Peale say it. "When you are climbing the ladder of success, remember the many hands helping you along the way. You may need those same hands on the way down."

Then I thought of Jack Havens. He had been faithful and committed to me, and he helped me so often. We had been very successful working on Nautilus and other projects. There was no doubt he understood my desire to be the athletic director at Ohio State and would not only accept that but help me attain it. But Cornell? I was not sure if that was fair to ask, because Nautilus was still winding down, and there was work to be done.

I did not interview at Cornell that weekend. I continued working with Jack Havens, evaluating and buying businesses, and with Ellen Havens in the banking business.

By now I should probably provide some perspective regarding Jack's place in the world of banking, not just in Columbus but around the country. One day I was visiting his home and he took a call from Henry Kissinger, who wanted feedback on a banking problem somewhere in the world. Yes, the Henry Kissinger who was secretary of state under presidents Nixon and Ford.

Also, about five years ago, Nancy and I took a vacation with friends to the Little St. Simons Islands, a privately owned island off the coast of Georgia, open to naturalists, bird-watchers, and environmentalists. A tall, bald man and his wife sat down beside us in the dining area, which had open seating. He was instantly recognizable because he was on television virtually every day during the 2008 banking crisis. It was Henry "Hank" Paulson Jr., former secretary of the treasury under President George W. Bush. He and his wife, Wendy, became frequent dining partners during our stay.

I am still not certain whether I was more impressed to learn Hank had talked with John F. Havens in the past or that the Paulsons owned the island!

Ohio State President Gordon Gee calling

Then, in 1994, Jack called and said, "You are going to get a call from Ohio State president Gordon Gee." Jim Jones was retiring, and it was about the athletic director position.

Instinctively, I knew the timing was not right. I was facing my fifth or sixth back surgery, my first ear surgery, and a hip replacement, all in a nine-month period. Simply enduring the procedures and recuperating seemed impossible, much less doing a twelve to fifteen hour a day job at the same time.

Gordon called on a Friday and went into his full sales mode.

"Rex, when I'm talking with Jack Havens, he brings your name up and talks for forty-five minutes. I have to end the conversation," he said.

Knowing Jack as a man of few words, who seldom talked for more than ten minutes at a time, I felt complimented.

"Didn't those [health] problems start here?" Gordon continued. "Why not get them solved here? No one else in the process is an All-American athlete from Ohio State with a doctorate in the field. You are needed here." He was aware it was necessary for someone to repair relations between the athletic department and former athletes.

I knew enough not to argue with him. Actually, it was fun to hear I had value from someone at Ohio State.

The following Monday, Dr. Manny Tzagournis called. His title was vice president for health sciences at the Ohio State University. He was essentially the top doc at the school. He had all my medical records and a plan for me to work full time and recover completely. It sounded very difficult.

I was never offered the OSU job, so I never turned it down. I believe I would have gotten it, but I knew I was not healthy enough to do it properly. Dan Heinlein asked me to endorse Andy Geiger, and I did. He got the job.

About a year later, I ran into Andy and asked him how the first year was going.

"Rex," he said, "do you know how many times I have eaten dinner with my family this year? Six times in one year!"

Not seeking the Ohio State job in 1994 was the right decision— one I have never regretted. I believe I would have enjoyed working for and with Gordon! We have always had great respect for and synergy with each other. But I wanted my family to know the full story of the experience seeking my dream job, then turning it down (sort of), because it had so many pieces and parts to say about my faith as a Christian.

At times you are treated unfairly, and I still battle resentment about that.

At times the second choice is better than the first would have been.

Some things happen that are better than you can imagine.

People are important, whether you are on your way up the ladder or on the way down.

Sometimes good deeds are rewarded, sometimes not.

Sometimes good deeds are rewarded later.

No experience is all good or all bad. Look for the good part and accept the bad.

When situations change, goals might too—or they might not.

Consistently applying the words of Christianity to life makes me think what hitting a baseball in the majors must be like. The average pitcher throws more than ninety miles per hour, some much faster. Pitchers can make the ball go up or down, side to side, bend or break sharply. You never know what is coming. Beyond hitting the ball, there are fielders all over the place to catch the ball. In fact, there are nine, but some days it seems like there are twenty.

The best hitters fail about 65 percent of the time. Many of the players in the Baseball Hall of Fame failed more than 70 percent of the time. The task is difficult.

A friend from Portsmouth, Ohio, Larry Hisle, struggled to make the majors for several years, but he finally became an all-star by reducing the very difficult task of hitting a baseball to one simple goal: "Take good swings at good pitches." After injuries shortened his career, he became the batting coach of the two-time world champion Toronto Blue Jays. In 1993, by taking "good swings at good pitches," Toronto players had the three highest batting averages in the American League: John Olerud, .363; Paul Molitor, .332; and Roberto Alomar, .326. Never before in the history of baseball had the top three batters been from the same team. Plus, Blue Jay Joe Carter knocked in 121 runs, all while following Hisle's advice.

"Humble and Kind"

With a song first released on an album in 2015, then released as a single in 2016, country singer Tim McGraw summarized my faith in five words: "always stay humble and kind." For me, it was the Christian equivalent to hitting a baseball by "always take good swings at good pitches," as it takes a very complex problem and condenses it into a brief message.

While I may never achieve McGraw's song in my lifetime, it is a clear standard for me as a Christian. Thinking about those words helps me see opportunities to do it. Sometimes those opportunities come when I least feel like rising to the challenge. Those are the times when it is most important to do so.

Someone failed to do what he promised, causing you delays or loss? "Always stay humble and kind."

The love of your life found someone else, and your pain is off the charts? "Always stay humble and kind."

Your child got in trouble at school for the 326th time this month? "Always stay humble and kind."

A loved one does not seem to be receiving the necessary care at a hospital? "Always stay humble and kind."

For me, "always stay humble and kind" is the clear, concise, Christian response to "take good swings at good pitches." For a challenge, make your own list of the times it is most difficult to "stay humble and kind." The "always" part can wait until the "humble and kind" part becomes more comfortable. You may find yourself adding to the list frequently.

Jack Havens

The words *humble and kind* are a good start in explaining the life of a man who personified them to me: Jack Havens.

Jack worked with giants of business and academia throughout Ohio and the nation, but he chose to remain in the background as much as possible. In my opinion, God sent Jack and his family into the life of the Kern family when we needed him the most. He "made some calls" to get me a position in the Ohio State athletic department after Ed Weaver told me there were none available. When Hugh Hindman told me there was no place for me in the athletic department, Jack chose me to work with his daughter, Ellen, in taking Nautilus exercise equipment to California. He helped us learn how to run a business, mentoring us for years while he was running several businesses himself and advising many others on their companies.

When we had completed our run with Nautilus, Jack introduced me to the world of finance and mentored me while I worked with him directly. He literally turned a banged-up former athlete into a businessman.

As if all that were not enough, he and his wife, Sally, were dear friends of our family until he died far too soon in 2017 at the age of ninety. Fortunately, Sally is still with us.

While Jack would not have wanted to be featured in this book, I would have tried to convince him to allow it. Fortunately, his daughter and our dear friend, Ellen Havens Hardymon, was anxious to discuss her father:

"My father contracted polio at the age of three and was unable to walk until an operation when he was twelve. At Ohio State, he earned a varsity *O* in track. That tells you how he attacked problems, both his own and the ones his friends brought to him for his advice. If you could only use two words to describe Jack Havens, they would be *problem solver*.

"He founded a number of businesses in central Ohio and served as chairman of Muirfield Village as Jack Nicklaus was developing that area. From 1980 to 1986, John G. McCoy asked him to serve as chairman of Banc One Corporation and coordinate their five-year plan of expansion. During, before, and after, Dad served on such corporate boards as W. W. Williams, Cardinal Health, Worthington Industries, Midland Life Insurance Company, Big Bear Company, Advanced Drainage, and Cornerstone International. He served on both the board of trustees and the Ohio State University Hospitals boards and helped launch the Arthur G. James Cancer Hospital.

"I first heard of Rex when he spoke to my eighth-grade class at

Columbus School for Girls. We really paid attention to that freshman football player from Ohio State!

"In the mid-1970s, I was an Ohio State student working out at the Nautilus facility in Worthington, a suburb of Columbus. The owner, Jim Carpenter, mentioned a franchise opportunity to sell Nautilus equipment in California. After doing the due diligence, I took the idea to Dad. He worked with Jim and me to investigate the situation. We decided that the equipment was good, it was a solid business, and it was priced right. Then Jim backed out the day we were going to sign the papers. We bought the franchise anyway.

"A friend of mine, Gary LeFevre, and I went to California to get started and realized I needed help. Dad knew Rex would be the perfect mentor and partner for the job, and he joined us.

"Rex was a rock star for what we needed. The Rose Bowls were fresh in the minds of every sports fan in California. His name recognition was higher in California than anywhere except Ohio, so he gave us immediate credibility. His friendly, sincere manner made a perfect impression on people. Plus, he worked very hard.

"Like myself, Rex had a steep learning curve on the financial side of running a business—business plans, cash flow, accounts receivable. Dad was always available. We never stopped learning from him. Even though Dad was a minor investor, he knew what it meant to me and to Rex, and he gave us his full support.

"Dad believed in Rex—for who he was and for what he could become. They were very much alike—they worked hard, were competitive, and never failed at anything. In business and life, they stood for honesty and integrity. You don't really 'win' in business; you succeed in business when both parties benefit. They understood that and saw the desire for mutual success with their business partners in each other.

"One other thing about Rex that people often miss is his wife, Nancy. She has meant so much to him and his success along the way. I like to say, 'Success comes in pairs,' and they are a perfect example.

Lasting Tribute

The admiration Nancy and I have for Jack is such that we established the John (Jack) F. Havens Scholarship Fund for track at Ohio State to honor the man who overcame polio to letter as an OSU discus thrower. Should there be a time when Olympic sports are phased back and scholarships are not provided, funding will go to the Arthur G. James Cancer Center—one of so many projects he helped guide while remaining out of the public eye.

Rex Kern (right), Ohio State quarterback, joins three other members of the Fellowship of Christian Athletics Foundation at a White House worship service Sunday. After the services (from left) are: Jay Wilkinson, Republican candidate for Congress from Oklahoma and son of Charles "Bud" Wilkinson, former University of Oklahoma football coach; John Erickson, Republican candidate for the Senate from Wisconsin and former University of Wisconsin basketball coach; Mrs. Nixon; Nixon; and Bobby Richardson, University of South Carolina baseball coach and former New York Yankee.

A newspaper article showing me with President Nixon. John Erickson had been the basketball coach at Wisconsin and became President of FCA.

Two of my favorite people! Ellen Havens Hardymon and Dr. E. Gordon Gee.

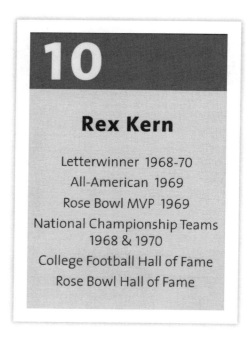

10

Rex Kern

Letterwinner 1968-70
All-American 1969
Rose Bowl MVP 1969
National Championship Teams
1968 & 1970
College Football Hall of Fame
Rose Bowl Hall of Fame

A concise summary of my career.

In Recognition
of Outstanding Performance

Rex Kern

has been named to

PREP ALL-AMERICA
BASKETBALL

1967

HIGH SCHOOL		COACHED BY
LANCASTER		GEORGE HILL
Lancaster, Ohio		

selected by

Coach & Athlete Magazine

co-sponsored by

Royal Crown Cola Co.
Columbus, Georgia

In Recognition
of Outstanding Performance

Rex Kern

has been named to

PREP ALL-AMERICA
FOOTBALL

1966

HIGH SCHOOL		COACHED BY
LANCASTER		EARL JONES
Lancaster, Ohio		

selected by

Coach & Athlete Magazine

co-sponsored by

Royal Crown Cola Co.
Columbus, Georgia

JOHN ERICKSON was an associate professor and head basketball coach at the University of Wisconsin for 9 years, and has served on the advisory board of the Fellowship of Christian Athletes.

REX KERN is presently a senior at Ohio State University, is quarterback for the "Buckeyes," and an active member of the Fellowship of Christian Athletes.

BOBBY RICHARDSON, former New York Yankee second baseman, is now head baseball coach at the University of South Carolina and is national representative for the Fellowship of Christian Athletes.

JAY WILKINSON, former White House Staff member, was an active participant in the Fellowship of Christian Athletes during his football-playing days at Duke University.

THE WHITE HOUSE

WASHINGTON

October 22, 1970

Dear Rex:

It was a special pleasure to welcome you and your parents to the White House last Sunday, and I want to thank you once again for your kindness in participating in the worship service. The occasion was a particularly memorable one for us. Mrs. Nixon and I were glad that you could join us for coffee beforehand, and we will be expecting great things of the Buckeyes this fall.

With every good wish,

Sincerely,

Richard Nixon

Mr. Rex Kern
1942 Iuka Avenue
Columbus, Ohio

Rose Bowl Hall of Fame induction, 1991. Michael kept a close eye on the statue, as he did all day, while J. R., Nancy, and I enjoyed ourselves.

Karl Rothermund, two-time Heisman trophy winner Archie Griffin, and I.

Nancy and I with our granddaughter, Alexis.

Nancy, John-Ryan, myself, and the co-captain of
the victorious Nittany Lion lacrosse team, Michael.

Back row: myself, Nancy, and our first grandson, Colby;
Amy and Heather. Front row: Michael and J. R.

My idol, John Unitas, the great quarterback
of the Baltimore Colts.

Tackling the great Leroy Kelly in our 20–3 1971
playoff victory over the Cleveland Browns.

Kevin Rusnak, Nancy Henno, and I at the 1969 Rose Bowl.

Mom helps me recuperate following shoulder
surgery after the 1969 Rose Bowl.

My dear friend Woody Hayes, who wrote,
"To Rex Kern, a great football player, an
unequaled leader and a super friend.
Your old coach, Woody."

My College Football Hall of Fame induction is recognized at the Horseshoe, with family, teammates, Archie, and our outstanding AD Gene Smith.

Members of our 1967 state final four baseball team,
from the left, Lenny Conrad (outfielder), Dick Daubmire
(pitcher), Coach Dick England, and myself (third base).

Coach England's basement: To my left, Connie England, Nicki Baltz,
Mark Baltz, my brother Keith, and Coach.

The poster on the door to my room at the Phi Delt house
was a daily reminder of our only Big Ten loss.

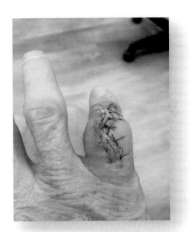

Grandpa Harley Kern had big hands, but his little finger was smaller than mine is now!

Kansas City Athletics

HUMBOLDT 3-9911   MUNICIPAL STADIUM, KANSAS CITY, MISSOURI 64127

June 19, 1967

<u>Certified Mail</u>

Mr. Rex W. Kern
630 Garfield Ave.
Lancaster, Ohio

Dear Rex:

As you know, the Kansas City Athletics selected negotiation rights to you at the recent Free Agent Draft Meeting held in New York City.

Under the rules of the Free Agent Draft it is necessary to start negotiations with you within fifteen days of the June Free Agent Draft Meeting.

This letter is merely to confirm that Mr. Dan Carnevale, our scout in your area, met with you and your father on June 16 and started negotiations with you. I realize, Rex, that you have a desire to go to college and we certainly want you to go to college, especially with the military situation the way it is. If you were to agree to a contract with the Kansas City organization we would give you your college education and would permit you to stay in school interrupted and play for our organization during the summer so that you would not be faced with a military situation by leaving college to play professional baseball. We are also in a position to offer you a lump cash bonus and I certainly hope that you will give Mr. Carnevale's offer further consideration as we would certainly like to have you playing for the Kansas City Organization.

I would also like to call your attention to the new rules of the Free Agent Draft as it now stands. If you do not sign a professional contract at this time and enter a four year college you will not be able to sign until at the end of your four years of college and at that time you will have finished your senior year and you will not have any bargaining power. We feel that you have a very fine future in professional baseball and that you very possibly could be playing in the Big Leagues within a few years.

If you have any questions concerning the offer made to you by Mr. Carnevale please do not hesitate to call me, collect, at the office here

CHAPTER 7

INJURIES AT OHIO STATE AND BEYOND

"I can do all things through Christ who strengthens me."
Philippians 4:13

I n the previous chapter, I mentioned I offered my athletic talents to God when I gave my life to Him, realizing that He had given those talents to me initially. As time passed, and I gained more information, my perspective on that gift changed.

In high school, I was a very good athlete against COL competition. Again, that was not my achievement, but my gift.

At Ohio State, I met many other young men who were very good athletes in their high schools. The most striking example was Jack Tatum, from Passaic, New Jersey. On our freshman team, Jack was possibly our best fullback, or halfback, or defensive back, or linebacker, or wide side defensive end. Considering there were four defensive backs and two linebackers, it is possible he could have started at any of nine different positions, over several teammates regarded as high school All-Americans. Jim Stillwagon did not have skills as diverse as Jack's, but he was a dominant middle guard and could have played offensive guard or linebacker.

When we moved to the varsity as sophomores, we saw films of and played against remarkable athletes, such as Jerry Levias of SMU, Leroy Keyes of Purdue, Ed Podolak of Iowa, Ron Johnson of Michigan, and O. J. Simpson of USC. The list grew during the next two years.

The point is, the more I knew about other athletes, the more impressed I was with their gifts. Not that my gifts were less, but rather, I was able to put my athleticism into perspective.

In the NFL, that perspective changed again. I was playing cornerback at the same time as Jimmy Johnson of San Francisco, Willie Brown of Oakland, Mel Renfro of Dallas, Jimmy Marsalis of Kansas City, and Dick LeBeau of Detroit. These men were better athletes and more experienced than me. It was a challenge to act like I belonged, much less to believe I did.

Eventually, I realized God had given me other talents as well. I loved to compete. I loved to work out, to practice, and to learn. Those skills could help me supplement my athleticism. If I studied and listened, the experience issue would take care of itself. I understood that other abilities expanded my gift of athleticism. I later realized those gifts would help me in other areas of life as well.

Even keeping those thoughts in mind, it was discouraging to think I was going to have to defend against the speed and deception of Paul Warfield; the hands and moves of Fred Biletnikoff; the size, speed, and strength of Charlie Taylor; the blocks of Gene Upshaw and Larry Little; and the power of Larry Csonka, Mike Garrett, O. J. Simpson, and many other athletes with similar skill and devotion to the game.

One thought erased all those worries: God was on my side. He would decide if I was going to be cut or successful; how long I would play and how well; and where my career would go after the NFL ended, sooner or later. My job was simple—trust in Him and work like crazy at something I loved to do. That thought enhanced my focus, decreased my concerns, and increased my joy.

A changing perspective on my athleticism in comparison to my peers was the second time I questioned exactly what this particular gift from God was all about. The first had been at Ohio State, when I had back surgery for the first time.

During the spring practice of our freshman year, my classmate Ron Maciejowski and I were fortunate that the two returning varsity quarterbacks, two-year starter Bill Long and Kevin Rusnak, were both playing baseball. This allowed each of us to get far more repetitions with the varsity players than we normally would have and to receive more coaching instruction while learning a new offense.

But toward the end of spring practice, I began to have considerable pain in my back and down my leg. When I was unable to get out of bed one morning, I told my roommate, Dave Cheney, "I can't move." When I called the trainer, Ernie Biggs, he wanted to see me. After he saw me, he sent me to Dr. Jud Wilson.

I had met Dr. Wilson after a freshman football game. We ran an option against the Indiana freshmen on a muddy rainy day near the goal line. I was hit around the six-yard line, put my left hand on the ground for balance, and dove into the end zone. I was knocked out and woke up a little later. I played the next series before realizing my left shoulder was hurt. After the game, he gave me two cortisone shots, and my arm was in a sling for a while.

There were no injuries during freshman basketball until the end of the season. What I thought was a hamstring problem had me hobbling around at times, but I made it through spring football, despite the hobbling.

Dr. Wilson initially diagnosed the problem as sciatic irritation. It was later described as a ruptured disc. He said an operation would be scheduled soon and that I would be ready for fall football. I asked if this was connected to what I thought was a hamstring issue. He said the hamstring was caused by the ruptured disc irritation.

I ended up having my first of seven back surgeries that summer spending about seven days in the hospital bed.

More than fifty years ago, back surgeries raised more concern than they do today, and they are no walk in the park. While they are not life threatening, there are potential consequences that are undesirable. Operations certainly can be career threatening, especially when your career includes getting hit by bigger, stronger, and nastier men who are moving at a high rate of speed with the expressed desire to inflict maximum pain and suffering.

To comfort my parents, Woody Hayes told them not to worry. If I never played for Ohio State, he would see that I graduated. While reassuring and appreciated by all of us, his words still made the risk feel very real.

I remember my first injury, though my age is not clear. It was certainly during the time when I was a redhead, stirring up trouble for something to do.

Anyway, I was pestering my brother, Keith, and one of his friends, Johnny Kiser. This went on over a period of several years—let's say I was five or six. When I saw they had had enough, I ran to the safety of my dad's barbershop. Just before I got to the door, I tripped on the sidewalk and hit my head on the corner of the cement step in front of the shop.

My father and his customer came outside to see what had happened. I remember someone saying, "He's going to be all right, but he will have to be sewn up."

Not exactly a man of the world when I graduated from Lancaster High School, I was somewhat less than that in grade school. When I heard "sewn up," my mind created a picture of my mother, sewing on a Singer sewing machine. That thing had a sharp piece of metal moving at a high rate of speed. How would I be hooked up to it? Would it hurt?

I also remember crying like crazy.

I was relieved when we got to the doctor's office, and there were no sewing machines in sight. It was five or six stitches—none by a Singer—and I slept at home that night.

After that incident, I only had a few normal injuries before Ohio State. There was a broken leg in the high ankle area in the eighth grade. I recovered from that despite crutch races in the school hallways with my friend Greg Woltz. There was also a broken clavicle on a play at the plate in an American Legion baseball tournament after my junior year. Coach Jones was pretty upset with Coach England, our baseball coach, until I was ready for football practice. Oh, and two concussions serious enough I had a special helmet made to use during my senior year of football.

While resting in Riverside Methodist Hospital, I decided there were two choices: Worry is always a choice, or it appears to be. Thoughtful deliberation is different than worry because there is a stopping point. You decide on the best course of action and act. Worry ends only if you decide to stop worrying. After thoughtful deliberation, I resolved to put the matter in God's hands while taking every action the doctors suggested—rest, proper exercise as my strength returned, good diet, and a positive attitude. I remember picturing myself walking along, holding Jesus's hand. It was a comforting thought then, and it continues to be today.

My first back surgery took place at the end of June 1968, at Riverside Hospital in Columbus. Later, doctors monitored my progress, accelerated by the weight equipment Woody sent to Lancaster. Within forty-five days I ran the mile and was cleared to practice, but with no contact! My doctors, familiar with countless back operations, used words like *remarkable* and *unbelievable* when discussing my recovery.

I saw it as part of a plan that I was beginning to understand. If I played my role to the best of my ability, things were under control and would work out. Maybe my healing would become a part of my testimony. As the hymn says, "Trust and obey."

The perfection of the plan proved to be true in a scrimmage near the end of two-a-days. I was wearing a gold jersey, which meant do not make contact. Woody was enjoying calling the option because we kept making first downs. There were times it seemed he was as happy beating Coach Lou McCullough's defense on Tuesday or Wednesday as he was Purdue's or Iowa's on Saturday. He was perfectly willing to accept the advantage that this time the defense was prohibited from tackling me. The defensive players were frustrated because their hands were essentially tied behind their backs, plus their coaches were yelling at them to play better defense. I saw their point and was not sure what this proved.

Woody was having fun and called another option. We ran it, and Jim Stillwagon had had enough. He hit me as if it were a game and flattened me. I felt like every bone in my back was broken.

Woody went berserk. He threw Wagon out of practice and took his scholarship away. Wagon went in to shower, telling anyone who would listen, "The heck with the Old Man. I should have gone to West Virginia." First Bill Mallory, then Woody went in to see him.

"Jim, you did the right thing," said Woody. Then, as only Woody could do, he put the responsibility on Wagon. "How are your mom and dad doing? How would they feel if you left Ohio State?"

Soon everyone was happy. Wagon did not disappoint his parents. Woody was not responsible for losing an All-American middle guard to West Virginia. Bill Mallory was not somehow to blame. Of course, the reporters never mentioned anything in the papers. They knew that if they did they would not be allowed to attend future practices.

As for me, I was fine. The man no one ever referred to as Dr. Stillwagon had probably prescribed the perfect treatment. Some adhesions were torn, and the healing process for my back was accelerated. Psychologically, I knew I could take a hard hit and was able to start the first game against SMU.

Looking back, I had not really had time to get into game shape. Incomplete recuperation may have led to various injuries that took me out of several games during the 1968 season.

One week before the start of the 1968 season, Woody wanted to scrap the I formation after spending all spring and fall on it and go back to robust—that is, running the fullback almost exclusively. Hugh Hindman, an assistant who had played for him at Miami (Ohio), fended off that hasty decision. Fortunately! (*A Fire to Win – The Life and Times of Woody Hayes* by John Lombardo, Thomas Dunne Books, St. Martin's Press.)

When we beat Southern Methodist, 35–14, there was a play that has caused a great deal of discussion over the years.

We were leading, 20–7, late in the second quarter. It was fourth and ten at their forty-one, and I felt we were ready to make a big play. When Woody sent in Mike Sensibaugh to punt, I waved him off and quickly called a play.

Of course, I did not know this at the time, but on the sideline people were expressing their opinions. Woody was wildly waving his hands. Mike Sensibaugh thought, *He's going berserk.*

Larry Zelina, out with an injury, said, "This is going to be interesting."

Bill Long, who had started at quarterback the previous two years, told Jim Roman, "I'm going in the next play."

Quarterbacks coach George Chaump thought, *Good, Rex. Good.*

In the huddle, Jim Otis said, "Rex is nuts."

None of them knew what Woody had told me in the spring. "Rex, it looks like you are going to be our quarterback," said Woody. "You are going to see what the coaches can't, and you must trust your instincts at certain times. You've got to decide what will or won't work."

As a naïve sophomore, I believed I had Woody's confidence. Looking back, if we had lost the ball on downs, I might have been buried on the bench, watching Long and Mace battle for playing time. If we had lost the game, at least my place in Heaven was secure.

The play was a disaster. I called for a short pass to Otis over the middle, but he was covered by both linebackers, and I was on my own. I was hit in the backfield, spun 360 degrees in the air, and fortunately landed on my feet. The box score reports I gained sixteen yards around right end for a first down. Then Woody called a time-out, Long went in for two plays, SMU called a time-out, Woody sent me back in, and I threw a sixteen-yard touchdown pass to Dave Brungard with thirty-five seconds to go in the half. SMU could not do anything, so the halftime score was 26–7, OSU.

Zelina was sitting by Ron Maciejowski during my run. He punched him on the leg and said, "It's going to be a long three years."

Later in the game, John Brockington, who got the start due to Z's injury, caught a thirteen-yard pass and ran for a forty-four-yard gain. Ron leaned over to Larry and said, "At least I will have company."

Looking back it is easy to see that many skilled offensive players, a new scheme by a creative quarterback coach, and unprecedented on-field play calling flexibility would mean exciting times for the Buckeyes and their fans for the next two years.

Back to my injury report.

Against Oregon, their defensive end gave me a hairline fracture to the jaw with his helmet. Today it is called targeting, carrying a fifteen-yard penalty and automatic ejection from the game. If it had a name then, it was probably *incidental contact*. I left the game and ate through a straw until the next game. For the rest of the season, I wore a lineman's face mask for practice and games. Ron Maciejowski came in and almost immediately hit Bruce Jankowski for a fifty-five-yard touchdown to end the scoring, 21–6, good guys. Woody told the reporters it was the longest touchdown in history, Pole to Pole.

Next came the game with top-ranked Purdue, which beat us 41–6 in 1967 and which Woody had prepared for since. I played through most of the third quarter until a running play, when Leo, Otie, and Brock all carried out their fakes. The problem was, one of them was supposed to block the Purdue player, who clobbered me for a loss of six yards. I left the game, and Woody sent in the senior and two-year starter Bill Long.

Facing third down and goal to go on the Purdue fourteen, Long dropped back to pass. He did not see a receiver open, but he did see a hole in the middle of the line. He ran untouched into the end zone on his first play, with 3:35 to play in the third quarter. It was also his only play of the game; I went back in the next series.

We won the game on Ted Provost's interception for a touchdown and Bill's touchdown, 13–0.

Our offense really clicked in a 45–21 win over visiting Northwestern. They stopped us inside, holding Otis to 48 yards on 15 carries, but that left me room to run—121 yards on 20 carries—and find Jan White—three catches for 97 yards—and Bruce Jankowski—four catches for 53 yards. When the offense rolls up 565 yards, Woody can accept the fullback being held down.

Our first road game of the season was at Illinois. At the close of our Friday walk-through, I noticed two Black men talking with first-year running backs coach Rudy Hubbard. *Who are they?* I wondered. Later, Rudy came up to me and explained.

"They are Illinois fans," he said. "They called me over and said, 'Which one's Kern?' When I pointed you out, they said, 'He can't be a homey. He has to be a brother to do all that fancy stuff.'"

That day, this redhead from Lancaster, Ohio, was proud to hear I played like I was "not white."

While working on this book, I was ecstatic to learn Coach

Hubbard had been selected to the 2021 College Football Hall of Fame class, largely on the basis of his success as head coach at Florida A&M for twelve years. He was the only coach from a historically Black college or university (HBCU) to win the Division 1-AA national title, now known as the Football Championship Subdivision (FCS).

As for the Illinois game, we played well for a half, when we led 24–0. Woody's halftime speech consisted of a lecture on Abraham Lincoln, who was born in Illinois. Why he did that, we never knew, but it gave us the impression that the game was in hand. It almost cost us; he never repeated that mistake the rest of the time we played for him.

They scored two touchdowns in the third quarter and one in the fourth, adding three two-point conversions to tie the score with 4:38 to play. After Zelina ran for a first down, I was knocked into next week and had to leave the game. Woody saw something in Long's eyes that made him uncomfortable, and he called for Mace.

Again, Woody chose the right man. Mace hit Z for a first down, then ran for one himself, then hit Z for a 44-yard bomb to the Illinois 4. Otie carried it in for a touchdown with 1:30 to play. Illinois returned the kickoff to their 27, then hit two passes for first downs. Things looked dicey until safety Mike Sensibaugh intercepted a pass on our 10-yard line and took it 33 yards, far away from our goal line. Mace took a knee, and we escaped, 31–24.

For our sixth game of the season, a fair Michigan State team came to Columbus. Our offense was moving the ball, with an 83-yard drive capped by an Otis plunge, a short drive to a missed field goal, a 41-yard drive stopped by a clipping penalty, and a 61-yard drive that resulted in my 11-yard pass to Bruce Jankowski for a second touchdown. We led, 13–0, early in the second quarter. Our running game was working, and I was nine of twelve for 138 yards. It looked like it was going to be a good day.

As the Spartans drove 71 yards for their first touchdown, I realized my ankle had been badly sprained during our drive. The medical staff looked at it, iced it, and wrapped it. I was out of the game.

After MSU made the score 13–7, Mace came in and took us 83 yards for an Otis touchdown. Who could ask for more than that! The 19–7 score carried to halftime.

Early in the third quarter, Michigan State scored a touchdown, immediately matched by a 53-yard Buckeye drive finished with a Mace keeper. The Buckeye offense stalled, and another MSU touchdown made the final 25–20. It was closer than we hoped, but the Bucks never trailed.

My ankle was much better, but the coaches must have thought another week of rest would be a good idea. Wisconsin had not won a game, and Mace had been outstanding in difficult situations all year. After the Badgers came Iowa and Michigan, two dangerous teams. It all made sense. I was not needed, because Mace started and had a great game, completing thirteen of nineteen passes for 153 yards and twenty-three rushes for 124 yards. Bill Long relieved him in a 43–8 victory.

I was back for Iowa and had a fair game. We won, 33–27, as Jim Otis rushed twenty-nine times for 166 yards.

Michigan: November 23, 1968

Every Michigan game is a big deal at Ohio State, but this game was among the biggest ever. We were second in the nation; they were fourth. The winner went to the Rose Bowl. The winner had a chance to win the national championship.

Most of all, *it was Michigan*. We wanted to make our best showing of the year, and every one of us had to be in top form.

With all this only days away, Tuesday morning I could hardly move. I was so sore and stiff I could not get out of bed. I called to my roommate, Dave Cheney, for help.

Before I knew it, Ernie Biggs, our trainer, had hurried over to the dorm. After that, there were doctors and frowns and worried conferences. Coach Hayes, ever the strategist, commanded that nobody was to know about what had happened. My condition was to be kept a total secret.

In a room filled with concern, I felt plenty myself. I also heard a voice that kept saying, "He is my refuge—my God in whom I trust." At a time when I had reason to be tense, I relaxed. I had experience. I'd been in God's hands before. I later learned there was a cracked vertebra in my back, which would eventually heal. With massage, my back loosened up. As a precaution, I did not participate in practice Wednesday, Thursday, or Friday.

On Friday night we went to a movie as a team, then returned to our hotel rooms, where hot chocolate and cookies were waiting as our snack. I had a nervous stomach, not unusual for the biggest game I had ever played, not unusual due to the fact I did not know if I would be able to play at all. The result was several quick trips to the bathroom.

Woody knocked on the door, mixing a bed check with a social call. He asked how I was.

"Ready to go, Coach," I replied.

"We're looking for a big game from you," he said to my roommate, fullback Jim Otis.

"If Rex stops going to the bathroom, and I can get some sleep, I will be ready," Otie replied.

Woody immediately called Doctor Bob Murphy to our room to check me out. As Dr. Bob began his checks, Woody had a solution.

"Jim, you need your sleep," he said. "You take my room. I'll stay here with Rex."

This idea did not have my support. Spending a night in the same room with Woody was not a comforting thought. I looked at Dr. Bob and shook my head, mouthing the words, "Please no." I used every form of nonverbal communication I could imagine when

Woody looked away.

Fortunately, Dr. Bob ruled that the change in sleeping arrangement was not necessary, though he did not clear me to play until the following morning. I was very relieved.

The next day we all played well. I played a full game without incident. I still don't believe the final score: 50–14, Ohio State!

When I talk to sports fans, I give them the bruising details—all power and guts—and then I talk about how football is not only physical but it's also mental. Football is decisions and strategy. It's capitalizing on sudden opportunities, knowing the right time for a pass or a run. It's being razor shape but at ease. It's being confident. It is trusting your teammates—and God.

We stayed on the ground. Otie led us with four touchdowns and 143 yards. Z and I added 92 yards and 96 yards. Ray Gillian pitched in 66 yards on five carries. We only passed nine times.

We led, 50–14, with 1:23 remaining in the fourth quarter. Woody elected to go for two. When asked why, Woody replied, "Because they would not let me go for three." That would haunt us fifty-two weeks later. For now, we were focused on preparing for the Rose Bowl.

"California, Here We Come"

We knew nothing about playing in a Rose Bowl but had complete confidence in our coaches. Woody's teams had won two Rose Bowls, after the 1954 and 1957 seasons. We were playing Southern Cal and Heisman Trophy winner O. J. Simpson, but our defense had stopped three very good tailbacks in Leroy Keyes, Ed Podolak, and Ron Johnson, so we had confidence in our players and their coaches. The offense thought it could score on anyone.

To my complete surprise, someone from the television show *The Dating Game* sent a telegram. I was invited to be the bachelor on their show and choose one of three bachelorettes for a "night on the town." The show would be filmed when the team was out for the Rose Bowl.

For a sophomore in college, this was a dream come true. I would have been excited to be one of three guys competing for a date with a beautiful girl, as I had been told Tom Selleck and Burt Reynolds were. As the bachelor choosing, though, I could not lose. I was guaranteed to have that date, and she was going to be beautiful!

Then the magic wore off. The real question was, "Does Woody tell me no, or do I just tell the guy instead of asking?' I knew what the answer would be.

The opportunity was too great to ignore. "I have heard no before," I decided. My other decision was when to ask him. Best time: after a real good practice.

The day came. Our practice that afternoon was outstanding. Woody was eating with the coaches in the cafeteria. I rushed in where angels fear to tread.

"Coach," I began, "I got a telegram from a representative of *The Dating Game*. They want me to be on the show when we go to California."

I might as well have been speaking Chinese. Woody was dumb-founded. A couple of the coaches tried to explain the show. The others were too smart to admit they knew anything about it. Of course, I tried to explain it.

When Woody was tired of being out of control, he said, "We're going out there to win a football game. I'd just call them back and say you are sorry, but we have to get better as a football team."

"OK, Coach," I said, and I got my dinner.

On the flight to Los Angeles, before the announcement for us to tape our ankles for practice after meeting with the media, Woody said to me, "Rex, you know that *Dating Game* you asked about? If it's not too late, I suppose it would be all right. Can you still do it?"

"No, Coach," I replied. "That is dead in the water."

At the time I was disappointed, though far from surprised. Soon I would be very happy not to have that inconvenient time commitment because I had more important things to do, and not just football.

Before that, there was a problem.

After a spirited workout in French Field House, turned up to ninety-eight degrees because Woody always quoted an admiral who said, "If you are going to fight in the North Atlantic, then train in the North Atlantic," the fullbacks and halfbacks hit the tackling dummy to begin practice. The quarterbacks were always excluded from this common practice. Why risk unnecessary injury?

That day, for some unknown reason, Woody said, "George [Chaump], bring those quarterbacks over here and let them hit the tackling dummy."

Let's pause the story here and consider some history. For one thing, quarterbacks never hit the dummy for a reason. Did that reason change? No. For another thing, I had been in the hospital six months earlier for back surgery and had been injured several times during the season. Was that worth considering? Probably so.

The question is, why didn't one of Woody's trusted confidants or trainers or other assistants ask him to take a step back and think about what he was doing?

Because no one did that in public, and almost no one did that in private. Woody always got his own way, so why risk being collateral damage when there was virtually no chance of a positive outcome? Being fired was a possibility. Usually those firings were forgotten, but why risk your job? Being ridiculed or demoted was a probability. Who needs that again? Look how much static George Chaump had received all year for taking the offense into the twentieth century with our new I formation, which the players liked to call "Rip" and "Liz," depending on whether our wingback lined up on the right or left side.

There were no volunteers to question the order. In fact, no one considered doing it.

I was the first quarterback in line and not about to ask any questions either. So I hit the dummy and went down in pain with a dislocated left shoulder. Woody said, "Oh, *unprintable* (five times)." Ernie Biggs popped my shoulder back into place, but I was through for a while. I could not practice and did not know if I could play in the Rose Bowl.

Looking back, I feel sorry for Woody. He could not control himself and pushed away everyone who wanted to help him.

Fortunately, Ernie Biggs and his staff rigged up a shoulder harness to protect me, and I came pretty close to working my way back into shape in California. Despite Ernie's efforts, in the last play of the third quarter, USC safety Mike Battle dislocated my shoulder when he tackled me. "Pull on my arm," I screamed at him. He walked away. Because I was so focused on the game, I was thinking about the clock being stopped and not needing to take a time-out. Ernie put my shoulder back into place. No one knew what had happened.

It was a well-played game by both teams. Total yardage: 366 yards for USC and 361 for us. They had 51 yards in penalties; we had 53 yards. We had a 21–19 advantage in first downs. We recovered all three of their fumbles and also recovered the only one we had. Mike Sensibaugh gave us a big advantage with his punting, averaging 45.37 yards to their 36.85 yards. We punted seven times; they punted six. So we exchanged punts six times and gained an average of 8.5 yards each time. That is the same as a 51-yard pass play or run from scrimmage!

I was voted the MVP of the game, due to the contributions of all my teammates and coaches.

My job was to direct the amazing assortment of weapons Woody had put together. On any given play, Jim Otis was a great choice, and we did know how to block twenty-six and twenty-seven, fullback off tackle. Brock and Leo were major threats outside or inside, and Z and Ray Gillian had to be accounted for as receivers or runners. I remember Ray had several outstanding plays in that game. Every single play, defenses had to defend future NFL players Jan White and Bruce Jankowski on pass routes. And I had Woody's full confidence to change the play when necessary. It was a great time to be a Buckeye quarterback.

Thinking back, calling plays for OSU in that offense was somewhat like being a Major League manager in the seventh game of the World Series in the 1960s and choosing between Sandy Koufax, Bob Gibson, Don Drysdale, and Juan Marichal as the starting pitcher. Even if I made a poor choice, good things were likely to happen!

There were many heroes on the team. The defense held USC to sixteen points, seven of which were scored with five seconds on the clock on a disputed touchdown. The Trojans had played seven top twenty teams during the year and were only held below sixteen once, never below nine. Wagon had nine tackles, Doug Adams eight, and Mark Stier added seven. It may have been Mark's best game as a Buckeye. He had suffered a shoulder separation on Monday and was not expected to be able to play very long. He was among the team leaders with twenty-eight minutes and also called the defensive signals. Tatum made six tackles and recovered an O. J. fumble. Urbanik hit their quarterback, Steve Sogge, to cause a fumble, and Stottlemyer recovered it. Sensibaugh and Anderson had interceptions.

Woody gave senior Bill Long the game ball for the outstanding job he did in practice imitating Sogge. Mace was the only other quarterback who could take snaps with the offensive starters, Red One. He was overworked, and his elbow became very painful. It still bothers him today. He never mentioned a problem to me at Ohio State, and I did not see a loss in effectiveness, but it might have been an issue.

On a similar note, when some subs went into the game in Pasadena, Mace understood why Long got the call at quarterback, but he still wanted to be part of the game. So he went in, tapped tight end Dick Kuhn on the shoulder, and replaced him. Mace got his name in the record book.

Also, the "presentation" of the award was different than the big production we see today. A stranger walked into the locker room, asked where I was, walked up to me, handed me the trophy, and said, "Congratulations, you were the MVP of the Rose Bowl."

I said, "This is not mine; it's everyone's." I doubt that anyone heard because they were all celebrating, and I was glad to rejoin them.

If the presentation of the trophy seems prehistoric, consider the ticket price. My parents sat in eight-dollar seats that day.

Fans who watched the game on television have told me that Curt Gowdy mentioned my ballhandling several times in the broadcast booth. Lancaster coaches John Holland and Earl Jones deserve the credit for helping me develop that skill, which was enhanced because the defensive players were focused on our many offensive threats. During any one play, five or six players might appear to have the ball when everyone carried out his fakes properly.

Before leaving the Rose Bowl, two other stories might be of interest.

First, I have very large hands. My Lancaster coaches told me how helpful that trait would be to control the ball and nearly hide it on my hip, and they had helped me develop the gift. When I first met Buckeye head coach Ryan Day, and we shook hands, he said, "Great quarterback with big hands."

Those hands also proved to be valuable in another competitive setting.

During my rookie year with the Baltimore Colts, one day I noticed big "Bubba" Smith—six eight, 285 pounds, and no fat—holding court with several of his defensive line teammates. This was a common event, but the topic of hand size caught my attention. Bubba's hand was much larger than his similarly sized teammates.

Always ready for a little competition, I joined the group to see if my hands matched up. Everyone was shocked to see that the five eleven, 184-pound cornerback had a hand as big as Bubba's, and from thumb to small finger, slightly longer. From thumb to small finger, my hand measures 10 1/4", from thumb to index finger, nine inches. I tried not to smirk as I left the group of giants shaking their heads.

Second, some five decades after the 1969 Rose Bowl, a Buckeye fan told me about watching the game with his parents. Noting that his mother seemed agitated, he asked why.

"I. can't. find. the. ball," she said through clenched teeth.

When he explained how much trouble the Trojan players must be having, she relaxed and enjoyed herself.

While working on this book, I discovered something surprising in "An Ohio State Man: Esco Sarkkinen Remembers OSU Football," by William Harper, published in 2000.

"Sark" had been an All-American end as a Buckeye from 1937 to 1939 and an OSU assistant coach from 1946 to 1978. Tom Harmon of Michigan, Heisman Trophy winner in 1940, called him the "toughest opponent" he ever faced. "Sark" earned five national championship rings and thirteen Big Ten championship rings as a Buckeye as well as the love and respect of the defensive ends he coached from 1946 to 1978.

Quoting Sark, "As was customary at the beginning of each season, we coaches gathered around Coach Hayes's office desk. We were asked for our individual predictions for 1968—by secret ballot. When the ballots were opened, the best prediction I recall was 7–2–1."

As freshmen, we knew nothing about Big Ten football, but we played against the 1967 varsity every day, and they went 6–3 that season. If we had been asked to vote, our predictions would have been closer to 10–0 than the coaches were.

We accomplished our goal of winning the Rose Bowl, 27–16, and ended up being voted the number-one team in the country to go with our Big Ten title. It was the first time any of those things had happened at Ohio State since 1957, and it was the first undefeated season since 1954.

More important for me, in the long run, I met a Rose Bowl princess who would become my wife. Nancy and I are a story for another chapter.

There is one more thing to mention about the spring of my sophomore year: I became a member of Phi Delta Theta fraternity.

Fraternity Row

Teammates Tom Backhus and Dave Brungard were Phi Delts, and another Phi Delt helped save my football career during freshman year. "Being in a fraternity gives you another group of teammates and broadens your base of friendships and contacts," Tom said. That was good advice, though time did not permit me to take full advantage of those opportunities.

After pledging, we had hell week, when this story took place.

A young man, who appeared to be a lawyer wearing a three-piece suit named Mr. William Friend, was introduced to the pledges. He had release forms for us to sign before we could go through hell week, which was necessary before we could join the fraternity. He passed out the forms and told us to sign.

As I read the form, it seemed we were relinquishing most of our rights under the Constitution. To paraphrase, it said, "Phi Delta Theta and the Brothers would not be responsible in the event of any injury."

The previous summer I had my first back operation and had signed several documents for insurance companies with a variety of stipulations. All the legal language was not fresh in my mind, but I had a strong suspicion I should not sign this paper. I asked to speak with Mr. Friend in private.

He was surprisingly understanding of my concerns and offered to remove one paragraph to which I objected, then another. Each time we initialed the paragraph that had been deleted. I thought, *Maybe they are just trying to scare us and do not want any pledges to drop out now.* So I kept objecting, he kept understanding, and we kept deleting.

Finally, we were both satisfied. The form I signed read, and I quote, "I, Rex Kern, delete, delete … signed, Rex Kern." I had completely agreed to nothing at all.

"Mr. Friend" had been a Phi Delt at Ohio University. Before that he went to high school with the former president of the Ohio State Phi Delt house, Rich Terapak, and they were classmates at the Ohio State law school. The whole thing was a hoax, yet a memorable part of our harmless hell week. They were, and are, loyal Buckeyes.

1969: Junior Year

The 1969 Bucks had a dream year for the first eight games of the season.

First of all, quarterbacks coach George Chaump had convinced Woody to use the I formation and the hurry-up offense, a remarkable feat. Second, George had a teaching method that allowed quarterbacks to learn quickly. He always said, "If they [the defense] do this, we do that." Week to week our game plan changed, and opposing defensive personnel and scheme could change greatly, but George made the whole thing as simple as a game of checkers. Soon Mace and I were thinking right along with him, figuring out countermoves, asking more intelligent questions, and learning the game plan more easily by the week.

In 1968, we set many OSU offensive records. In 1969, we broke them. We finished second in the country in tempo, running an average of 84 plays per game. We still hold the school record for running 101 plays in the opener with TCU and against Illinois. The days of "three yards and a cloud of dust" appeared to be over. Only six lettermen were lost on offense and defense combined, and thirty-nine returned. We were preseason number one by every poll, and stayed there until that fateful day in Ann Arbor.

The previous year's team made a huge impression on fans and media alike because it was so different from every other Ohio State team—and because it won the national championship. The truth is, for eight games, the 1969 team was much better. Even counting the clunker up north, the offensive statistics for the 1969 team far surpassed the 1968 team:

	1968	1969
Rushing yards/game:	301	308
Passing yards/game:	138	185
Total offense/game:	439	493
Total points:	323	383
Points allowed:	150	93

The offense scored 60 more points in one less game. Again in 1969, the defense was an under rated team strength, significantly reducing points per game from 15.0 (10 games) to 10.3 (nine games).

Of the first eight games, we were ahead at the half by three or more touchdowns seven times! The only exception was a two-touchdown lead over Washington, 21–7. Only three of the eight teams even scored in the first half. Washington and Purdue had seven points each, and MSU trailed, 34–14.

One might think that an up-tempo offense that was scoring rapidly would put the defense under pressure. That is part of the logic behind "three yards and a cloud of dust"—the other team can't score if we have the ball. The faster we score, the faster they have the ball. Also, if a team is winning by large margins they are playing substitutes early, with more points scored by the opponents against less experienced players.

So, despite reasons that the defense should have declined as the offense improved, that did not happen. The offense improved from ninth in the nation in scoring to second, while the defense improved from nineteenth in points allowed to seventh.

With a chance to become healthy after the 1968 season, I only had one injury in 1969 until the night before the Michigan game. At Northwestern, early in the fourth quarter, leading 21–0, I jammed my right shoulder. Unable to raise my arm above my shoulder in front of me, I came out of the game. At the time it seemed like a temporary thing, but even today I have a calcified knot in my right shoulder. The final score was 35–6, OSU. Mace came to the rescue again.

What happened before the 1969 Michigan loss was not exactly an injury, but it was one of the worst medical issues of my Ohio State career.

Friday, November 21, was a cold, drizzly day in Ann Arbor. When we were stretching, my back had gotten wet from the water on their artificial turf. I started to have back spasms, but my back was not a problem during our light practice. After practice Woody told me that ABC wanted to interview me about the Heisman Trophy and asked me to speak with them. Normally he would have told anyone interfering with our schedule to take a hike, but he asked me, and I agreed to his request. I stood around in the cold and damp until ABC arrived, late.

When I went to bed that night, I felt fine. When I woke up Saturday morning, I could not move. My back had completely tightened up. I was rooming with Leo Hayden and told Leo, "Call Woody and tell him I can't get out of bed." Leo tried, but Woody just said, "Don't bother me, just tell him to get out of bed." Eventually Woody understood the magnitude of the problem and summoned the medical team. Some trainers came to the room and started treatment with light heat. Then, they transported me to the hotel conference room where the players were getting their ankles taped and preparing for the game.

When we arrived at the stadium to begin our pregame work, the doctor said, "This will relax you and reduce the spasms." About that time Mike Sensibaugh walked behind me and later told me he almost passed out. "That was the biggest, longest needle I have ever seen," he said. I remember being glad I had not seen it myself.

We will return to the 1969 Michigan game in the next chapter. This chapter is based on my injuries over the years. There are two more to address from 1970 and five after my Buckeye career ended.

The first 1970 injury was a torn quadricep muscle in my right leg. There was a significant indentation and a big gap on the leg. That took almost two weeks to heal.

The second showed up after a game. I was normally the last player to leave, partly because I was tired, partly because there were several medical checks to be made. While I was in the shower, George Chaump said, "What is this about?" It looked like I was pregnant. "It" turned out to be a lower left abdominal tear, a ruptured lower abdominis psoas muscle. The psoas muscle is located in the lower lumbar region of the spine and extends through the pelvis to the femur.

Ernie put ice on it and the swelling went down after a while. The back brace I was already wearing probably gave me some support and relief. I continued wearing the brace as a precaution through the rest of the season.

Neither injury caused me to miss any game time.

As for the injuries after Ohio State, the first was when my buddy

Jim Stillwagon gave me two broken ribs in the defensive backfield at the Coaches All-American Game in Lubbock, Texas, already discussed in the chapter on Faith. Wagon was a "hitter" to friend and foe alike. All our OSU teammates were glad he was a Buckeye, for what he meant to our team and for the harm he caused our opponents. I saw both sides.

I had two concussions in the NFL. The most serious was when I tackled O. J. Simpson at the goal line. I broke an inner ear bone, which led to two operations. The other came when Oakland's outstanding guard Gene Upshaw knocked me into the nickel seats on a sweep. At the risk of bragging, I am proud of the fact that Bill Curry, Colt center, told me that his close friend Upshaw described me as his toughest cornerback to block.

The most frightening injury took place in a 1972 preseason exhibition game at Oakland. Nancy came up from her parent's house for the game. She saw the injury and had to wait somewhere between an hour and two until she could learn that it was not as serious as it looked.

I was at cornerback, and Gene Upshaw, an All-Pro for a reason, hit me head-on, spun me around, and another player hit me in the back. These plays happen all the time on a football field. Typically, you go on to the next play. This time I wanted to get up but could not. It was like that feeling when your leg is asleep, only it was from my waist to both feet. My lower extremities were numb. The medical people carted me off the field, being very careful because they did not know what had happened.

I was unusually concerned during this injury because this time I was also thinking about Nancy, sitting in the stands, trying to cope with the uncertainty and lack of information.

I do not remember whether the collision took place in the first or second half, so I can't estimate how long Nancy sat there, wondering how severe the problem was. I later learned she tried unsuccessfully to get information from the locker room, then decided to return to the hotel to await the team. However many hours it actually was, it must have seemed like forever.

During my second year with the Colts, I was holding for our placekicker, Jim O'Brien, who had kicked a Super Bowl game-winning field goal for the team after the 1970 season, when I broke a finger playing defense. I kept playing cornerback, but my career as Jim's point after and field goal holder was over because my finger, splinted and wrapped, was not flexible enough to hold for kicks.

Finally, I dislocated my left thumb at the wrist during the 1972 season. I was able to play with it in a cast, but it kept dislocating inside the cast. Surgery was required to place one pin in the wrist and a second in the thumb. I missed the remainder of the season.

Seventeen Surgeries

To the best of my knowledge, I have had seventeen surgeries: seven back, two total hip replacements, a shoulder surgery, two ear operations, a dislocated thumb, prostate surgery, and two minor ones. On August 13, 2021, doctors completed major reconstruction of my right little finger, the seventeenth. My best guess is about six concussions, two each at the high school, college, and NFL level. Technology has greatly improved since I played, so the improved accuracy of labeling a concussion now might result in a higher number. There were rehabilitations for most of the operations and several other injuries.

In addition to those who have been mentioned, I must give thanks to "Moose," Dr. Moustpha Abou-Samra, who saw our family through five back surgeries—one for Nancy and four for me. Now retired in Ventura, California, Moose will always be SPECIAL TO US!

Also, from the time I began to work with Jack Havens, he was an inspiration to me as I dealt with the operations and rehabilitations that resulted years after injuries.

He had contracted polio at the age of three and was twelve before a revolutionary surgery allowed him to walk again. Though there were consequences with his health for the rest of his life, he lettered in track at Ohio State and appeared to function normally, largely because he decided that was the way it was going to be.

One day I was the only one in the office in Columbus. Jack was at a meeting of the Ohio State Hospital board; his daughter Ellen was at a meeting; and Annie Leighty, his loyal secretary of thirty-five years, was running errands. When the phone rang, I rushed to answer it. Jack believed the phone was to be answered by the second ring, and we should get down to business right away.

It was Jack, who asked to speak to Annie. After I explained she was out, he said, "Ask her to cancel all my appointments for tomorrow."

"I'll do that," I replied. "What happened?"

"Some guy in a pickup truck ran over my leg," said Jack. "The bottom portion of my leg is pointing south—the top north."

I knew Jack had health issues, and I knew he had a plate with a ninety-degree angle in each leg attached to his foot to protect his Achilles tendon, so various possible problems came to my mind. But Jack thought most questions were a waste of time, so I just said, "Is there anything I can do?"

"No," he replied. "The emergency squad is on the way. They will be here soon and take me to the hospital. I'm fine."

That night, Nancy and I visited him at the hospital. Two or three days later, he walked into the office wearing a boot.

As mentioned, I decided that injuries were a part of athletics and that both were a part of my Christian faith. Many times, while preparing for operations or going through rehabilitation, I asked myself, "Is it worth it?" That was usually a very short conversation because it always was worth it. I loved sports so much that I did not regret the injury. I was too busy doing everything I could to get back on the field or the court or the diamond. That perspective—that belief—made me a quick healer, which was certainly to my advantage. After a while I began to see injuries as what pastors call "sermon illustrations" for my Fellowship of Christian Athletes talks. Instead of focusing on the pain or the inconvenience, I asked, "Would this be a good example in that talk?" or "Is this the beginning of a new talk?"

On the other hand, many people have asked me the same question: "Was it worth it?" I answer "yes" for two reasons. First, as I have written, it was the cost of God's gift of the athletic ability that provided the experiences and allowed me to meet the people I have encountered along the way. Second, I look at the injuries and the operations as tuition for three Ohio State degrees. I would not have attended college without an athletic scholarship!

A man named Dr. Viktor Frankl was an Austrian holocaust survivor, neurologist, psychiatrist, and author of thirty-nine books. In his most famous book, *Man's Search for Meaning*, he discusses his experiences in a German concentration camp.

As he reports the pain, the horror, and the dehumanization of that experience, readers gain a new perspective on the problems we face.

Then Dr. Frankl provides hope for all of us when, speaking as a man who has endured far more than most of us ever will, he writes, "Everything can be taken from a man but one thing: the last of the human freedoms—to choose one's attitude in any given set of circumstances, to choose one's own way."

Choosing an attitude of a positive future at a time when all the apparent facts showed nothing but misery and horror sustained Dr. Frankl and some of his friends. Those who "faced the facts" were much less likely to survive.

Also, there is a story titled "The Parable of the Chinese Farmer" that examines events from the standpoint of good or bad. Here is the version told by Alan Watts, British philosopher and writer from craftdeology.com:

Once upon a time there was a Chinese farmer whose horse ran away. That evening, all of his neighbors came around to commiserate. They said, "We are so sorry to hear your horse has run away. This is most unfortunate."

The farmer said, "Maybe."

The next day the horse came back bringing seven wild horses with it, and in the evening everybody came back and said, "Oh, isn't that lucky. What a great turn of events. You now have eight horses!"

The farmer again said, "Maybe."

The following day his son tried to break one of the horses, and while riding it, he was thrown and broke his leg. The neighbors then said, "Oh dear, that's too bad."

The farmer responded, "Maybe."

The next day men came to conscript people into the army. They rejected his son because he had a broken leg. Again, all the neighbors came around and said, "Isn't that great!"

Again, he said, "Maybe."

The farmer steadfastly refrained from thinking of things in terms of gain or loss, advantage or disadvantage, because one never knows. In fact, we never really know whether an event is fortune or misfortune, we only know our ever-changing reactions to ever-changing events.

In another, longer version of this fable, the refrain is, "Maybe it's good; maybe it's bad. Who can say?"

Either way, in what we see as "good" times, and in what we see as "bad" times, it is important to remember that times will change, and often so will our perspective of whether those times were good or bad.

I am fortunate to be able to remember the "good" far more clearly than the "bad," that the "bad" often contained "good" or led to it, and that it was worth going through the "bad" because the "good" was not far away.

I wish the same experience for every reader.

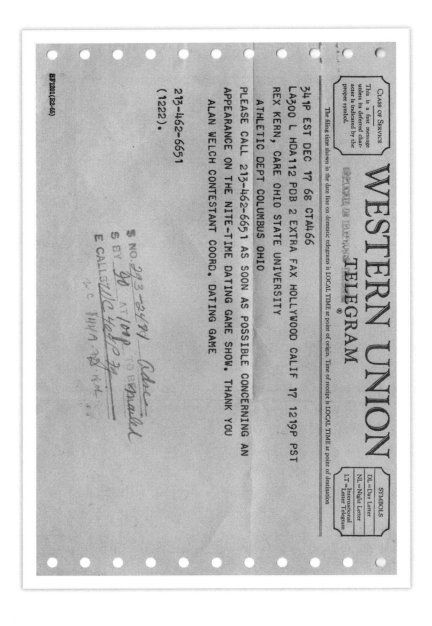

A telegram inviting me to appear on *The Dating Game*.

This picture with Lou Holtz was taken after our Rose Bowl
win in 1969. I asked him to sign it much later, before he was
inducted into the College Football Hall of Fame in 2009.

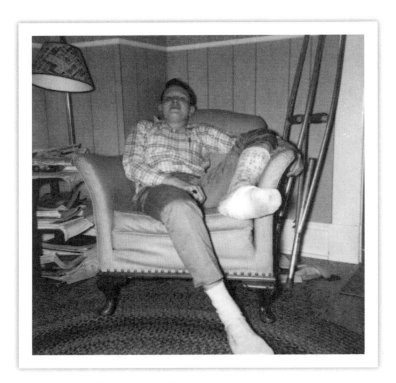

That's me, resting up for my crutch races
with Greg Woltz in the halls of eighth grade.

CHAPTER 8

THE 1970 SEASON: SENIOR YEAR AND BEFORE

"It didn't have to be that way."
Buckeye Super Sophs

The Super Sophs and I played at Ohio State in 1968, 1969, and 1970—three different seasons. Looking back, the experience can best be described as two different eras.

From the SMU game to open the 1968 season until the 1969 Michigan game was the era of change. George Chaump was given the opportunity to bring the Ohio State offense into the modern age of football, attacking in different ways with an unprecedented variety of weapons, making the opponents defend the entire field. The success was undeniable. As the players gained experience, the success increased. The result of the era of change was a record of

18–0, achieved in such dominant fashion that coaches and media outside Columbus were talking about the Buckeyes as one of the greatest teams of all time.

This is the part of our three years fans remember so fondly.

After the Michigan game was the era of regression. The offense stopped improving and relapsed into a version of the Buckeyes from the early 1950s to 1967. The 1970 team should have been outstanding and undefeated, but it was more workmanlike than great. The opportunity for great was lost after the 1969 Michigan game.

Those statements require some explanation.

First, let's examine facts to support the concept of the two eras:

	1968	1969	1970	1967
Rushing yards/game:	301	308	312	208
Passing yards/game:	138	185	87	86
Total offense/game:	439	493	399	293
Total points/ game:	32	43	29	16
Rank:	9/119	2/122	18/123	77/118
Points allowed/game:	15	10	12	13
Rank:	19/119	7/122	11/123	30/118

The first three columns show the offensive and defensive achievements in 1968, 1969, and 1970. The offensive numbers surpass the 1967 team by far. The bottom two rows show national rank of points scored and points allowed. For example, the 1968 team scored 32 points per game, which ranked ninth in the nation among 119 Division I teams. The 1969 team was greatly improved despite the Michigan result, the 1970 team had a sharp drop-off, and the 6–3 1967 team was not at all comparable.

Assuming the idea of two eras is clear, let us explore what happened on November 22, 1969, in Ann Arbor and what happened as a result of that game.

The final score: 24–12, Michigan. That was also the halftime score.

The story of the game is commonly wrapped up in one word: *interceptions*. Four of my seventeen passes were intercepted; my six completions gained eighty-eight yards. When Mace came in for me in the fourth quarter, he was unable to turn things around. Two of his ten passes were intercepted; his three completions gained forty-nine yards. Our team stats were bolstered by Mike Sensibaugh's eighteen-yard completion out of punt formation. That sustained a drive too late in the fourth quarter to make a difference, especially when the drive ended in an interception. We also lost a fumble. Seven turnovers are enough to lose two games, much less one.

That paragraph was no fun to write. Who decided to write this book, anyway?

There is no doubt in my mind that Michigan was the superior team that day and deserved to win that game. Here are some relevant facts:

1. Michigan was strong that year. In September, they lost to Dan Devine's Missouri team, which beat four top-twenty teams and finished sixth in AP. Missouri was very good! Michigan also lost their rivalry game to Michigan State, though that was absolutely *not* Bo Schembechler's rivalry game in 1969.
2. Twenty-two Michigan players in that game were drafted by the NFL. Their personnel was outstanding—very underrated at the time.
3. After losing to MSU, Michigan won four straight heading into our game, scoring 178 points and allowing 16. That is an average score of 44.5 to 4, about as hot as a team can be. We were averaging 46 to 8 after eight games. The matchup was much closer than people realized.
4. Michigan safety Barry Pierson was the star of the game, with

three interceptions and a sixty-one yard punt return to set up one of their three touchdowns. He was named AP Back of the Week, and rightfully so. He gave the credit to Coach Schembechler and his staff, saying, "Bo told us that from day one. He showed us how we were going to win it, and that's exactly how we won it. I give most of the credit to Bo and his staff. They had that thing figured out perfectly." After the game, Pierson said, "When their wingback went in motion, the running backs did not carry the ball. Either the quarterback or the wingback did. No motion—watch the running backs. That knowledge made my job easy." (As quoted in the *Detroit Free Press* article by Orion Sang, November 25, 2019.) As for Pierson's comment, I remember thinking Bo was in our huddle all day. Every time we called a play, they had two men where the ball was going.

5. Bo played for Woody at Miami (Ohio), coached under Woody in 1951 and 1952, then came back to OSU for five seasons, 1958–1962. He knew everything about Wayne Woodrow Hayes. He prepared for Ohio State like Ohio State had prepared for Purdue in 1968—every practice. Esco Sarkkinen's book quotes Bo as telling his coaches, "The first thing I told them is, 'The objective of our entire season is to beat Ohio State … I even installed Ohio State's premier play, 26 and 27, (fullback off tackle left and right) in our offense so our defense would learn how to defend it. There were no surprises on game day."

6. Michigan had twenty-one Ohio players on their roster. Some did not like Woody, or they would have been Buckeyes. Some were rejected by Woody, which they resented. Every Michigan player knew that the previous year, when asked why he had gone for two points when he was ahead 50–14, Woody had said, "Because I could not go for three." Earle Bruce believed, "It was Woody's fault we lost to UM in '69. It was

a mistake to go for two in '68." Jim Mandich, a tight end from Solon, Ohio, who went to Michigan because at Ohio State "I would be an outside tackle," said, "Our attitude that year (1969) was revenge. They had embarrassed us and rubbed it in. We were plenty angry." The great Paul Brown, who had won a national title as OSU coach in 1942 and was almost offered the Ohio State job ahead of Woody, said, "When you win, say nothing. When you lose, say less." Woody knew many quotes, but that was the one he needed to apply on November 23, 1968.

7. All three Michigan touchdowns came after kick returns which gave them good field position—two kickoffs and Pierson's 61-yard punt return. The Pierson punt return set up a 3-yard "drive." On the opening kickoff, Tom Campana returned the ball 31 yards, but our drive stalled on Michigan's 11. After Larry Zelina returned a punt 36 yards to their 16, Jim Otis scored the first touchdown of the game. Their punter averaged 41.7 yards per punt; ours averaged 27 yards. We were outplayed in the kicking game.

8. Our defense held Michigan scoreless in the second half after making mistakes in the first. Afterward, our players talked about defensive changes the coaches had introduced just for this game, and that they were allowed to return to past techniques at the half. As strong as our defense was for eighteen games, was there a good reason to change from what worked so well? Would it have been better to continue to improve something that had proven its value or start over?

9. I had four interceptions, and Mace had two. When I was talking to him recently, which means more than fifty years later, Ron mentioned that Woody had come up to him on the field before the game and said, "Rex is hurting and not doing well. Be ready to play 90 percent of the game today." My back had tightened up, and I was given a shot of what

I always assumed was a muscle relaxant. I remember being in a dreamy, slow-motion state. Was I too relaxed, mentally or physically? Was my reputation as a fast healer from the 1968 season—particularly the 1968 Michigan game and the 1969 Rose Bowl—misinterpreted as someone whose back could heal in a few hours? That is idle speculation. With twenty-twenty hindsight, I wish a healthy Maciejowski had been on the field to start. Five of our interceptions were in the second half, when we were trailing 24–12. Again, our defense was remarkable. But the stress on the defense from the turnovers and the influence of Michigan's kicking game caused the offense to be in terrible field position the entire half. We had the ball eight times in the second half. The first time was on our two-yard line. We also tried to start a drive from our ten. We did not begin a drive in better position than our twenty-three that half. Michigan's defense, like ours, was too good to allow long drives.

10. I wonder if Woody really believed any former assistant could beat him. That is not a fact, just a thought.

After reviewing all these points, my conclusion is that there were many reasons we lost that game—physical and mental. I also believe the Buckeye players and the coaches shared the responsibility for the loss, while the Michigan coaches and players deserved the congratulations.

While I do not know which points were most responsible for the loss, or to what degree, there were many factors to identify and address.

In difficult times, Woody had a way of ignoring facts and reverting to his core beliefs. Even after eighteen straight wins with "that new-fangled offense," he decided that offense was the problem in Ann Arbor. He forgot the success we had previously. He forgot that Michigan knew we had to pass in the second half and could anticipate it, and he decided the passing game was the problem. His changes to the offense would result in our 1970 offense being cut back almost to 1967 levels.

It is true that the 1970 offense was far superior to the 1967 offense, but that is due to the difference in talent level. John Brockington and Leo Hayden were first-round NFL draft choices, and Jan White, Larry Zelina, Bruce Jankowski, and Ron Maciejowski were also drafted. The impact of change in scheme is clear when talent is more or less constant.

1970

In 1970 our offense consisted of Brock running twenty-six times a game; Rick Galbos and Jim Coburn, our backup fullbacks, five more. That means we ran the fullback thirty-one times in an average game. Also, Leo carried thirteen times, and Mace and I added fifteen more. White and Jankowski caught fifty-two balls in 1968 and twenty-nine in 1970. Larry Zelina, another draft choice and a potent threat as a runner or receiver, had fifty-six touches on offense in 1968 and thirty in 1970. Three proven producers talented enough to attract NFL interest hardly needed to be defended.

It was no wonder that when Brock and I saw Northwestern coach Alex Agase at the Hula Bowl, he said, "We were so afraid of your team after the 1969 season. We knew the talent; Woody shot himself in the foot. We thought we had a chance to beat you."

We beat Northwestern in Columbus, 24–10. Brock carried the ball forty-two times; Leo and I split thirty more carries. Jan had one catch, and Bruce had none. Z did have six carries for thirty-nine yards and two catches for twenty-nine yards. Those three had so much more to offer. If our defense had not stopped the Northwestern passing game, they might have beaten us. As Agase suggested, it did not have to be close.

But I am getting ahead of myself. The era of regression began long before the 1970 football season.

I do not remember the change taking place in spring practice. At the time, that seemed relatively normal. There was the rug placed on the entry to the practice field with the 1969 score that we passed over twice a day.

1969

MICH 24

OSU 12

1970

MICH

OSU

There was the emphasis on Michigan, as there was every year, but it was fairly comparable to the emphasis on Purdue in the spring of 1968.

The first time I noticed that things were going to be different in this new era was after basketball coach Fred Taylor called me. He had been contacted by the Army to take some college athletes on a tour of hospitals in Vietnam. As I recall, he mentioned Jim Plunkett and Archie Manning. He hoped I would go with them.

I told Fred I was very interested in going and would get back to him as soon as I ran it by Woody. I did not say I thought it would be a slam dunk, but that was my thinking. Woody had been to Vietnam four times by then. I considered myself a loyal American, but I was beginning to wonder if American leaders were right about fighting in Vietnam. This trip would allow me to learn what was happening as well as support the troops. Ever since my friend and high school basketball teammate Terry Webb was killed in Vietnam, I had felt a personal connection to the men—my age and even younger—who were serving there.

When I asked Woody for permission to go, he said, "We should talk about that. Let's go in my office."

The Talk

After we sat down in his office, he said, "I think you should tell Fred you can't go. It probably would have been fine if we had not lost that last game, but that really changes everything."

That discussion was a perfect example of what it was like to "talk" with Woody at times. He did not ask for an opinion, or even additional facts. He just reached a conclusion, and things were settled. I never said a word, and our "talk" was over.

I was stunned, disappointed, and more than a little angry. I certainly had no idea this was my first glimpse of what the 1970 season was going to be like.

I still regret missing the experience. Fred passed away in January, 2002. I never spoke with him at any length after telling him how disappointed I was at not being able to go. In thinking about this for the book, I contacted his oldest daughter, Janna Taylor Roewer, to see what she might remember about the trip.

"I think it was Dad and four players," she recalled. "I do not think Archie Manning went, but Jim Plunkett for sure. Also, a Georgia Tech basketball player named Rich Yunkus. I do not remember the other two players. They saw soldiers brought in right off the battlefield. Dad was pretty shaken up by the experience. He was very quiet when he got back. I think he was gone about a month."

I could have served my country and heard stories from men who were serving in a far more committed way; gotten to know Fred, the first coach to recruit me; become friends with Plunkett and possibly learned about Stanford before the Rose Bowl; and talked basketball with Yunkus, who would average thirty points per game during the coming basketball season. That is a lot to lose, plus other experiences that can't even be imagined. It did not have to be that way.

Weeks later Woody said he had reconsidered and that it might be OK for me to go. Of course, it was too late. Of course, he knew it would be.

But missing the trip brought another idea to the forefront—something that had been on my mental back burner for some time.

My relationship with Nancy Henno, the Rose Bowl princess, had been deepening since the 1969 Rose Bowl champs had left for Columbus. I had been to California twice. She had been to Columbus once, and we had talked two or three times a week by phone. She had transferred to Ohio State in the fall.

The thought was to land two jobs working in construction out there. I would go out for the summer with Bruce Jankowski; stay at the Phi Delt house at USC; and work out all summer, with Bruce running routes for my passes. He could meet Nancy's friends and all the other "California girls" he could find, and I could achieve my twin priorities of being ready for the season and spending a great deal of time with Nancy.

Everything seemed to fall into place. Nancy was all for it; Bruce was all for it. I found two construction jobs for the summer, providing money and exercise for us.

At the end of spring practice, the starters were invited to Woody's house for a cookout. We knew it was more than an invitation, but not what was on the agenda.

After we ate, Woody asked us to go in turn and report how we were going to prepare for the 1970 season. Bruce was one of the first to speak. "The same way I have the last three summers: work out hard in New Jersey."

Surprise did not cover my reaction, which included shocked and disappointed as well.

Bruce had not said anything to me about the change, and I thought everything was pretty much finalized. Now major changes were required, and in short order. I was in a daze, thinking about what to do.

Strangely enough, we did not speak about what had happened for years.

When I finally asked, Bruce said, "Woody called me into his

office and said, 'Bruce, you are thinking about continuing your career in the NFL after this year, aren't you?' I nodded slowly, wondering why he was bringing up professional football. He never mentioned that when we were in college. Woody then said, 'Then I think you better change your plans to stay in New Jersey for the summer and work out there.' I was scared. What was he threatening to do? If I asked for clarification, he might explode, and that could not mean anything good. I am sorry it worked out that way."

I told him I understood. In hindsight, lots of things happened during the Michigan game and throughout the 1970 season that required understanding.

California, Here I Come

My summer in California was terrific, though very different than I had planned.

Rather than staying at the Phi Delt house, the Hennos invited me to stay with them. We learned a great deal about each other and enjoyed the process.

Before going there, I went to a Fellowship of Christian Athletes camp in San Diego, where I met Bob Chandler, the fine receiver who played against us in the Rose Bowl. USC went back to the Rose Bowl after the 1969 season to play Michigan. Bob was named MVP for scoring the only touchdown in the Trojans' 10–3 victory.

We talked about working out together over the summer. We found a field not far from either of us, tried it, and continued all summer.

He explained their pass patterns to me so I could throw to him. I explained our patterns to him, and I threw while he ran them. USC had a down year, with a record 6–4–1, or we might have met in the Rose Bowl. I could have provided some useful information to our defensive staff if we had played USC. For example, Bob told me that 80 percent of their pass patterns were based on the jet cut, which Woody judged to be "terrible" when George Chaump suggested it to him. Their staff would have laughed at Bob if he told them the routes we used.

Bob caught more passes and gained more yards in his senior year than he did in his first two seasons combined. He went on to a twelve-year NFL career, made All-Pro twice, and won a Super Bowl. We were teammates the year I played for the Buffalo Bills, 1974.

Bob Chandler passed away far too soon at the age of forty-five.

There was another change as well. My second week out there, while driving to my construction job, a crazy California driver cut in front of me on my one-hour drive to work, causing an accident. I was not hurt, but I decided that as much as I needed the money that drive was not worth the risk.

The Test

After working with Bob all summer, I got a call from George Chaump the day before I was to fly to Columbus.

"Woody wants you to work out as soon as you get back," he said.

"Fine, George," I replied. "I fly back tomorrow. Do you want to schedule something for the next day?"

"What time will your plane get in?" he said.

Maybe I should have seen something coming, but I had been a civilian for three months. My self-protection mode had not been activated. I just answered the question and said my early morning flight would be arriving in the early evening.

"OK, Woody and I will meet you at Ernie Biggs Practice Facility an hour later," he said, and hung up.

Clearly, he expected me to state the obvious fact that I would be tired from flying all day, needed at least one day to recover from jet lag, and wanted to wait a day or two before the workout. He was on orders from Woody, had the answer Woody wanted, and that was that. If I had been scheduled to arrive at one o'clock in the morning, the workout would been scheduled for two o'clock in the morning.

Fortunately, the plane was not late. I arrived on time after a nine-hour flight. Woody and George were waiting. I did some stretching and a few calisthenics. Woody was anxious to get started. I expected to have a few throws to warm up, someone to tell me when the test was going to start, and the pressure to begin.

After my first throw, Woody threw his hands in the air and yelled, "George, I told you he did not work out a single *unprintable* day out there. There goes our whole *unprintable* season."

And Woody stormed out. George and I looked at each other in total disbelief. After being disciplined to work out all summer, this was the way my 1970 season began. Welcome back to Columbus.

The Undefeated, Disappointing Regular Season

The players were excited about the regular season, aiming for the type of spectacular improvement we had from 1968 to 1969. The national media ranked us number one and did not spare the superlatives. *Sports Illustrated* claimed the prize in that department, writing something like "Rex Kern may win the Heisman Trophy and not play enough to letter."

In the opener, Texas A&M held Brock to 77 yards on nineteen carries, but we still rushed for 415 yards and won, 56–13. Duke fell, 34–10, as Leo Hayden, Brock, and I all went over 100 yards.

In the Big Ten opener at Michigan State, I went out after a roughing the passer call in the first quarter, then out for good in the third. Neither Mace nor I passed well, but our defense was stout in a 29–0 win. When Minnesota came to the Horseshoe, Brock had a huge day with 187 yards on twenty-eight carries, while Leo and I added 152 more. I was nine for fifteen, passing for only 74 yards. OSU, 28–8.

At Illinois, Woody talked to us about Lincoln on Friday rather than during halftime. That worked out better than two years prior. We won, 47–29, as the defense had an unusually bad day. Darrell Robinson rushed for 187 yards on forty-three carries, and the Illini offense totaled 431 yards. They held Brock in check—twenty-one carries for 76 yards—but the rest of us took advantage of our opportunities to outrush the home team. Jan White grabbed five passes to help me to a nine-of-fifteen day as we out passed them too.

The first half of the season went pretty much as we hoped. After five games, we were averaging thirty-nine points a game, with a high of fifty-six and a low of twenty-eight. The second half showed an abrupt change. For the next five games, we averaged nineteen points, with a high of twenty-four. Woody decided to practice for Michigan, and we buttoned up, turning a race car into a Model T.

Brock carried forty-two times for 161 yards against Northwestern; Leo and I added 136 more. All the passes were short, except for obvious passing situations, but we won, 24–10. At Wisconsin, before a record crowd for Camp Randall Stadium, we won 24–7. It was not as intimidating as it is today, but the fans had a habit of catching extra-point kicks, passing them up the rows, then out of the stadium. I remember the players speculating about what became of the balls. Of course, today there are nets behind the goalposts to catch the balls.

In 1970 we had a game at Purdue the Saturday before Michigan. It was snowy, windy, rainy, and sleeting—just a miserable day. Gary Danielson, who played twelve years in the NFL and is now the college football color man for CBS, had two completions in twelve attempts. Purdue had three first downs the entire day. Our receivers told me how difficult it was to keep their footing and to catch the ball.

All year long the entire team had wanted to open things up. I certainly agreed with that, but this was not the day to do it. We could give the ball to John Brockington, who gained 136 yards, and Leo Hayden, 63 yards, and get home with a victory. Anything else was a gamble.

For some reason Woody wanted to gamble. He kept sending in delayed passing plays to either Jan White or Larry Zelina. The first few times we ran that type of play I saw that Purdue prepared for both plays, and their players were pointing out the coverages. Those plays could not succeed, so I changed the call, usually to a conservative Brockington run. Finally, Chuck Bonica, who was bringing in the plays, said, "If you don't stop changing the plays, he's going to kill me."

I said, "Chuck, in my huddle, I call the plays." I called another run, probably by Brock.

When I came off the field, Woody said, "If you change one more play, you will be sitting beside me."

I did, and I was.

Mace came in at the end of the third quarter and bailed us out again. Here's the way he remembers it:

"Woody called 98 Hook for the umpteenth time, but Purdue was sitting on that move all day. I told Bruce Jankowski to run a post route, and it was wide open."

That 52-yard pass got us to the Purdue 27, where we missed a field goal. Our defense stopped them, Mace scrambled for 23, Hayden rushed for 15, and Freddie Schram kicked a 30-yard field goal to put us ahead, 10-7.

Purdue lost the ball on downs, and we escaped.

Did Woody take me out because he was mad at me? Because I was wrong to change the plays, which I had been told to do before my first game as a sophomore? Because he thought Mace would come through again? Because he wanted his orders followed regardless of the consequences? I do not know.

What I do know is that Mace made an important adjustment at

the line of scrimmage, threw a big pass to Bruce to change field position, and made two fine runs to improve it. The defense was outstanding all game. Purdue only had 71 yards on offense; their score came on a kickoff return. Of course, Fred Schram kicked a winning field goal.

Mace: "Wins" and "Saves"

I have spoken about what Ron Maciejowski meant to our football teams for fifty-some years, and I intend to do it for fifty more, if possible. Here is an attempt to show his on-field contributions in a new way.

Baseball pitchers and football quarterbacks are often compared for the influence they have in a game. Pitchers get credit for a win if they are pitching when the winning run scores, and they register a save if their team is ahead when they enter the game, then finish it. Quarterbacks are team players, but the concept of wins and saves helps quantify Mace's value to us.

In 1968 Mace came into the Illinois game tied 24–24 and led the team to victory. He also started the 43–8 Wisconsin game. There are two wins. Against Oregon and Michigan State, he earned saves. Very few Major League pitchers win 20 percent of the team's games and save 20 percent as well. More importantly, I doubt we would have won the title without him.

In each of the next two years, Mace added a win and a save. In 1969 Northwestern was a save, and Wisconsin was a win. In 1970 Michigan State was a save. He entered the Purdue game when it was tied, 10–10, and directed the drive that set up the Schram field goal—a Buckeye win.

As a major contributor to our 27–2 team, he had four wins and four saves. Mace was absolutely indispensable to our success.

★ ★ ★

The way he took me out of the Purdue game, it was obvious that things were still not right between Woody and me. I had developed an ulcer, chewed Maalox all day, and my weight was down to 173 pounds. (When I went to Baltimore, Tom Matte told me he had an ulcer playing quarterback for Woody. When Cornelius Greene graduated, he told me the same thing. What a coincidence!)

When Nancy said, "You've got to talk with him," I did not really listen to her.

I just said, "He won't listen to me." I regret that today, but not because I believe he would have listened. I do not. My regret is that I cannot say, "I tried, but he would not listen." Today I see it as my responsibility to have tried. Back then, I did not.

For our final OSU-Michigan game, both teams went in unbeaten. It was the first OSU-UM game since 1905 that two unbeaten, untied teams were playing for a Big Ten title. Both the Rose Bowl and a possible national championship were at stake. For us, so was revenge for what happened in Ann Arbor last November.

We won, 20–9. Despite the fact that Michigan was fifth in the nation in rushing defense, we ran sixty-five times and passed twelve. Leo Hayden led us with 117 yards on twenty-eight carries; John Brockington had 77 yards on twenty-seven carries.

It was the only game against our rivals in which I had good health and a full week of practice to prepare. We had 329 yards of total offense and eighteen first downs.

Our defense was outstanding, holding them to ten first downs and 155 yards of total offense. Stillwagon had twelve tackles, and Stan White had an interception, a fumble recovery, and eight tackles. Woody called it "the greatest game in Ohio State history." We were happy and relieved.

Shortly after the celebration was over, players started talking about the Rose Bowl. The seniors had been there two years ago.

Woody had dominated everything. He kept us on a tight leash, and that was fine. We did not know anything, he thought, so we might be too young to trust. We understood what had happened.

This time we were winners of twenty-seven out of twenty-eight games, had proven we could be trusted, were Big Ten champions again despite being restricted on offense, and wanted to be number one in the country again. We wanted to be considered one of the great teams of all time, with a record of 28–1. Even though we hoped to prove our position by using all our weapons to attack on offense, we were resigned to grinding it out as we had since September. We accepted that. We wanted these things almost as much as we wanted to breathe, and we looked forward to working hard to earn them.

Plus, we wanted to have just a little bit of fun while we did it.

The Promise

Nothing drastic, but we did not want to fly across the country, go through media day, have our pictures taken, answer questions for hours, then have a hard practice. We understood having a ten o'clock curfew on game week, but we wanted some freedom before that. We agreed to do all the two-a-days the coaches needed, we just wanted to relax before we started. The captains asked to meet with Woody.

Woody told us we could not go a few days early to see the sights, because that was against Rose Bowl rules. We had to fly in and meet with the media the same day. Other than that, he heard us out and said, "I'd like to do that."

The seniors were happy. The others had no idea why but decided that must be good. We could not have been in a better frame of mind to go, do what had to be done, and do it together for one last time.

Maybe an hour after the plane took off, our trainer got on the public address system. He announced that Bucks and Red One—first-team defense and offense—should get ready to be taped. There would be a full practice after meeting with the media.

There was an audible sigh on the plane. Jan White tapped me on the shoulder and said, "You've got to talk with him."

Again, I said, "He won't listen to me." Again, regret.

The media took longer than expected. Everyone wanted time with Jack Tatum, who had been named the UPI Defensive Player of the Year, despite every offense avoiding him whenever they could. Woody wanted to start practice and was upset. Predictably, he blew a gasket. We had a hard two-and-a-half-hour practice. The players were on edge.

The captains met and decided we had to face Woody, but it could not be in private. That approach had failed. It had to be in public, but still within the team. We decided that after practice a meeting would be best—seniors and coaches only.

Let me interrupt this story for a back story.

Two years earlier, Phil Strickland had been late for a meeting before the 1969 Rose Bowl. When a meeting started, the door was locked. Phil knocked. Earle Bruce, his position coach, was nervous because he coached the guards and was responsible for them. Someone opened the door, and Woody shouted, "No, he's going home. Earle, get him on a plane."

It never happened, but the point was made that it could.

Returning to senior year, the four captains decided to meet with Lou McCullough, the defensive coordinator and assistant coach for six years. Jim Stillwagon, Doug Adams, Jan White, and I started telling Lou what had happened. "He lied to us ... it's two weeks until the game ... he's treating us like sophomores ... he tells us not to make a fist too early because when the fight starts it won't have any power, but that is just what he is doing."

Lou said he agreed with us.

The captains decided to have the most indispensable player of the four be the person to face Woody in order for it to be difficult for Woody to send anyone home. We chose Jim Stillwagon, our Outland Trophy winner, the most outstanding lineman in the nation. He could not be replaced.

As the next team meeting was winding up, Wagon stood and said, "There is one more thing. Sophomores and juniors can be dismissed. We would like to talk about the schedule."

Before Jim got too far, Woody erupted. "I'll be. I'm the winningest coach in Rose Bowl history."

At this moment, Lou stood up and said, "By God, Coach, I don't know what got into them." He walked out.

"If you guys don't like it," Woody continued, "I will put you on a plane and send you home."

Phil Strickland jumped out of his seat and said, "All right, boys, let's go."

The rest of us followed his lead and stood.

Woody immediately said, "We can work this out." There were genuine negotiations. But the hurt feelings lasted much longer. It did not have to be that way.

To top it all off, the next practice Woody announced he had studied the offense Darrell Royal was using at Texas—the triple option—and that he was going to put that in for the Rose Bowl.

We had the best offense in Ohio State history in 1968, and it was much better in 1969. The only reason that what we had worked on for three years was not even better in 1970 was that our coach stopped us from running it. Now he was going to install something new for one game. *What is going on?*

History shows that Stanford won the Rose Bowl, 17–27. In truth, the game was called on account of mutiny. Only the remnants of a game were seen in the stadium and at home. Today we know we should have done better, but we have yet to decide how we could have done it.

The "Almost" drive

In the middle of the third quarter, we led, 17–13, but had been pinned down on our own six-yard line by a punt.

We responded with five first downs: Brock carried twice for the first one; Leo Hayden went around right end for twenty-three yards; Brock picked up another on third and one; Jan White drew a pass interference call for the fourth; and I ran around right end to put the ball on the Stanford twenty-nine, first and ten.

Brock gained six but runs by Leo and Rick Galbos left us fourth and one to go on Stanford's twenty-yard line. Our drive of 6:21 had ended the quarter. During the break, plays were discussed, and 27 was called—Brockington over senior left tackle Dave Cheney, who was All-Big Ten, and our senior All-American tight end, Jan White. I felt confident we were going with our strength.

When the clock started, Stanford had guessed correctly about our plan. They had an extra player in that hole. The play was doomed, and I had to adjust. The choice was clear. I had been coached that when this happened I was to call the same play to the other side by shouting, "Railroad." It was my job to make the change clear to everyone. Somehow I failed! It was only after forty-five years at our first reunion for the 1970 team that I learned neither right tackle John Hicks nor right end Bruce Jankowski heard the "Railroad" call. They made their blocking assignments for 27, the original play, and Brock was stopped cold.

Instead of us riding the momentum of six straight first downs into the end zone to add to our lead, Stanford had the ball, first and ten. Heisman Trophy winner Jim Plunkett led his team on a thirteen-play eighty-yard drive for a touchdown and a 17-20 lead, then scored again to win, 17-27.

I will never forget that play, because it was my job to convey the change to ten teammates, and only eight got it. Eighty percent at this moment was not good enough. If I could have one do-over from my entire athletic career, that would be the one.

After the game, Woody described it as "an afternoon of missed opportunities." When we saw that quote, we thought of an earlier afternoon when he missed the opportunity to keep his word to us as well as our inability to adjust to that.

To top off the entire story, Stanford coach John Ralston approached Jim Stillwagon at the Hula Bowl with a book under his arm. He showed Wagon a copy of *Hotline to Victory*, written the previous year by Wayne Woodrow Hayes. It included all our plays, signals, and formations.

"Every one of our coaches got a copy," Coach Ralston said. "This is how we prepared for you guys."

It did not have to be that way.

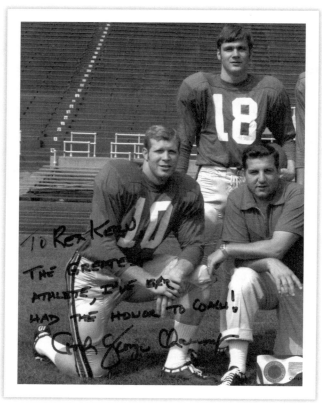

Quarterback coach George Chaump made it easy for
Mace (18) and I to learn the offense every week.

CHAPTER 9

WOODY STORIES

"His mission was not to produce players for the NFL, but to produce players who could produce in society."
Daryl Sanders, OSU 1960-61-62, All-American offensive tackle.

As the Ohio State team was preparing for the 1951 Rose Bowl, there were rumors that head coach Wes Fesler was considering retirement, even though the former Buckeye three-time All-American and Phi Beta Kappa member seemed perfect for the job.

Despite that distraction, Ohio State beat California, 17–14, to win the Rose Bowl and finish sixth in the country. When the Bucks lost the famous "Snow Bowl" to Michigan at the end of the 1951 season to miss an outright Big Ten title and finish fourteenth in the country, Fesler did resign, citing "excessive pressure for winning football games."

As Ohio State, then referred to as the "graveyard of coaches," was looking for its fifth coach in ten years, Fesler was announced as the new coach at Minnesota on January 23, 1951. His salary was $14,000—$1,000 less than he was being paid at OSU.

The Associated Press polled sportswriters around the state for their recommendations for the new Buckeye coach. Former Ohio State coach Paul Brown, whose Cleveland Browns had won four titles in four years in the All-American Conference and were preparing to move to the NFL, received sixteen of twenty-nine votes. Massillon High School coach Chuck Mather was second. The Ohio High School Football Coaches Association, which had played a major role in Brown being selected by Ohio State in 1941, strongly supported him again. In a poll by the *Columbus Citizen*, Brown received 2,331 of 2,811 first-place votes. OSU freshman coach Harry Strobel was second. Milton Berle, Lassie, Lana Turner, and Ed Wynn received votes. The man who was chosen to lead Ohio State on February 18, 1951, received no votes in either poll.

Woody Hayes had led Miami (Ohio) to a 9–1 record and a victory over Arizona State in the Salad Bowl. It was his second year coaching the Redskins, after three years coaching at his alma mater, Denison.

With such a beginning, no one could have forecast that he would coach twenty-eight years, twice as long as any Buckeye coach, before or since; win five national championships, the majority of the eight won in school history; or win thirteen Big Ten titles. The smart betting was that he would be fired the first year.

So Woody got a job no one thought he could get, and he kept that job when no one believed he could. In twenty-eight years, Woody did plenty of things no one thought he could do.

Woody was an admirer of several important historical figures, from General George Patton to President Abraham Lincoln to General George MacArthur to Winston Churchill, the prime minister of the United Kingdom during World War II, then again from 1951 to 1955.

Just before World War II, the soon-to-be prime minister Churchill described Russia as being "a riddle, wrapped in a mystery, inside an enigma."

That paints an interesting picture, but Mr. Churchill would have needed several more words to describe Coach Hayes. Here are a few I have heard his players use: authoritarian, arbitrary, generous with his time and money, short-tempered, ultracompetitive, hardworking, schizophrenic. And I am just getting started.

Woody was also personable, persuasive, a teacher, a reader, a speaker, dictatorial, controlling, sensitive, insensitive, stubborn, opinionated, explosive (intentional, for effect), explosive (out of control), emotional, dedicated, friendly, abrasive, caring, contradictory, inspiring, loyal, shortsighted, farsighted, unapologetic, without prejudice, inflexible, and Republican—except when his former player Ben Espy ran for city council as a Democrat. Then loyal trumped Republican.

*　*　*

Randy Hart, my teammate at Ohio State, became a notable defensive line coach with several colleges, beginning as a graduate assistant in 1971 and 1972 for Woody and including working from 1982 to 1987 with Earle Bruce at Ohio State. Randy's longest time in one place was at Washington, where he worked for five head coaches over twenty-one years. When the sixth coach wanted his own staff, Randy moved to Notre Dame for one year.

Then he received a surprising call from the Stanford coach, former Michigan Wolverine quarterback and present coach Jim Harbaugh!

Hart suspected a prank, but Harbaugh convinced him the interest was genuine. So Randy put together a PowerPoint presentation on defensive line play and flew to Palo Alto.

Upon Randy's arrival, Harbaugh asked to hear some Woody stories. Randy told a few and tried to show his presentation. Harbaugh insisted on more stories, so Randy complied, then tried to get to his presentation, but Harbaugh asked for more.

Randy finally said, "It's been two hours, and I have to catch my flight back. Can I hit a few high points on this presentation?"

"No, don't bother," replied Harbaugh. "I decided to hire you before I called. The job is yours; I just wanted to hear Woody stories."

They worked together one year. Hart got used to Harbaugh sticking his head into his office first thing in the morning and saying, "I need a Woody story to start my day." Randy always had a new one and always asked for a Bo story in return. The stories had a remarkable resemblance.

Harbaugh left to coach the San Francisco 49ers after one season. Hart stayed at Stanford until retiring after the 2015 campaign.

The Ones I Lived

Here come some Woody stories. Some I experienced; some I have heard many times. All are true, to the best of my knowledge, though many are contradictory. Are you enough of a psychologist to put them together? The subject of psychology takes me back to my freshman year, which can give us a start.

Most of the way through fall quarter freshman year I was failing psychology. Part of the problem was I had not yet learned to study and part of the problem was I did not yet value excellence in the classroom. I was certainly not on a path to a doctorate, more on one to becoming ineligible.

Woody had a solution. He and four selected coaches would tutor me before the final exam. When Woody had a solution, everyone got in line or else.

I would meet with each coach from eight to ten in the morning. Each coach would tutor me on psychology. At the end of the week,

I would be able to pass the subject. The facts that none of the coaches knew what was emphasized in the class, or whether it was an essay or multiple-choice test, were not considered.

"Be in my office at eight Monday morning," Woody said.

I walked in with my psychology book, and he took a book off his shelf that was about 3" thick. The first paragraph was about the Oedipus Rex Complex. He said, "I'll be. You know, that was the problem with a player on my team in 1956. I should have done this and that to help him."

Two hours later he slammed the book closed. He had not stopped talking, much less asked me a question. "That was a great session," he said. I remember thinking, "I'll get the Oedipus Rex question right if it is on the test, but what about the other ninety-nine?"

The other coaches, while interesting and entertaining, were no more helpful. At least their agenda did not include being center stage for two hours.

My salvation in psychology came from the Phi Delta Theta Fraternity house, where I was being rushed. I had met Mel Kosanchich, the Rush Chairman, during Rush Week and Mel was taking the class as an elective. An engineering student with a photographic memory, he had no trouble with the subject.

With Mel's guidance, I got a C in the course. I must have aced the final because that was a big improvement.

Of course, Woody took great pride in telling everyone what he did. I did not correct him. Because I owed my football career to them, I became a Phi Delt.

★ ★ ★

One of the conditioning tests for Woody's teams to begin fall practice was a mile run in Ohio Stadium. It took place around the track—which then went around the field in the horseshoe, when the south end was open, and the name fit.

Who would you guess ran that mile with the group until he got to the south end, left the group, and hid out of sight for three laps, then rejoined the group for the last half-lap?

Here is a hint: He was so outstanding in the 1968 Purdue game while defending All-American LeRoy Keyes all over the field that he was named defensive lineman of the week by one wire service and defensive back of the week by another. Jack Tatum is the answer. He never got caught. If he had been, he would have to be punished, but he was too valuable to the team.

* * *

Earlier we discussed Woody's high graduation rate and high percentage of advanced degrees as well as his immediate action to improve those figures. Here are some other stories comparing what he did at Ohio State to what other colleges were doing.

After arriving at Colts training camp in 1971, I decided to see how many Colts rookies had graduated from college. Remembering that they might have returned later and gotten degrees, this is what I found in the fall of 1971: There were seventeen players drafted—five from Big Ten schools, three from other national football powers, two from the Ivy League, and seven from other schools, including one from the MAC. Of the seventeen, four had graduated from college when they arrived at Colts camp, including me.

In contrast, there were thirteen drafted from our senior class at Ohio State that year. When they arrived at pro training camps, seven had graduated. Others graduated later. So, seven out of thirteen, 54 percent, for Ohio State, compared to four out of seventeen, 24 percent, for a random mix of football schools.

Also, from the days at my first Colts camp, I was talking with two of our highest draft choices, both from football powers. Someone asked the question, "What are you going to do if you are cut?"

My immediate answer was that I hoped to work in the Ohio State athletic department and work toward a masters' degree. They both said something about construction.

At the time, I was reading about what was going on in college football and believed they had redshirted, taking five years to play four. Could it be they had not graduated after five years?

I tried to ask a nonjudgmental question along the lines of, "What the heck did you do for five years?"

They both commented that they were enrolled.

At Ohio State, being enrolled was the beginning of a long, hard process involving going to class, reading, doing homework, studying, and taking tests, with the intention and expectation of earning a degree. I changed the subject.

When the Buffalo Bills informed me that I had failed my physical and would have to retire, I was taken to the airport with two free agents just out of college who had been cut. They were talking about which teams might give them a tryout, desperate to find a way to get into the league.

After four years of pro ball, I wanted to reassure them that they had other choices, so I asked what their degrees were in.

They looked at me like I had three heads.

"We didn't graduate from college," they said. "We played football."

It seemed ironic to be leaving the NFL the same way I arrived, with college student-athletes who were not students. Thank you, Ohio State. Thank you, Woody. Thank you, Fred Taylor. Thank you, Nancy.

★ ★ ★

Freshman football was everything I had hoped. Still, after the varsity beat Michigan, 24–14, on November 25, I could not wait to hit the hardwood and begin my basketball career. I did not know it at the time, but several years later, in *The Golden Age of Ohio State*

Basketball: 1960–1971, Coach Taylor said he believed I could be an All-Big Ten caliber basketball player at Ohio State. I just wanted to play—and win.

Several weeks later, Woody walked into St. John Arena as the freshmen were warming up for basketball practice. He caught my eye and signaled me over.

"I'm going up to Avon Lake to watch a guy we are recruiting play basketball," he said. "He is a wide receiver who can help us. I want you to go with me. Get changed."

"Coach," I said incredulously, "I'm sorry. I can't miss practice without Coach Taylor's permission."

Woody left in a huff, and I thought the matter was settled. But a few minutes later, he came back and said, "Let's go."

Being a naïve freshman, I assumed he had spoken with Coach Taylor and received his approval. If I knew then what I learned later—namely, that Woody did not get anyone's approval—I would have asked and made sure. Back then, I did not. I just changed clothes as quickly as I could.

The player was Dick Wakefield, who signed with OSU and became a fine receiver for the Buckeyes. In fact, do you remember the play in Ann Arbor in 1971 when Woody tore up the yard markers because he believed a Michigan player interfered with a Buckeye trying to make an important catch? Thom Darden landed on top of Dick, clearly making contact before touching the ball. It was a remarkable play by Darden, but it was pass interference first. Films show that Woody was correct, though it cost fifteen yards and some negative publicity.

We went to the game. I learned Wakefield was an impressive athlete and hoped he would be a Buckeye. I also learned that Woody was a dreadful driver. It was good to be home.

The next night, having started every freshman game, I was surprised not to be in the starting lineup. As the game progressed assistant freshman coach Rod Myers told me, "Word came down from above that you are not to play tonight."

What exactly happened the previous night? Certainly, Woody did not get permission, or I would not have been punished. Had Woody waited a few minutes, then come back thinking I would assume things had been worked out? If there had been a misunderstanding, what could it have been? I had known Fred for a couple of years and was certain Woody did not intimidate him as he did many others at OSU. Also, I believed that Fred would not punish me for something unless he believed I was at fault.

As a freshman, I did not know how to handle it. Now I would go to Fred, explain what happened, say that I understood his decision but wanted him to know the facts, and promise to communicate directly with him in the future. At that time, I would have reiterated to him that I was very serious about my basketball future at Ohio State.

I never did ask Woody about that situation. Certainly, his plan was for me to meet Dick Wakefield, but was it also to create distance between Fred and me? Did he want to make certain I chose football over basketball? I do not know, but that was the result.

After the football season we had in 1968, the success and the length, it is unlikely that I could have played basketball. The basketball Bucks had played eight games before the Rose Bowl and started the Big Ten season on January 4. Plus, they had four returning starters. Even if the football team had not won the Big Ten, the basketball season started a week after the Michigan football game. It would have been difficult for me to catch up on a team with experienced players. Also, the shoulder dislocation I sustained during the misguided tackling dummy experience needed attention.

So the Woody-Wakefield incident probably had no impact on my athletic career, but I consider it important for two reasons: First, it seems Woody was willing to mislead me to get the result he wanted. Second, what he did cost me was a relationship with a fine man who would have been a willing friend and mentor for life. Coaches Jones, Hill, and England at Lancaster worked together so I could play three sports in high school and were all significant contributors to my life. Woody Hayes and Fred Taylor both would have been as well, but Woody did not share.

★ ★ ★

Woody was not a scientist by nature. When someone made a suggestion, Woody would ignore the idea for as long as possible. If he ever did evaluate it, the test would be set up to confirm Woody's original opinion.

George Chaump was our quarterbacks coach. He was the epitome of the phrase "humble and kind." In 1968 he coached the best offense Ohio State had ever had. In 1969 he improved it. The previous six years he had posted a 58–4 record as a high school coach and won six straight Central Pennsylvania championships. Woody referred to him as "the high school coach trying to change the way we play on offense." Woody made George's job extremely difficult.

George had been trying to convince Woody to use a play George called "better than 26 and 27" for several months. It was a direct challenge that Woody finally accepted one day in practice.

The play was called "jet cut," which my summer workout friend Bob Chandler had told me was the basis for 80 percent of USC's passing offense. Our speed receiver would run directly at the cornerback, make him retreat to defend the long pass, then the receiver would sharply break to the sideline. The quarterback passed when the defender was running away from the ball, so the receiver had separation. It was very difficult to defend.

Ron Maciejowski and I would be throwing to Bruce Jankowski and Jimmy Lee Harris, a 9.5 track guy who backed up Bruce. We would be attacking some of the best defensive backs in America—Ted Provost, Tim Anderson, Mike Sensibaugh, and Jack Tatum.

To begin the test, Mace and I completed nine straight passes. We were throwing well, and the guys were catching everything. I thought I saw George smile. I was confident this play was going into the playbook.

Then Mace threw one just off Bruce's fingertips. Woody erupted as if a referee had blown a call or an out-of-town writer had called his offense obsolete.

"That's the play you have been telling me about?" he yelled. "That's *unprintable*." And he stalked away. The experiment was over. Woody was right again. In this case, one piece of evidence beat nine.

* * *

Woody had a nickname among his quarterbacks in 1969, carefully selected to reflect his volatile personality and absolutely *never* mentioned in his presence or close enough for him to hear it. Ron Maciejowski, Kevin Rusnak, and I referred to him as "Schizo."

Our ringleader was Kevin, who was funny and always into something. I say that with admiration because Mace and I were seldom far behind. One day we were warming up before practice, throwing balls into a net, when I noticed our position coach, George Chaump, come on the field. Immediately, he said, "Rex, where are Mace and Kevin?" Out of the corner of my eye, I had seen them hide inside the tarps used to cover the field. By that I mean there were containers over the tarps so the tarps could be laid on the field quickly. The containers were about 2.5 feet in diameter. Kevin and Mace were inside the empty tarp containers. Because George would not be upset, but Woody would be upset and blame George, I told him.

Remembering George on his hands and knees, imploring them to "get out of there before Woody comes out" always brings a smile to my face.

Woody was at a barbershop in an Arlington shopping center when a fan stuck out his hand.

"Hello, Coach," the man said. "I just wanted to thank you for the joy you have brought to my wife and me. We go everywhere together and have not missed a game in twenty-five years."

"Where is she now?" Woody said.

"She is at Riverside Hospital. She has not felt well for a while, and we wanted to get the problem fixed."

"Sorry to hear that," said Woody. "What room number?"

The man answered.

That night, the man went home, had dinner, and went to visit his wife. As he got close to her room, he heard Woody's voice and his wife laughing.

That story certainly did not come from Woody. The source was a stranger who wanted to tell me what Woody had done for his wife.

* * *

I was invited to a dinner for Archie's class. Then President Jennings was there and noticed a group of players seemed to be avoiding Woody, scattering when he approached. Jennings asked Archie about it. Archie said, "Those are the players who didn't graduate."

* * *

When I graduated from Ohio State for the third time with a Ph.D. in 1983, Woody and Anne Hayes hosted a lunch for our family—Nancy and I, my parents, my brother, Keith—as well as for Jack and Sally Havens and Larry Zelina. Anyone who knows Woody would guess it was at the Jai Lai on Olentangy River Road, and they would be correct. It was a kind and generous gesture by a dear friend.

Former Players

The book *1968: The Year That Saved Ohio State Football* by David Hyde has a detailed story about the way Woody stressed education—especially law school—for players long after they received a bachelor's degree and stayed involved in their careers as well. It was useful in explaining what I already knew about Bill Pollitt.

Bill was a year ahead of the 1968 Super Soph class, but he played the wrong position. He was a middle guard, and the best in the country was in our class, Jim Stillwagon. Bill earned two letters, mostly as a linebacker. No one was going to play very much behind Wagon.

Bill got his BS in education in 1970 but was not certain he wanted to teach. He was a graduate assistant for Woody in 1971 and 1972. Apparently, a little bit of "The Old Man" rubbed off on him, as Bill decided he wanted to be a lawyer

The problem was, Bill's law school test scores were in the bottom 2 percent. Even Woody's appearance at Pollitt's interview with the dean of the OSU law school was not enough. The dean explained that the average score among OSU students was 600. Pollitt could be admitted with a 500, but not a 396.

Every other law school to which Pollitt applied turned him down. The last chance was Capital University. Woody could not attend the interview, but he sent a letter of recommendation. The assistant dean told Pollitt, "You should go to trade school. With these scores, you are wasting our time, and we're wasting yours."

When Pollitt reported to Woody, he erupted, trashing his office. Then Hayes asked two questions: "*Unprintable*, do you want to go to law school?" and "Will you make it?"

Bill answered that he did, and he would.

"You'd better," Hayes said. "Because if you screw it up, you'll not only screw it up for yourself. You'll screw it up for every player who comes after you. My word won't mean anything."

Three days later, Bill Pollitt received a letter of acceptance from

Capital Law School. He ranked fourth in his class after the traditionally difficult first year. He graduated and became a Columbus city attorney. In 1996 he was appointed judge in Franklin County Municipal Court, to which he was reelected six times and annually ranked by the Columbus Bar Association as one of their most respected judges. One year his campaign slogan claimed he was "The only lawyer to bring down O. J. Simpson," which he did on a kickoff return in the 1969 Rose Bowl.

"Here I was, a reserve player who didn't help him win anything," Hyde quoted Pollitt as saying, "and he changed my life. Nobody can say anything bad about Woody Hayes in front of me. He gave me an opportunity no one else would have."

Franklin County judge H. William Pollitt passed away on August 13, 2020 due to COVID-19.

★　★　★

Rod Gerald was recruited from Dallas, Texas, as a quarterback. In his freshman season, he backed up Cornelius Greene, then started in 1976 and 1977. As a junior, he led the team to a Big Ten cochampionship and was voted first-team All-Big Ten. The team's 9–3 record was very deceiving—the three losses were all to top-five teams: Oklahoma, Michigan, and Alabama in the Sugar Bowl. In the final AP poll, the team ranked eleventh in the nation.

During his senior year, Rod was moved to wide receiver. He did not graduate and moved back to Dallas, where he had drug issues. Woody badgered him about completing his degree and also went down to speak at a benefit OSU alumni organized at his request.

From 1984 until early 1987, Woody kept after Rod. In March, Woody called and demanded Rod give him a commitment to return. "But then he died (March 12, 1987)," Rod said. "A week after, Anne [Hayes] called and said, 'Rod, I know what Coach wanted. I want you to see things through.'"

Three months later, Rod was in Columbus. In 1989 he graduated from Ohio State. At the time, he said, "I've made a lot of strides. I have a wife and two kids, I have my degree, and I have a job. I've been completely free from drugs and alcohol since 1985. I'm here because of Coach Hayes and his tenacity."

★ ★ ★

"Woody was the most emotional guy I have ever seen, and he got madder than hell at his players. He'd get so emotionally involved and explode. He'd punch kids and yell at them, but off the field he was like a father to them. He was really like two different people," noted Ara Parseghian, player and assistant coach at Miami (Ohio). p. 73, *A Fire to Win – The Life and Times of Woody Hayes* by John Lombardo, Thomas Dunne Books, St. Martin's Press.

"The man is 98 percent good and 2 percent explosive. Unfortunately, he explodes 98 percent of the time in public." Ara Parseghian, again.

★ ★ ★

"I know he found out that a former player's wife was suffering from brain cancer, and the medical insurance had just about run out. Woody agreed to be roasted, with all the money going to help pay the leftover medical bills for this woman," recalled Steve Myers (1972-1973-1974).

"We hated him, but we adored him," said George Rosso (1951-1952-1953).

"Woody would be a great coach if we could lock him in the locker room so he can't get out with the team on Saturday," said Bo Rein (1964-1965-1966).

Dick Schafrath (1956-1958) said, "Woody Hayes is the best thing that ever happened to me outside my family, my wife, and kids."

Woody's trips to hospitals to see people—those he knew and those he did not—were legendary. He often took players with him unless they had a test the next day.

* * *

Woody quizzed the quarterbacks on play calling by announcing down and distance, then asking for the play call. When the situation was third and forty-five, the right answer was "Robust 26, fullback over left tackle."

Woody's reaction was, "Great call. We'll catch those linebackers on their heels. Great call! Great call! You can call that play any time." (Ron Maciejowski and Rex Kern.)

In his biography, *Bo*, Coach Schembechler wrote, "He made mistakes. His temper was, at times, inexcusable. But he shaped me and everything I do with a stamp of passion and strength. He was a remarkable coach, a teacher, a winner. I will miss him forever." Bo played for Woody, coached for him, and coached against him.

"Woody is a God-fearing man. It's nice to know he is afraid of somebody," said Archie Griffin (1972–1973–1974–1975). Arch said this at a roast, which might mean it was a slight exaggeration.

* * *

Bo Schembechler told this story from his senior season at Miami (Ohio), when he played for Woody. The team was returning from Phoenix, Arizona, where they had defeated Arizona State, 34–21, to win the Salad Bowl. They had to make an unscheduled stop in Nashville to wait out a thunderstorm.

"It was after midnight, and we were hungry," remembered Bo. "After we got to the airport lobby, Woody found the manager of the restaurant, who was getting ready to close."

"We've got to get these guys something to eat," Woody explained.

The manager pointed to Boxcar Bailey, star fullback of the team and the only Black man on the Miami team. "That guy's not going to eat here," said the manager.

Woody stared at him and said, "What do you mean he's not going to eat here?"

"We don't serve his kind."

It was January 1, 1951, and America was a long way from "the land of equality."

"If that guy doesn't eat here, then none of us will eat here," replied Woody.

Embarrassed, the manager suggested he could eat upstairs.

"Fine. We'll all eat upstairs," said Woody. The manager said there was no room.

"Wearing a stare I will always remember," Bo concludes, "Woody tells the guy, 'Then Boxcar and I will eat together upstairs, and the rest of the team will eat downstairs.'"

The Woody I know would have preferred to take the team to another restaurant, but he realized the unlikelihood of finding one open at that time of night. The Woody Bo knew "won us all over that night." (From *I Remember Woody* by Steve Greenberg and Dale Raterman.)

* * *

Greg Lashutka (1963-1964-1965), former mayor of Columbus, recalled, "Woody's legacy was not wins and losses; it was the lessons he taught us. Everyone, whether they liked it or not, got a minor in history from Woody."

John Hicks (1970-1972-1973) said, "A lot of people who were in his life are a lot better off today. He simply made people better, and you can put football aside. It was his commitment to life, period."

Randy Gradishar (1971-1972-1973) noted, "Woody studied

families, mostly the parents, as much as, if not more than, the kids. He wanted to see what kind of family structure there was."

* * *

Carmen Cozza played for Woody and Ara Parseghian at Miami (Ohio) before becoming a college Football Hall of Fame coach at Yale, where he won 179 games in thirty-two years.

"I used to kid him [Woody] that I thought my name was *unprintable* until I was a senior. He had a way of getting into your face. When he laughed, I laughed. When he cried, I cried. When he got mad, I hid."

* * *

Jim Stillwagon spoke for all of us after the 1971 Rose Bowl game, when he said, "Not to take any credit from Stanford, because they played well, and they beat us, but we had beaten ourselves in the smashmouth two-a-day practices Woody ran for two weeks before (the game). He was wound up so tight with a bowl game on the line. We were getting taped up on the flight into Los Angeles so we could hit the practice field the moment we landed, and Heaven forbid he would let us enjoy any of the rewards of the Big Ten title. He said participating in events like Lawry's would only make us soft."

Though he was upset, Wagon remained a loyal Buckeye, not mentioning that Woody had promised us there would be no practice on arrival day that year.

* * *

Dick LeBeau played running back and cornerback at Ohio State in 1957–1958–1959, before a fourteen-year Hall of Fame NFL playing career as a cornerback, then spent forty years as an NFL assistant and three years as a head coach. He was highly regarded for his defensive innovations and the performance of his defenses. He worked actively as a coach until he was eighty.

One day, in 1966, he stopped to talk football with Woody to show what he had learned and get the current thinking of a coach he admired so much.

They spent three hours together. When asked how it went, Dick said, "He just does not get it; he can't get it. The game has passed him by. When he looks at the blackboard, there is a blank stare in his eyes."

Woody was only fifty-three at the time, but he was head coach at Ohio State for twelve more years, controlling the offense while relinquishing almost full control to defensive coordinators Lou McCullough and George Hill.

What if the athletic department had recognized the decline, which was so obvious to LeBeau? What if Woody had been convinced to rely more on his outstanding assistants and oversee the offense as he did the defense? Or at least to give the ideas proposed by his assistants a fair chance of success?

My answer is, it would have required a period of great upheaval. But suppose men he admired joined together and persisted? If Woody had let them help him, his final years could have established him as one of the greatest college coaches of all time.

Does that sound like an overstatement? His actual record in his last eleven years included eight finishes in the top eleven in the country and six in the top five. His teams won three outright Big Ten titles and shared six more. They went to nine bowl games, winning three. That is a great record for any coach and any university.

Yet Woody's players and assistants will tell you they were not allowed to be at their best in important games because their offenses were stripped down, and their hands were tied. My teammates and I are certain we would have won the 1971 Rose Bowl if we had been permitted to play our best. Archie Griffin's class played in four Rose Bowls; the only time they won was when the players and coaches threatened to revolt unless Woody made changes. During their fourth season, they lost to UCLA, 10-23, which they had beaten in the regular season, 41–20, *at UCLA.* Every year Woody got so tight against Michigan that the offense was constricted, and the defense played under pressure.

If Woody had supported George Chaump and guided his efforts with the backing of the university, I feel a couple more Michigan wins, more Rose Bowl championships, and possible big victories here and there would have meant multiple added national titles. With three more, Woody would have eight titles to Nick Saban's seven and Bear Bryant's six. It could have happened.

Woody on Woody

Woody used to say, "I am not a hater. You cannot be a hater in life. But I despise them. That is OK." I never understood the distinction between hating and despising, and I never heard him explain it.

To defensive end Mike Radtke—whose wife, Marti, was expecting their first child any time—Woody said, "Now, I want to say one *unprintable* thing. Women have babies every day of the year, and we only play SMU once this year. Your wife better not screw up this game for us." After a 35–14 victory, Mike got the game ball from Woody and twins from Marti.

"As the youngest, I don't think there is any doubt I was spoiled." Woody, *A Fire to Win: The Life and Times of Woody Hayes,* by John Lombardo, Thomas Dunne Books, St. Martin's Press . . . straight from Woody, by way of *Quotable Woody,* by Monte Carpenter: "I can do your job, but you can't do mine" to an OSU professor . . . Woody once remarked, "Be careful what you say. Not a one of them [the media] wants you to win. But I don't expect you to carry a chip on your shoulder like I do" . . . "The great thing about football

is that when you get knocked down, you get up and go again . . .
Blame is safer than praise . . . The most valuable gift you can give
anyone is your time."

* * *

In his first book, *Hotline to Victory*, Woody wrote, "We must never
allow the defense to bunch up against us ... force our opponents
to defend the width and depth of the field." Too bad he forgot
that in 1970.

"When you get fancy, you get beat. You may score some spectacular victories, but can you win the championship?"

"They couldn't beat me with two Michigan coaches, so they had
to come down here and take a coach that I trained."

"Paralyze their resistance with your persistence."

"The bowl games are only supposed to be a fun reward." Yes,
another one he often forgot.

* * *

"You can never pay back, but you can always pay forward."

"I don't apologize for anything. When I make a mistake, I take
the blame and go on from there."

"If this offense was good enough for [Amos Alonzo] Stagg, its
good enough for me." Stagg was a legendary coach, with a 314–
199–35 record, but he retired in 1946 at the age of seventy.

"You don't make a mistake by going straight ahead—three yards
and a cloud of dust offense. I will pound you and pound you until
you quit."

"The five big mistakes in football are the fumble, the interception, the penalty, the badly called play, the blocked punt—and
most of these originate with the quarterback. Find a mistake-proof
quarterback, and you have this game won."

⋆ ⋆ ⋆

"I've had smarter people around me all my life, but I haven't run into one yet that can outwork me. And if they can't outwork you, then smarts aren't going to do them much good."

"RHIP: rank has its privileges."

"When you are winning, you don't need friends. When you are losing, you don't have them anyway" ... "The will to win is not as important as the will to prepare to win" ... "Football is an avocation. Education lasts a lifetime" ... "When you are winning, you don't need friends. When you are losing you don't have them anyway" ... "An athlete without an education is heading for a bad situation."

⋆ ⋆ ⋆

When Ohio State beat USC to win the 1955 Rose Bowl, Woody listed five Big Ten teams he thought were better than the Trojans. With one unsportsmanlike comment, he made enemies on the West Coast for twenty years.

Woody's Assistant Coaches

George Chaump introduced the I formation to Ohio State in 1968—three years before Mike Garrett of USC had earned a Heisman Trophy running in the I. Two years later, O. J. Simpson finished second as an I back; he won it that season. Woody vehemently opposed the concept. He called it the lighthouse formation because the defense always knew where the ball was going by watching the lead blocker, the fullback. We had several successful tailbacks at Ohio State, from Dave Brungard to John Brockington to Leo Hayden, but the best was to come later. Archie Griffin won two Heisman Trophies, the only college player to do that, and he did it in the I. Fans should be glad the assistants sided with George and convinced Woody to make that change.

* * *

Here's a story from *Ohio State '68: All the Way to the Top*, by Steve Greenberg and Larry Zelina. Defensive coordinator Lou McCullough described how Woody decided which players were on offense and which ones were on defense:

"When I first came to OSU (March 1963, from Iowa State)," McCullough begins, "Woody would identify the thirty-three best players, take the first twenty-four for offense, give me the rest for defense. Every year I told him he could not have a good defense unless the defense had some of the best players. Before the '68 season, he told me we would alternate picks. I said, 'Will you remember that?' And he did!"

That is how Lou had three sophomores—Jack Tatum, Mike Sensibaugh, and Tim Anderson—in our defensive backfield in 1968. In prior years, they would have been on offense. In the five preceding years McCullough coached for Woody, Ohio State finished in the AP Top Twenty only once—ninth in 1964. Thank you, Lou!

Tate, Baugh, and Tim probably thank him as well, as all three had fine NFL careers. By the way, Baugh, who sadly passed away in April 2021, still holds the Ohio State career record for interceptions, with twenty-two!

* * *

After learning that Woody claimed twenty-four players for offense before making the rest available to Lou, and remembering from my years as a Buckeye just how intense those practices were, I wondered how the two different platoons compared on game day against opponents.

According to the data posted on the website **www.sports-reference.com**, the defense was far superior.

At the time, there were between 120 and 118 major colleges playing football. From 1963, when Lou took over the defense, until 1968, when athletes were divided more fairly, OSU's defense never ranked lower than thirty-second and never higher than sixteenth. Over five years, their average ranking was twenty-seventh. The offense ranked anywhere between fifty-sixth and ninety-eighth. The average was seventy-third.

Since the athletes on offense were better, and the results were worse, maybe the scheme on offense should have been reconsidered.

* * *

According to Esco Sarkkinen, "Woody loved votes. Many times we assistant coaches would vote yes, and Woody would vote no. Woody's no vote wiped out our eight yeses."

Earl Bruce worked under Woody as an undergrad assistant (1951–1953) and assistant coach (1966–1971), eventually becoming head coach (1979–1987): "[Working for him was] like being in the Marine Corps. It was a great experience, but I'd never do it again."

* * *

Lou Holtz, assistant at Ohio State in 1968 and head coach at various schools for thirty-six years afterwards, won a national title at Notre Dame (1988). He finished his college coaching career with a record of 249–132–7. "At times you would absolutely want to strangle him. There were other times you admired him, you always respected him, but after you left you absolutely loved him. Woody cared."

* * *

Bill Mallory was assistant to Woody (1966–1968) before taking his first head position at Miami (Ohio) in 1968. "Woody said he wanted to talk with me before I left. So I went to see him, and he said to me, 'Remember what's number one with these young men. Education. See that they get that education.'"

★ ★ ★

"Woody had a way of showing up in the middle of a conversation," recalls my friend and teammate Randy Hart. "And most of the time the conversation was about him. When Woody came into the coffee room, the first coach to see him immediately shouted, 'Whiplash.' The pressure was really on Friday nights, because Woody was never satisfied that we were prepared and always wanted a coach to reassure him. When the phone rang, no coach answered. The caller knew to let the phone ring once, hang up, and call back. As for his visits to our rooms on Friday night, the only time a coach answered his door was after one knock, two knocks, and three knocks, in succession. Woody did not knock like that."

★ ★ ★

In his book *Wins, Loses, and Lessons*, Lou Holtz discusses his first staff meeting at Ohio State in the spring of 1968. There was a fight when Woody accused an assistant of not spending enough time with an athlete on academics. The assistant "respectfully disagreed," and Woody "went after him, grabbed him by the shirt, and started a tussle." Holtz had never seen anything like that, and wrote, "The man had what counselors today would call 'anger management issues.' Later that day, Woody resolved another matter by throwing a film projector through a glass door."

Before accepting the job at Ohio State, Holtz had asked Woody to speak with current assistant coaches. At first he was told the other assistants were not available. When Holtz persisted, Woody said they were all busy, except Tiger Ellison. By chance, Lou and Tiger walked out of the room together when the meeting ended.

"Tiger," said Holtz, "I thought you said Coach Hayes was a good guy, a great leader?"

Ellison chuckled and said, "Hey, Attila the Hun was a great leader. Doesn't mean you'd have him over for dinner."

Holtz concluded the story by writing, "Tiger had never said an unkind word about anybody in his life."

The athletic department responded to the damaged projector by issuing an edict that all film projectors in St. John Arena be chained to the tables.

Writers

As a writer for *Sports Illustrated* in the 1970s, Doug Looney did the impossible. Despite the rejection and the avoidance he received from Woody, he earned Woody's tolerance. Not respect—after all, Looney was an out-of-town writer—but at least he gained some limited access in Columbus. His view of the Ohio State–Michigan series, as a journalist, was that it was a wonderful confrontation between two giants—the schools and the coaches.

"They [Woody and Bo] coached their worst in those games. They would get so uptight. Not only did they perform nervous, so did their players," Looney said.

* * *

Prior to the 1969 Rose Bowl, Woody and the famous *Los Angeles Times* sportswriter Jim Murray had a one-sided conversation over several days. Murray wrote about Woody, and Woody ignored him. The players tended to agree with the writer, who thought the

Ohio State players should have been allowed to attend the annual Lawry's Beef Bowl with the Southern Cal Trojans and should have been allowed to speak with the reporters long enough to finish a sentence.

After our 27–16 victory, we especially enjoyed Murray's final words: "We didn't know if the Ohio State team could use forks, spoons, and knives, or if they could even talk, but the nation found out they sure could play football!"

* * *

"Next year, of course, Woody would have a chance to make it six (national championships, figuring the upcoming game with Michigan game was in the bag), given the good health of Rex Kern and Jack Tatum." Dan Jenkins, *Sports Illustrated*, November 24, 1969. Sports writers, like kids, say the darndest things . . . "'They shalt not pass,' is for him both an offensive and a defensive admonition." Ron Fimrite, *Sports Illustrated*, December 4, 1972.

Anne Hayes

Anne Hayes married Woody in 1942. "It certainly hasn't been a calm and peaceful marriage. But I don't think I would want to be married to anybody else. I have to fight eighty-five to one hundred football players for attention, but that is better than one skinny blonde. I don't get upset when I am at a game and some fan calls him an *unprintable*. Why should I? I've called him that myself. After one game, Woody said he would take me to dinner and the movies. He took me to dinner all right. The movies were four hours of game films."

Woody's temper

At times Woody displayed his temper in a calculated manner, with the intention of establishing or maintaining control. For example, at practice he would throw his watch on the ground and stomp on it. He kept a box of cheap watches in a drawer in his office and put one on before practice when he expected a show of frustration might be necessary. When a situation arose that "required" a show of temper, but he had forgotten to bring one, he borrowed a watch from a student trainer or someone he could trust and used it for his demonstration. The next day that person found a new watch on his desk. Stitches in hats were cut so hats could be easily torn during a "megaton." Also, during meetings with his coaches when he felt he was losing control of the meeting, he might fire the coach who had raised an uncomfortable point. If necessary, the other assistants told the coach he was expected to act as if he had not been fired.

Other times, Woody lost his temper without intent. When these explosions took place at practice or in meetings, players and coaches did not mention them, and local media who saw them did not report them. When they took place in public—the Gator Bowl, the Rose Bowl, yard markers at the 1971 Michigan game, sportswriters, photographers—they were recorded. The list of public displays grew and was fully reviewed with each further outburst.

★   ★   ★

John Brickles, head coach at New Philadelphia High School where Woody had his first coaching job as an assistant, recalled, "He lacked patience. Woody had a hard time controlling himself and drove the kids too hard." *A Fire to Win – The Life and Times of Woody Hayes* by John Lombardo, Thomas Dunne Books, St. Martin's Press, p. 24.

Gator Bowl, December 29, 1978:
The Punch or "Just another punch"?

Most Buckeye fans associate that game with Woody punching a Clemson linebacker named Charlie Bauman, who had intercepted an Art Schlichter pass late in the televised Gator Bowl game.

The exact situation was third and five on the Clemson 24-yard line, fourth quarter, 2:30 to play. Schlichter was playing very well at the time, having connected on sixteen of nineteen passes for 205 yards and was OSU's leading rusher with 70 yards.

After the game, Athletic Director Hugh Hindman, who played for Woody at Miami (Ohio) and was an assistant to him at Ohio State for seven years, confronted him privately in the locker room and told him that Ohio State president Harold Enarson would be advised. Hayes was offered the opportunity to resign but refused, saying "That would make it too easy for you. You better go ahead and fire me."

The next morning, Woody was fired, and Enarson said, "There isn't a university in this country that would permit a coach to physically assault a college athlete."

Every athlete, coach, and administrator who had been at an Ohio State practice in the past twenty-eight years, and every local journalist who had been allowed to view practice, knew that was not true. Ohio State had permitted Woody to hit players since he was hired in 1951. The line among the former players was "Woody hit every player who ever played for him harder than he hit Charlie Bauman." Some players added, "Except for Rex Kern (because I was often hurt) or Jim Otis (whose father was a fraternity brother of Woody's at Denison and a friend since) or Archie (because he was Archie)."

Woody had been a boxer since before he went to college and still packed a punch. Players soon learned to stand on his left side if it was absolutely necessary to be close to him at all. Woody's right hand was not much of an issue, but his left hand, fully extended after reaching across his body, was powerful.

Woody always stood in the offensive huddle in practice. Out of habit, when we played SMU in the first game of the 1968 season, we automatically formed our huddle for twelve men after the kickoff. We all laughed, closed the huddle, and got on with business, glad Woody was on the sideline.

One day Mace was with the first team in practice and made two mistakes. First, he was on Woody's right, and second, he was relaxed. When Woody felt the need to vent his anger, he punched Mace just above his belt. While Mace was struggling to get his breath, Woody yelled at him for not calling the next play more quickly. Mace was unable to say, "Coach, I can't breathe."

★ ★ ★

The vast majority of Woody's punches were not intended to hurt the player, but rather to make a point. They were aimed at parts of the body that were protected by padding, but Woody's aim was not perfect. My guess is that players were hit during most practices for twenty-eight years at Ohio State.

David Hyde, who did a fine job with *1968: The Year That Saved Ohio State Football*, reported that Woody hit an Iowa player during the 1966 game OSU won, 14–10. The way Hyde put it on page six, the player was "hit, or grabbed, or something. It was not captured on television or film … did not make the newspapers."

The following Monday, the week of the Michigan game, Athletic Director Dick Larkins, a strong supporter of Woody's—to whom his 1973 book, *You Win with People*, was dedicated—entered the football office and delivered bad news. Hyde writes, "Woody," Larkins said, "The athletic council has met and asked for your resignation."

Hayes didn't flinch. "Is that all you've got?" he asked.

Larkins nodded.

"OK, go back to the athletic council, tell them I'm not resigning, and that they are wasting my time."

There was nothing done by anyone. There was nothing even mentioned by anyone. Apparently, the Gator Bowl was the second time Woody was fired. I always wondered why Woody refused to resign; now I know the strategy had worked in the past.

Returning to the Gator Bowl, I have always felt that part of the cause of the frustration that led to the punch was that it involved a forward pass. With only 146 yards gained on the ground, and almost half of that by Schlichter, a pass would have been reasonable to anyone. But Woody was the coach who repeatedly resisted throwing to Paul Warfield, Jan White, and Bruce Jankowski! Woody may have felt intense regret at the play call.

Plus, Woody had moved his first-team All-Big Ten quarterback, Rod Gerald, to receiver in order to attract Art. Would the coach have preferred to have a senior throw the ball or a freshman? More regret.

When OSU began to recruit Art, quarterbacks coach George Chaump asked me to call him and promote the program. This was a player they wanted. I told him I would be glad to call.

After I introduced myself on the phone, I found I was speaking with Max Schlichter, Art's father. He asked why my completion percentage had declined in my senior year and other questions about being the quarterback at Ohio State. Then he told me the grand plans the family had for Art, from starting as a freshman to being the number one pick in the NFL Draft to success in the NFL. The very personal agenda Max outlined was not one that would fit in with the Ohio State players and coaches I knew. I never had the opportunity to speak directly to Art.

When I gave my report of the conversation to George, and my recommendation not to continue to recruit him, George said, "Oh no, what is Woody going to say?"

I still do not have an answer to that question, but I do know my advice was not taken. Art Schlichter set many offensive records at Ohio State and was in the top ten voting for the Heisman Trophy three times. The team was 36–11–1 when he was there, with one

Big Ten title and a 2–2 record against Michigan.

After Art was taken fourth in the 1982 NFL Draft by the Baltimore Colts, his career went off track. He was suspended for gambling one year, played three, and started only six games—all losses. He never got control of his gambling problem. He served time in prison for theft and corrupt activity and was released in August 2020. He has been diagnosed with "fifteen to seventeen" concussions as a result of football, which have led to Parkinson's disease and dementia.

Aftermath of the Punch

A little more than a year after the punch, my good friend and business partner Jack Havens, then president of the Ohio State Board of Trustees, called me. After the infamous Gator Bowl, he was afraid Woody would be fired. Now he thought it was time to look to the future, and he had a plan.

"Rex," he said, "do you think you could arrange a lunch for us with Woody?"

"I think so, Jack," I replied. "I will try."

When the three of us met at a restaurant north of campus, on Olentangy River Road, there I was, looking at two power guys.

"Woody," Jack said, "We need you at Ohio State. You have too much to offer to the students, the school, and everyone who loves the university."

Woody was stunned.

"That is very kind of you, but I am not ready now," he replied. "I'll let you know."

Time passed. When Jack told me that he had gotten Woody back to the university and that he had an office in the ROTC building, I stopped to see him—sort of welcome him back. What a disappointment.

Woody would not have accepted anything too fancy. It would

have made him uncomfortable; he probably would have avoided the place. But the university had not even requisitioned a desk!

I told Jack, who immediately saw that Woody had a perfectly adequate office of his own on campus. The man deserved nothing less and would have accepted nothing more.

Over the next six or seven years, we saw the best side of one of the most important men in the lives of every player he coached, whether at Denison, Miami (Ohio), or Ohio State. Freed of his perceived need to control, dominate, intimidate, and manipulate to maintain and expand his position of power, Woody excelled when he lost his power. With a base of operations but no need to try to improve the fullback off tackle play, he had time to remind his players to finish their degrees, provide counsel as requested, ask about their wives and children, teach military classes, do the public speaking he loved, chair fund raising drives for important causes, chat with students and simply be a kindly old grandfather to anyone who needed that type of man in his life. And don't we all?

My favorite memory of Woody's last act came when our youngest son Michael, age five or so, and I traveled from California to Columbus for a Buckeye game.

For us it was not so much a family outing, not a father and son event, but two guys, two buddies on an adventure. It was his first plane ride, first Buckeye game, first trip with all my attention focused on him. I was enjoying these experiences with him and enjoying providing them for him.

Before we left he had heard many "Woody stories," the good and the not so good. During the trip I retold a few and offered some new ones. On the way to the game, I mentioned some more.

In those days I was allowed in the press box. On the elevator up I said hello to familiar faces and introduced Michael to a few whose names I remembered. When we got to the press box, I said, "Is Woody here?"

The attendant nodded and pointed to the end of the front row.

I recognized him, of course, but he had aged in the past months. I bent over and said to Michael, "There's Woody—in the black cap with the block *O* on the front. Do you see him? Why don't you go say hello?"

Michael sprinted as only a five-year-old can when he sees a life-long friend, jumped in Woody's lap, and gave him a 100 percent hug. Woody returned that hug with the sincerity with which it was given and smiled in a way I had never seen in the three or four lifetimes we had gone through together.

With one hug, my son had given two men a thrill. Woody had received the love, appreciation, and approval he always wanted but feared would make him "soft." I saw Woody when he was truly "soft." It was a beautiful sight.

The public highlight of Woody's final act came March 14, 1986, when he was asked to give the commencement speech to graduates of the Ohio State University. He called it the greatest day of his life. He discussed paying forward, history, war, getting fired, and, of course, education.

On March 11, 1987, against the advice of doctors, Woody asked someone to drive him to Dayton so he could introduce Bo Schembechler at a fundraising event. After staying for Bo's comments, Woody went home. The next morning, when Anne tried to wake him, he was unconscious. He died of a heart attack, March 12, 1987, at the age of seventy-four.

Woody's funeral was held on March 17, 1987 at First Community Church in Grandview, a suburb of Columbus. Friends and admirers began to gather at one-thirty, though the doors did not open until two-thirty for the four o'clock service. The church, with a seating capacity of fourteen hundred, was packed. Former players and assistant coaches sat at the front. Former President Richard Nixon gave the eulogy. A friend of Woody's since they met after the 1957 game against Iowa, President Nixon quoted the Greek philosopher and playwright Sophocles, who wrote, "One must wait until the evening to see how splendid the day has been."

Though Woody was not a perfect man, he accomplished a great deal and improved the lives of almost every one of his players and many others during his life. When he put aside his perception of the need for control and power, and accepted "softness" in others, occasionally even himself, his "evening" was one to celebrate.

Woody and Ohio State behind the Scenes

While researching this book, I spoke with Daryl Sanders, who had called me the day after the Gator Bowl in 1978. He told a fascinating story about the months after that game, which few Buckeye fans have heard.

Sanders was a Buckeye tackle in 1960, 1961, and 1962, on teams that won a national title (1961) and compiled a 21–5–1 record. After being selected twelfth in the NFL Draft, he started every game for the Detroit Lions for four years before retiring to go into business.

"I was watching the Gator Bowl with two Ohio State teammates and our wives at the Seven Springs Ski Resort near Pittsburgh," Sanders recalled. When the event took place, the three former players—Dave Tingley, Dan Connor, and I—each said he had been whacked by Woody in practice and we instinctively laughed at the recollections. There was no replay and very little discussion by the announcers of what had taken place. Soon we realized this was an opposing player in public, not a Buckeye in practice.

"It became clear to me that I needed to be with Woody. We were not especially close, not like I was with Bo Schembechler, my line coach, but I knew Woody needed someone and was not certain who it would be. Despite the fact that we had the room for three more nights, my wife and I were in the car at eight the next morning.

"Of course, this was before cell phones, so we gathered limited information from the radio. We stopped, and I called Dan Heinlein, president of the alumni association and a personal friend. 'Has anyone spoken with Woody?' I asked. 'No, but everyone is worried,' he replied. *Worried about him or about their jobs?* I remember thinking. Dan and I discussed ways to make first contact with Woody. Dan brought up Rex Kern as a favorite of Woody who might have some good ideas of how to approach the Old Man. Rex agreed that something should be done that day. Rex suggested I go to Woody's house with Archie. Rex said we know it would mean a lot to Woody, and he would be more welcoming if a Black and a white player showed up together. After some discussion, we agreed not to get more players so we would not overwhelm him. We knew Woody was hurting but had no idea how he was coping emotionally. Was he angry, distraught, or at his limit of coping ability? We thought it made more sense to show up and show our care and personal support for him.

"Archie was glad to join me. We met at the corner of Woody Hayes Drive. We felt tension and trepidation and believed that feeling was common with everyone involved—Woody, Ohio State, and his players. I said, 'We need to pray first.'

"For fifteen minutes, we said a mutual prayer, alternating turns speaking. The essence of the prayer was for the right thing to happen and for us to serve Woody.

"When I knocked on the door, Woody answered rather quickly. He looked at me, and over at Archie, standing next to me, and said, 'Well, come on in.'

"It was about one in the afternoon. We sat there for seven hours. Woody's wife, Anne, did not join us. Once we heard a cough; I assumed it was her. There was nothing to drink or eat. There was never a period of silence. Woody talked about 80 percent of the time, discussing people, coaches, football, and games—everything but the incident.

"When it seemed appropriate to leave, Woody said, 'I have a

second phone that is confidential—let me give you that number.' As we left, he said, 'Don't talk to anybody,' which I understood to mean media, but not players.

"That night I filled a legal pad with notes. What are your options? What is important to you? What protection do you have? What risks are there?

"At nine the next morning I called Woody and said, 'I have been thinking about the situation. We need to get on the front end of this. I have a list of questions to discuss and need to gather some information.'

"'Come on over,' he replied.

"When Woody signed his first contract he was aware of Ohio State's reputation was the 'graveyard of coaches.' His contract made him a professor, now tenured. His pension was protected. This was wonderful news to me and led to additional questions.

"'Wait a minute,' he said, and called to Anne to join us. Woody had no concern for money. He would write checks without knowing how much was in the account, and not cash other checks. Anne had an arrangement with the bank branch manager that when Woody had an overdraft she should be called, and she would stop in and transfer the money from savings.

"I started to suggest what he might consider important, such as a title of professor emeritus, classes to teach, an office, some level of income, in addition to what was guaranteed, being welcomed at The Faculty Club ...

"After three or four hours, I had a sense of what was important to him and was ready to negotiate on his behalf.

"Dan Heinlein and I met twice. Dan said the university required a letter from Woody authorizing me to be his representative. At the time, I owned a Cadillac dealership, had my secretary type one up, and Woody signed it.

"The next step was to talk with someone on the athletic council who was identified as their go-to guy for terms and conditions. He was cocky. His attitude was that they did not want to do anything more than necessary, that Woody was fired and should just disappear. It was clear he would not be a part of any reasonable solution.

"If it was going to be a fight, I needed to learn what I did not already know and build up alliances in the interest of fair play. I reached out to people of influence whom I respected, Jack Havens being one.

"Then, I got a call from Dan Heinlein. He said, 'You should not have gone outside the loop.'

"My immediate reply was, 'You made me.' I proceeded to raise Cain, explaining the unacceptable attitude I had encountered. If I created the impression that I was willing to go farther 'outside the loop,' that was fine.

"Dan called back and said that President Enarson wanted to meet with me. I hoped he would be the ultimate decision maker, and he was.

"President Enarson told me that Woody would receive three-fourths of his salary for life. I asked what that was and was told he had made $43,000 for the previous twelve months as coach.

"'May I ask a question?' I asked. 'What would you have paid him if he had been represented?'

"'What the governor was paid,' Enarson replied.

"'So you took advantage of him!'

"'No, he didn't care,' said Enarson.

"'You did not protect him! I and my alumni friends resent what you did to Woody!' I wanted to be intimidating. I have been in business all my life and resent people who take advantage of others.

"'There was nothing we could do,' Enarson replied.

"'What you should have been doing was sitting down two years ago. You could have worked together to face the obvious fact that he was getting older. You could have stated your needs and he could have expressed his thoughts.

"Shortly after that meeting, Woody showed me a letter from Enarson thanking him for not suing the university after a sponge had been left inside him during an operation. A lawsuit would have brought a huge settlement, because he had to be operated on again to remove the sponge.

"The thing is, Woody loved the university and those guys had jobs with the university. I'm not sure you fire a man like that before breakfast. Woody knew the power that he had, and that people who wanted to fire him needed a good enough reason. My problem was I did not know how much latitude the university had. In the end he got what was important to him, things like being able to teach, rights and privileges at The Faculty Club, an office, and a secretary. He had a great final act to his life.

"One thing which helped Woody make the transition from coach to teacher was that in the spring, two Hollywood producers appeared. Howard Koch and Gene Kirkwood had been in on the fabulously successful movie *Rocky* with Sylvester Stallone, and they wanted to do a movie on Woody.

"The famous writer Budd Schulberg was involved as well and came to Columbus. Woody and my wife and I were part of a small group to see a private screening of *On the Waterfront* with him. Imagine watching Marlon Brando as Terry Malloy saying, 'I coulda been a contender. I coulda been somebody,' while sitting with the man who gave him those words!

"Other writers came in as well. I gave them a list of about twenty players to talk with about Woody. The project obsessed him for about twelve months. We talked about it almost every day. It was his diversion after 'the event.'

"I remember when Woody met with Schulberg, Woody said, 'I give you freedom to paint me as I am, warts and all.' (He was quoting Oliver Cromwell, British military leader and politician who actually had visible warts in the seventeenth century and wished the portrait to be accurate.)

"The final signing of the documents took place at Chasen's, the famous restaurant in West Hollywood. Rex and John Brockington were there. Woody enjoyed being the center of attention after all that had happened.

"When the scripts were completed, Columbia Pictures decided not to produce the movie. Still, it was a valuable bridge for Woody and a fun experience for many of us. More importantly, we had signed a contract which provided $100,000 up front for him. He and Anne could live several years on that amount of money. A friend in New York knew someone in the movie business who thought that was a good deal.

"Along the way, Budd Schulberg's wife had asked me, 'What do you get out of all this?' When I told her I was doing it for Woody, she thought I should get something and got on Columbia Pictures. They gave me a contract for $15,000—$5,000 immediately and the remainder when the movie was released.

"Here's the way I see Woody: Great coach; humanitarian; would never lie, cheat, or steal; cared about his players, first string or last, able to help him or not," concludes Sanders. "When he heard one of his former players had tragically run over his own child, immediately Woody left to be with him. Nothing else mattered—distance, schedule, even football."

* * *

When Woody Hayes was fired by the university, the first team to reach out to him was the Dallas Cowboys—namely, head coach Tom Landry and talent scout Gil Brandt. They invited him to come to a game, be honored, sit in on meetings, have access to their operation. They had no obligation to do that, but they did have a sincere commitment to caring about a person at a difficult time in his life. I later spoke with Gil, who told me Woody enjoyed the complete access they gave him and had a wonderful time.

So What Do I Think about Woody?

One of the problems with writing a book is that the author is expected to reach some conclusions. When the subject is Woody Hayes, truly a "riddle, wrapped in a mystery, inside an enigma," that is quite a challenge.

Coaches who worked as his assistants have various points of view. Those who coached against him have others. Writers who covered him had others. Anyone who was charged with supervising him has a different perspective.

As a former player, I will try to explain my own, while acknowledging it has changed with time. It certainly may differ sharply from another player.

I believe Woody changed depending on your relationship to him, which kept changing over time for players. Having known him as a recruit, as a player, and as a former player who had graduated, I feel I knew three different people.

Woody the salesman: As a recruiter, Woody was a salesman. He was selling education, first to parents, second to their boys who had the background and intelligence to graduate from college as well as the size and athletic ability to help him win football games—lots of football games!

His deep and sincere belief in the importance of a college education helped him make many "sales" to parents and talented recruits. He also provided tutoring, motivation, and monitoring, headed by what he called "our brain coach," designed to help true student-athletes work to earn that education. If the athlete was not enough of a student while playing, Woody kept after him for years and even decades to complete his degree. In short, Woody believed in what he was selling and did everything he could to see that the customer got what he was sold.

Along the way, Woody worked to recruit "good kids from good families." This provided him with the type of people he wanted to be around at practice and on trips; who would compete under pressure; who would be good teammates for each other; as well as a large pool of lifelong friendship possibilities for his players.

If athletes met the criteria for athletics, academics, family, and personal character, race did not matter to Woody. He said a football team was like a piano, which needed the black keys and the white keys, playing together. Although some Ohio State alumni opposed his early recruitment of Blacks, the 1954 national championship silenced those critics. Bobby Watkins, Jim Parker, Jim Roseboro, and Jack Gibbs on that team, as well as players like Leo Brown, Aurelius Thomas, and Don Clark right behind them, looked darn good in scarlet and gray.

During recruiting, a time when parents were correct to question the sales pitch they heard from coaches, Woody delivered. He worked to make the sale good for the parents and the athlete, whether the young man turned out to be a star or a fourth-stringer.

Woody the coach: Woody the coach ruled his team like some fathers of the 1950s, the ones who made the rules with no discussion, made decisions with no debate, used their temper to silence questions, and saw no reason to change. The only explanation then was as follows: "Because I am the man of the house."

All his players learned life lessons from Woody—many to copy, others to avoid repeating. Lessons of both types have been valuable to us since graduation.

The football skills learned at Ohio State were not taught by Woody, but by our position coaches. He hired very well and most of my peers feel we were well taught by men like Hugh Hindman, Lou McCullough, Esco Sarkkinen, Earle Bruce, Bill Mallory, Tiger Ellison, Lou Holtz, George Chaump, and Rudy Hubbard. Some became successful head coaches in their own right, some remained as assistants, but all taught us what we needed to succeed in the Big Ten and, for those who had the desire and ability, the NFL. Woody recognized coaching talent and attracted it to the university, including a graduate student who became a Hall of Fame coach at Michigan, Bo Schembechler.

Woody managed the program and micromanaged the offense. Those were definitely not his talents. His vision was in the past, not in the future. When Woody was stressed, his fallback was to run the fullback. He ridiculed new ideas from his coaches and players alike rather than exploring them impartially. My teammates and I believe his conservative offense and need for control cost us an unbeaten season in 1970. The defense almost achieved that with their outstanding play, but there were two games they needed help from the offense. When we scored forty-eight points at Illinois in a 48–29 win, their efforts were supported. When we scored only seventeen points in the 17-27 Rose Bowl loss to Stanford, we did not help them out. Had the offense not been so limited all year, and had Woody not implemented the triple-option offense two weeks prior to the Rose Bowl, reducing Leo Hayden's ability to contribute, we believe we would have won our second Rose Bowl game. The result would have been a 28–1 record for the Super Sophs and recognition as one of the greatest teams of all time.

Other players from other eras have similar stories.

After graduation, Woody became a loving, caring grandfather figure. (If you did not graduate, Woody remained the father figure, repeatedly reminding you to "get that taken care of.")

If you called or stopped for advice or counsel, his door was open. If you needed a letter of recommendation, it was done. If he heard you had a serious problem, he dropped everything, including sacred practices, to come to you immediately.

To summarize the summary, he was a Hall of Fame coach who would have been better by accepting and implementing changes for the outstanding offensive talent he recruited. His Hall of Fame record as a coach—238–72–10, with thirteen Big Ten titles in twenty-eight years and five national championships—was exceeded by his greatness as a man and a friend.

Of all my memories of Woody, the strongest comes from the last time I saw him.

I was living in California and called him when I was in Columbus. He said, "Let's go to lunch," and decided we should go to The Faculty Club on campus as always. He insisted on paying (as always). He suggested, requested, insisted we return by way of Woody Hayes Dr., which our friend Jack Havens had been instrumental in initiating and completing.

Because he was frail and unsteady, I got out and went around the car to help him get out. I said, "Coach, I want you to know how much I love you," and kissed him on the cheek.

He smiled and said nothing.

A kind letter from Steve Hayes, son of Woody and
Anne and a longtime judge in Columbus.

Office of the President Emeritus

110 Enarson Hall
154 West 12th Avenue
Columbus, OH 43210-1390

Phone 614-292-2992
FAX   614-292-2124

December 3, 2001

Mr. Rex W. Kern
4675 Winterset Drive
Columbus, Ohio 43220

Dear Rex:

What a great idea. I would be delighted to contribute whatever I can and would be honored to do so. As you know Woody and I became fairly close during the early 1980's and I consider him to be not just a great football coach but a great academic and a great citizen as well.

Let me know if I can help.

Sincerely,

Edward H. Jennings

Reply from Ed Jennings to my letter concerning
a possible book on Woody Hayes.

Office of the President Emeritus

110 Enarson Hall
154 West 12th Avenue
Columbus, OH 43210-1390

Phone 614-292-2992
FAX   614-292-2124

May 20, 2002

Rex W. Kern
4675 Winterset Drive
Columbus, OH 43220

Dear Rex:

Perhaps my favorite experience with Woody occurred several years ago at a reception honoring one of his many championship teams. While I do not recall which team it was, the reception was at least twenty years after the fact, putting the team members at least in their early forty's. During the reception, I noticed that there were about five or six men who would not go near Woody. Indeed, these men made it a point to avoid him if he came close. Obviously, this got my curiosity up and so at the close of the reception I asked of a good friend, who was also a team member, why such behavior was exhibited from grown men who were clearly proud of their membership on the team as evidenced by their presence at the reception. Perhaps they had a falling out with Woody during the intervening years. No, said my friend, those men are the players who, to this day, have not graduated and knew without a doubt that Woody would confront them for their having not graduated in no uncertain terms. Woody would have not only embarrassed them but would have insisted that it was not too late to complete their degree.

Few members of the public understand that Woody was totally committed to the education of his players and their future success outside of football. In addition, Woody was a complete member of the academic community and a respected military historian that generated great respect among the faculty. In many ways he was a throwback to the days when in order to be a football coach, one first had to be a faculty member in the academic community. We would do well to follow his example today.

Sincerely,

Edward H. Jennings
President Emeritus

For Woody's players, here it is one more time: "I hate those sons of *unprintable.*"

CHAPTER 10

FAMILY LIFE

"My dad did not have different public and private personalities."
J.R. Kern

"A few things I learned from my parents: integrity, cooperation, faith, hard work (but no cutting corners), treating people with respect, persistence, timeliness. When it is all said and done, all you have is your name."
Michael Kern

When my wife, Nancy, had heard enough about the fun I was having with this book, calling old friends, hearing about others, and emailing others, she said, "When am I going to have a turn?"

When I told her that her turn was coming up, she said, "What am I going to say?"

I almost said, "That's what it is like when you ask me about my feelings," but I thought better of it. My goal was for her to participate, not for us to disagree. I was certain she would have some great memories and sound advice for the future generations of the Kern family. Besides, the fact that she is the heart and soul of our family earns her much goodwill.

Rose Bowl Princess Meets OSU Quarterback

"The Rose Bowl Court had nine activities before the Ohio State team arrived," recalled Nancy Henno Kern with the help of a souvenir copy of the Queen and Court Schedule from 1968. "Our tenth was to greet the team at the airport, December 20, which was a Friday. We were properly escorted by Tournament of Roses officials.

"It was a rainy day, so the greeting was brief, and we raced to find cars, which Chrysler had provided for the team. I spotted an open door and jumped into the back seat with two players. Dave Foley was in the front, Ted Provost was beside me, and on his left was a redhead named Rex Kern.

"I was an OK football fan but had tried to do a little homework in order to be able to participate in conversations. Having seen a list of the players and their hometowns, I said, 'Which one of you is from Lancaster?' a small California city not far from my home."

"That's me," I (Rex) said quickly. I had already noticed that this girl was very attractive, that if Ted had been a good teammate, he would have let her sit between us, and that now she was way on the other side of the car. All thoughts of *The Dating Game* were gone, at least the television show.

"How do you like being back home?" Nancy asked. Rex said he had never seen a palm tree before. That led to a conversation between us about Lancaster, Ohio, and Lancaster, California. Almost immediately, he was teasing me, with that ornery smile of his working away. That made me uncomfortable because we had just met, and he was not allowing me to deflect. Still, his sense of humor was hard to resist.

"I was going to football practice soon, did not know when I would see her again, and was a man on a mission," said Rex. "Plus, I did not feel like I was talking with a stranger."

"We all returned to the Huntington Sheraton from LAX Airport. The Ohio State team was out by the hotel swimming pool; we were on a bridge above. For some reason we were instructed to throw California oranges down to them. It was not difficult to spot a certain redhead, so I threw mine to Rex. I later learned that some of the defensive players objected to the oranges and said, 'This is the Rose Bowl, not the Orange Bowl.' The players threw the oranges back in a hailstorm. Members of the court realized we were in for some fun with this team.

"A few days later, the court, the players, and our Tournament of Roses escorts went to Disneyland. Rex and I walked around with Kevin Rusnak and Carol, a princess he had met. The Tournament sent a photographer with us. He was also a stringer for the *Los Angeles Times*, at least one Japanese paper, and a military paper. Our picture popped up in several places a few days later. After five hours to talk and play, it was clear there was a mutual interest between us."

Rex later added an important conversation during those hours.

"One of the subjects we talked about was school," he recalled. "When I said I was 'satisfied with Bs and Cs,' a look of disappointment came over her face. I knew I had said the wrong thing. Her opinion, expressed if not stated, had an impact on me that Woody's, my parents', and my teachers' never had. I did not settle for anything less than my best in competition. Why would I do that in school?"

"Sometime during the week, I remember hearing that Rex was on the cover of *Sports Illustrated*, and I was curious to see it," Nancy said. "I asked my dad to take me to the bookstore to buy a copy, my first *SI* purchase.

"The Queen's Coronation was held at the Huntington Sheraton. I went with a date, but by now I was far more interested in Rex.

"I remember telling my date I was having back problems and had to walk around. This gave me a reason to wander around the lobby, hoping to run into Rex. Either way, we met several times that night. Finally, my mother had had enough of me disappearing periodically. She found us, pointed her finger at me, and said, 'Nancy, get back there with your date.' Then she looked at Rex and said, 'You, young man, get up to your room.'

"Rex had practices and curfews, but we did see the floats before the parade with Kevin and Carol, and Rex was able to call two or three times. I was busy attending functions. At the CBS TV City affair, I danced with a television star, Lawrence Welk. His show, featuring 'champagne music,' was on for thirty-one years. In 1968, he was sixty-five years old, which seemed much older than it does now.

"My family came for the Rose Bowl and participated in some of the festivities," said Rex. "At the Big Ten dinner, when I spotted Nancy, I asked my brother, Keith, to go over and give her an OSU garter that someone had given to me. I was looking to make connections.

"One other thing Nancy forgot to mention," added Rex, "was my first attempt at a kiss at the floats. I bent over, tried to kiss her on the cheek, and she said, 'What are you doing?' Incomplete forward pass for number ten.

"I said, 'I just wanted to kiss you on the cheek for bringing us to the floats.'

"Not a great start, but I was undeterred. Woody often said, 'We will paralyze their resistance with our persistence.' I would be persistent. Rather surprising that I was successful, since I was taking romantic advice from Woody Hayes, huh?"

Post–Rose Bowl

"The team returned to Columbus on January 3, so we were able to spend the day after the Rose Bowl victory together for a picnic at the beach. And he was able to formally meet my parents, after his brief confrontation with my mother earlier," noted Nancy.

Rex added, "I remember that night she drove us to the top of the city of Altadena, where there was a beautiful view. Just as I was thinking, *This is a perfect make-out spot*, she put the car back into gear and drove down the other side of the hill. But that was all right. I was beginning to think very long term. I remember telling my mother I had met my wife to be."

"Rex's dorm had a phone that had been rigged so you could call long distance for free," Nancy remembered. "So we talked two to three times a week. By now my mother realized how much he meant to me, and she became my coconspirator. I did not want Rex to be making all the calls, so my mother and I broke into my father's supply of silver dollars, which I used to pay the phone company for some calls. We did not want all those calls appearing on the phone bill!"

Nancy and Rex were ahead of their time. Seven years later, a British group, 10cc, released a best-selling song titled "The Things We Do for Love."

"Rex came out to visit over spring break and once in the summer," said Nancy. "He stayed at our house and quickly won my parents over. The subject of going to the same school came up. At first it seemed logical to me for him to transfer to USC or any of the local schools. When I understood his loyalty to Ohio State and his teammates, plus the transfer rule about sitting out a season, I realized transferring would have to be my decision.

"September, 1969, I became a Buckeye. Rex picked me up at the airport, took me to my dorm, and left for football practice. My difficult transition began.

"I knew what it was like to be a college student, of course, after one year at Pasadena City College, but I had no idea what it was like to be an Ohio State student-athlete. In addition to becoming a serious student himself, Rex had practices, meetings, travel, and games. I hardly saw him. Plus, my roommate was blind, so we could not mix and socialize as I assumed we would. Except for the games, the fall was very difficult. Since I knew who he was, I tried to be patient and sympathetic. Oh, and he was tired most of the time as well.

"After the football season ended, he took me to a basketball game. I had been looking forward to time together—and a little attention—and he did not say a word.

"At halftime I said, 'I came from California to Ohio to spend time with you. Football is over, and we are together for an hour, and you still don't talk to me. If this is what it is going to be like, I can go back to California.'

"He listened to me, explained he had been playing basketball since fourth grade, and was literally playing and coaching this game in his head. I said, 'Tell me what you are seeing!' The important thing was, he heard what I was saying and began to understand my point of view. The second half he frequently pointed out intricacies of the game as they occurred. Then we went to get something to eat without football or basketball being mentioned. I started to feel like I belonged in Columbus.

"Another thing that helped my transition was going through sorority rush and joining the Pi Phis. They were the only girls who introduced me as Nancy Henno, not Rex Kern's girlfriend. I certainly wanted to be that but also to continue to figure out who *I* was as well as have multiple groups of friends along the way.

"Looking back, I find it interesting that Rex and I did not talk about faith very much at that time. My attraction to him was his kindness, his honesty. I went with him to churches and heard his messages, but when he spoke about surrender I rebelled. Why should I surrender? I felt a lot of conditions and expectations as a child, and surrender was not appealing. But there was that time when I was about eight that my father did not want to go to church. Mom did, and when we got to church I had a feeling of warmth, of acceptance, and love from God.

"That background came to mind because it was at the Pi Phi house that I saw a piece of paper on the floor. It was "The Four Spiritual Laws:" 1. God loves you and has a wonderful plan for your life. 2. Humanity is tainted by sin and is therefore separated from God. As a result, we cannot know God's wonderful plan for our lives. 3. Jesus Christ is God's only provision for sin. Through Jesus Christ, we can have our sins forgiven and have a right relationship with God. 4. We must place our faith in Jesus Christ as Savior in order to receive the gift of salvation and knew God's wonderful plan for our lives. Each point cited scriptural justification.

"That made sense to me. God is too big to be defined by human beings using human words, however. I prayed. My conversations with Rex became deeper and more profound.

"Good fortune can result even from bad housekeeping.

"As a result of our conversation at the basketball game and the growth of my faith, our relationship grew. Having Rex in California the following summer and seeing him get to know my parents—and them him—made for a wonderful three months.

"Rex has already discussed the communication gap between himself and Woody Hayes. It was sad to see because there was no reason for it other than Woody's inability to trust Rex, which had no basis. Rex and Bob Chandler trained all summer. The 1970 season should have been a long celebration with a happy ending. But Woody softened after Rex graduated and was an ally until he passed away. Rex's friendships with his teammates are even stronger now than they were then."

Marriage

"We were married in California in January, 1973. I adored Rex's parents, who were so welcoming to me in the early days and especially made a point of looking after me when Rex was in the NFL. His father ran the family. His mother was very tough, physically and mentally. Trenton was not one for giving sympathy, though I certainly experienced it personally when my back started acting up again.

"As for lessons about marriage for future generations, I would say marriage really does get better with time if you respect each other; share opinions, beliefs, and ideas honestly and openly; trust each other, which helps avoid jealousy; appreciate yourself and each other; and remain individuals as much as a couple.

"I get unconditional love and acceptance from Rex, which enables and even inspires me to return it. I respect him as a man's man, and I enjoy him being sweet to me. He is the most reliable person you will ever meet, and he's so gentle. We laugh so much; it seems as if we always have.

"We got through some difficult times when Rex faced health challenges—operations, rehab, and pain—or when he became overscheduled. I was always glad to share responsibilities (Rex: "That is an extreme understatement. She did a wonderful job."). But there were times his health would not permit him to do his share. My father was a traveling salesman who was gone a lot. When he got back, he wanted to be in control of the family, even in the areas that my mother enjoyed doing. This caused stress in our family. I remembered those lessons and tried to make changes in responsibility go smoothly.

"Most athletes are conditioned to ignore pain, so they are not taken out of the lineup. Rex had that mentality, and I did not want him to have to deal with unnecessary pain. Over time I convinced him to try new methods to relieve his pain. It was always a struggle for both of us—me to convince him, him to venture out to new modalities. He was conditioned to accept the situation and block out the pain. Today he says he feels better than ever, and he seems to enjoy our walks.

"I am looking forward to seeing what our sons have to say."

Rex: "Before we do that, there is one thing to mention about our wedding. I was especially concerned about Ohio friends and teammates feeling they had to travel to California and incur the expenses of airline tickets, hotels, and the rest for our wedding. If I had it to do over, I would find a way to explain, 'We would love to have you, but we understand if distance makes that too difficult.'"

★ ★ ★

J. R. Kern was born on November 19, 1975. He was born on Nancy's birthday!

"Most of the people I meet in Columbus who ask about my Dad bring up the Rose Bowl game or a Michigan game or the Purdue game or Woody—everyone wants to talk about Woody and Rex. It is almost always something about sports and Ohio State football. I have heard the stories, so I can talk with them. But to me, Rex Kern is someone very different than the twenty-two-year-old these people know or heard about years ago.

"I grew up in California. My Dad was retired when I was born, after four years in the NFL. My Dad and I were interested in the same hobbies: sports, fishing, and business. When we watched a game, I learned more from him than from the guys on television. When we played catch in the backyard, sometimes he offered some advice. Other times we just enjoyed each other's company. He was very good at deciding whether to coach or be a friend.

"Most of the time what we had in common was business.

"That started at the dinner table, when he would mention a business opportunity, a development along the way, a friendship with a business partner, maybe a personnel issue. I began to see myself as an entrepreneur, much like him. He saw that and encouraged me to try out my ideas, see what worked, then decide how to adjust when something did not go as expected. He struck a good balance between guiding me and letting me find my own path. When I needed help, he was always interested and available.

"So I was entrepreneurial as a child.

"In fifth or sixth grade, I thought about publishing a neighborhood newspaper. We talked about it, then Mom and Dad bought a software program to help me put my thoughts on paper. It was about the neighbors, sports, school—that sort of thing. I produced it. At one time, half the neighborhood paid for subscriptions.

(Rex: If I could interrupt, and I can, here's a quick story about JR in Little League baseball, playing on fields with fences at nine or so. Their starting pitcher had control problems one day, and JR was brought in around the third inning, no one out, bases walked full. Strikeout, strikeout, strikeout. No high jinks when he walked in from the mound, just a big smile. He was far better at that pitching business than I was.)

"We had orange trees and tangerine trees in our backyard. When other kids were going to the beach or playing, I was selling homemade fruit juices from eight to three on a street corner on Saturdays.

"In middle school, our family had a big-screen television. I asked permission to turn the family room into a movie theater. I would rent a movie, show it on the big screen, and make it an experience for the people who bought tickets. I hired a friend to work our concession stand.

"We lived in Ventura, so, of course, we were Dodgers fans. One night a friend of Dad's who was a team booster invited us to a private event. Tommy Lasorda, the manager, was there. I remember Orel Herschiser, star pitcher, and Steve Sax, second baseman, being there as well. I think I still have an autographed ball from that night.

"But what I really remember is they passed out little Dodgers pins that were collectors' items—the kind you could clip on a cap or a shirt. I collected every one that people did not want. That night I went home with about thirty-five pins. The next day at school, I started selling them for something like three or five dollars.

"Dad fostered my natural creativity by asking questions. For example, he might say, 'What will you do if ...' or 'How much do you think people would pay for that?' or 'Why would people buy from you if they could buy it over there?'

"When I was in ninth grade, he owned a small apartment building, about sixteen units. I did the books for him. Of course, he looked over my shoulder to make certain all the rules were being followed, but he made me feel like a partner and discussed business decisions with me. He showed me the importance of saving money for maintenance, and saving for future expenses became a habit in my personal life.

"I always had jobs too—from odd jobs to working in the pizza shop, working in the yard, helping neighbors, reffing youth basketball.

"About the same time, he had me checking the paper for stock prices. That grew into evaluating companies and considering buying stock in them. Late in high school and early in college, I was investing my own money in stocks. Now my sons are doing that.

"People assume that because he was a professional athlete he made a lot of money. In the 1970s, the pay was peanuts compared to today. (Rex: My original three-year contract with the Colts was for $17,000, $19,000 and $21,000, plus a $3,000 signing bonus. When my contract ended, I signed a one-year deal for $35,000 with Buffalo.) There are many pro athletes who were paid far more than he was who are in bad shape financially today. Dad's success is due to his resolve to save money and his ability to invest well.

"Plus, he is a very smart guy. He has three degrees from Ohio State and has several professional certifications, such as the Series 6 and Series 7 licenses, which are required to sell securities. His Certified Financial Planning license required a six-hour test and enabled him to help people prepare a financial plan for life.

"You asked the most important lessons my Dad taught me about business? OK. It's not how much you make. It is how much you save. Saving money allows you to have it when you need it, like to replace a car or repair the roof. Also, money saved can be invested to make more money for living or for giving. So develop skill at investing. Get a good education. Just as important, do not stop learning. Regardless of the field you select, the world will always be changing. Your competitors are learning and will pass you if you do not continue to evolve. Have faith in Jesus Christ. He will help you through all life's challenges and make the successes even better. Stay firm in your faith. Represent your faith because actions speak louder than words. Be humble. I felt little pressure as a kid because my Dad was not a legend in California. When we came back to Columbus, we were met by news cameras at the airport, and I saw myself on the news that night. I noticed the way people in Columbus saw him and the way he reacted. The man I saw on camera was the same man who helped me publish a neighborhood paper and who honored me by having me keep the books for his apartments. He did not have different public and private personalities. My Dad taught my brother and me that we should always give back, not just through tithing at church but by helping people less fortunate than ourselves. This book is a way he is giving back to the people who have befriended him and guided him since Lancaster. He taught us to have a servant's spirit.

"My parents encouraged drive. Work your hardest, do your best, have a work ethic and a passion for what you do. My mother was a wonderful example of this. She organized the family and took care of each of us while also working part-time or full-time jobs. She helped Dad cope with the physical ailments and surgeries he went through. She did physical labor when Dad could not, removing tree stumps, shining the kitchen floor, keeping the yard immaculate. Again, actions speak louder than words.

"Be a leader and lead by example. Most young people want to

fit in with their group; our message at home was to step up and lead. It was not to receive attention; it was to contribute as much as you could while finding the best possible way. There is a need for leaders in the world today, so the advice is even more profound than when I learned it.

"Enjoy life. If you enjoy your work, you will never work a day in your life. But life has to be more than work. My parents enjoyed me as a child, which made me feel loved and valuable. My kids deserve the same thing from me, and I want the same feeling my parents had too. I married a woman with many wonderful qualities, so I want to be sure to enjoy my marriage. Today kids get caught up in what society tells them, which is often unrealistic and unachievable. Set your own goals, but remember to include being happy.

"In business, to be a good deal, something must benefit both sides. Be honest, be fair, serve people rather than using them. Be an example for your faith. Besides being the right thing to do, the more people who want to do business with you, the better opportunities you will have.

"After graduating from Ventura High School, I decided to see what Ohio was about, so I went to college at Ohio State. My plan was to return to California after graduation. When I fell in love with my wife, Heather, after we were married I took her to California, hoping she would love it. She thought Ohio was a better place to raise a family. She was right. We never left and have found everything we could want in Dublin, a Columbus suburb. Our oldest son, Colby, is a senior at Dublin Coffman. Our youngest son, Chase, is a sophomore. Both play lacrosse. Chase plays basketball too.

"I graduated from Ohio State in 1998 and became a licensed real estate broker the same year. My mentor, friend, and partner, Todd Kemmerer, and I are principals at Capitol Equities in Columbus, where we transform commercial real estate and provide great advice to our clients.

(Rex here: John-Ryan did not mention he was a preferred walk-on to the Ohio State basketball team. Before the 1995 season, it looked like he would back up Doug Etzler at point guard, but he called to tell me he had a chronic back problem. I urged him to take care of his back and not play to please me. He made a wise decision to stop playing, and his back is fine today. Hopefully I will continue to lead him in back operations, 7–0.)

* * *

Michael Kern was born April 23, 1979.

"Like my brother, JR, I grew up in California. We both played basketball, baseball, and volleyball. I also ran track and played football.

"There was a family rule that you were not allowed to play football until high school, but my friends had been playing and wanted me to join their Pop Warner team in middle school. I got permission and went to practice. They had lost their quarterback, knew Dad had played pro football, and wanted me on the team.

"My first day of practice I found out they had no clear backup at quarterback. While the coach was deciding who to try, my friends said I should go in. Their logic was, 'Your dad played quarterback. Why not?'

"The coach took a chance and put me in.

"On the first play, the coach gave me instructions. He might as well have been speaking Greek. To say the least, the play did not go as planned. The coach said, 'No, no, no, you're not doing it right.'

"Not lacking confidence, I said, 'I know what I am doing. My Dad played professional football!'

"It turns out you may inherit genes, but not experience or knowledge."

(Rex: At the risk of interrupting my son, there is another story about his childhood to include. In the Kern household, we celebrated our children's birthdays pretty much like everyone else, with presents and a party. We also used the phrase, "You can do anything you want on your birthday," until this happened.

Our youngest son, Michael, who believed he could play quarterback because his father had played in the NFL, was celebrating his birthday by riding his bike around the neighborhood. I imagine he was about eight years old. One block over from our house, he was apparently riding recklessly or working on a stunt, because our friend Paul Feurborne, a physical therapist, thought Michael was in danger and shouted, "Hey, you can't be doing that."

Michael immediately replied, "I can do anything I want. It's my birthday."

Paul, thanks for looking out for our son and keeping us advised. Rest assured, we were more careful with our verbiage on birthdays.)

"Unlike JR, who is three years older, we moved to Columbus after my freshman year in high school. We lived in Upper Arlington, about two miles west of Ohio Stadium, where football is a big deal. I went from Little League in Ventura to police escorts to the stadium before games in Ohio. (Rex: Michael was kind not to mention that Lancaster teams were 0–3 against Upper Arlington when I was a Golden Gale.)

"As a sophomore, I learned a lot about football. I played on the reserves and some on special teams, wide receiver, and safety on the varsity.

"After football season, I expected to play volleyball, as I had in California. My teammates had other plans, saying, 'Guys in the band play volleyball. You're going to play lacrosse.' I did not know it at the time, but there are 144 high schools in the state that play lacrosse, ranking Ohio in the top ten states in the country. Also, Arlington once had a sixty-one-game winning streak and has won sixteen state titles.

"Among the other things I did not know about lacrosse were how to catch the ball and how to throw it. Dad helped with my basic skill development when we played catch in the backyard; however, he grew frustrated with the throwing part. Rather than using a stick, he used a baseball glove to catch. I wish we had pictures!

"Purdue was the first college to contact me for football my junior year. Notre Dame and Michigan State contacted me after my junior year, when I was starting at wide receiver and safety.

"Senior year, while a captain on the football team, I gave a verbal commitment to Penn State for lacrosse. The next night during dinner, Ohio State coach John Cooper called. It was my first contact from Ohio State. He said, 'We want to get you on campus—show you what we have to offer.'

I said, 'I gave my word, and that is not done lightly in our family.'

He seemed surprised, but he realized my decision was final.

"Some of the Arlington people, including my head football coach, had trouble with the decision. After all, they had been Buckeye fans all their lives and assumed I would go there if I had the opportunity.

"I had taken the recruiting process seriously and thoughtfully. I liked football, but I really loved lacrosse for games and practice. Plus, I knew Dad's history of injuries and wanted to be extremely active throughout life, including playing with my kids. I liked the small town of State College too.

"I would not trade my Penn State experience. My roommate as a freshman was a Penn State legacy. His parents had graduated from there, and his father played lacrosse. Soon I was an expert on the history. Before that, during my second week on campus, Coach Joe Paterno called my room. They had shown some interest in football, and he welcomed me to campus. That earned instant credibility with my roommate. My teammates were great guys to be around, and we remain friends today. Plus, my only injury was a broken hand, which was not sports-related.

(Rex: If I could interrupt my son, I had zero issues with Michael's decision to play lacrosse or to go to Penn State. He was thoughtful about the decision and right to follow his heart. My only problem was trying to throw the dang lacrosse ball with that stick. As he said, I adjusted. One of my favorite memories of Michael's athletic career was throwing passes to him and Arlington's other starting wide receiver, Carl Backes. I told them that on curl routes to always turn toward the sideline, where there are fewer defenders. One game Michael caught a pass in front of a back who was an Ohio State recruit, turned toward the sideline, and outran the back to the end zone! I am also proud to report he was selected first-team All-Ohio as a safety in 1996.)

"I came back to Colorado to get my master's degree at Denver Seminary, and I met my wife, Amy, after college in Colorado Springs. We have been married seventeen years and have two children: Caleb, sixth grade, and Lexi, fifth. Amy is in real estate and has been quite successful building her portfolio and her reputation as a top realtor in the Denver market.

"Two or three years ago, I took Caleb to an Ohio State football game. We were on the field. When the smoke machine went off, he almost lost his mind. Lexi and Caleb both play on competitive lacrosse teams and love acting in their local theater program.

"For now, she is undersized for lacrosse, but she is a bulldog.

"I have been in the construction business for fifteen years. My company's name is Elevate Contracting & Consulting LLC. We own, rehab, and repair commercial multifamily apartments and condos. I have a passion for consulting like I did for lacrosse. It is fun to make a complex process into a logical progression leading to an optimal conclusion for the client.

"The question is, 'What did I learn from my parents?' So many things.

"To mention a few, integrity, cooperation, faith, hard work (but no cutting corners), treating people with respect, persistence, and timeliness. When it is all said and done, all you have is your name. Of course, I learned about keeping your commitments, which is an advantage in business.

"One other thing that does not exactly fit the question is that I learned my Dad could not have done all the things he has done without my Mom. She contributed so much in so many ways, from the times she was a leader to the times she was in the background, filling essential roles. Their marriage gave me a model of what I wanted my own to be, and it helped me recognize the qualities I appreciate in my wife and the mother of our children.

"Got to go. Mom just pulled into our driveway. They live about two miles away—certainly another blessing."

★ ★ ★

The comments from our boys brought a couple of stories to mind. Their references to leadership resulted in an entire chapter, as you will see. Both were captains of their high school teams, John-Ryan basketball and volleyball, Michael football and lacrosse. Michael was also a captain at Penn State for the lacrosse team.

Our teaching them to be stewards of money reminded me of being about seven years old, going to the bank with my mother, and seeing her withdraw fifty-two dollars from her account. I was stunned. We were rich!

"How do you get so much money?" I asked her.

"It is called a Christmas club," she began. "For fifty weeks, I put in a dollar each week. If I do that, the bank gives me two more dollars, and we have fifty-two dollars for Christmas presents."

The whole thing sounded like magic to me. If you do a little bit every week, pretty soon it is a lot, and the bank gives you more on top of that. When I got my first paper route, I remembered that story and made regular trips to the bank.

Two battles that all parents face revolve around bedtimes and curfews. Nancy and I worked together to set fair times and stay consistent.

I learned from my father that they were constants, not variables.

If I was supposed to be home at 10:00 p.m., 10:01 p.m. was a problem, and 10:00:30 p.m. might be.

John-Ryan was a good basketball player at Ventura High School. As a freshman, he played "up" with the junior varsity. Most of his teammates were one year older.

One night he put on his coat and said, "I'm going out with the guys. I'll be home at midnight."

"What time is curfew?" I asked.

"Eleven," he said, then added some logical reasons for this being an exception.

"Ten thirty," I said.

"But, Dad—" he began, adding even stronger reasons for making an exception.

"Ten," I said.

Being a very intelligent young man, he said, "Dad, can we go back to eleven?"

"See you at eleven," I replied. He understood that we did not go back to eleven; we never really left.

When it came to loyalty, they learned about my father's story of the fireman's step ladder: "Remember the people who help you up the ladder of success."

Also, longtime Buckeye football fans need to know about the contribution Nancy made to the team, especially a certain star tailback named Jeff Logan, who was struggling with Spanish.

Nancy had a double major in Spanish and business in college, and she was teaching Spanish at Perry Middle School in Worthington, close to our home. When she heard of Jeff's problem, she offered to tutor him. That extra help was all Jeff needed. He passed the course and later graduated. After playing two years behind Archie, he led the sixth-ranked team in the country in rushing with 1,248 yards and added 606 yards for the eleventh-ranked team as a senior. Yeah, Nancy!

Finally, one last story about Betty Henno, Nancy's mother, a great sports enthusiast. When we had gotten to know each other, and she was no longer ordering me to my room, we had fun talking about Buckeye games.

After defeating Alabama and Oregon to win the national championship in 2014, they were rolling along the next year through ten games, until ninth-ranked Michigan State visited the number three ranked Buckeyes on a windy, rainy November day. Betty called and asked my opinion. "Tough game," I told her. I called her at the half, the game tied, 7–7, and she practically screamed, "What's wrong with that coach? Why don't they run Zeke?" Rather than tell her that Urban Meyer had a bias about running the quarterback like Woody Hayes did about running the fullback, I just agreed.

In the second half, it got rainier and windier, and Urban got more and more conservative. J. T. Barrett kept running into a brick wall, and I knew Betty was getting agitated. Ohio State had 132 yards total offense. The Spartans scored twice at the end of the game to win, 14-17.

When I called to console her, there was no answer. I told Nancy. We were both concerned. We were living in California, not far from where she grew up, so we drove down.

Nancy did not want to go in. I found Betty on her bedroom floor. She had passed away from a heart attack.

Sometime later I went on a Buckeye Cruise for Cancer. Urban was on the cruise. When we talked, I told him the story, ending it by saying, "You killed my mother-in-law."

He was speechless and walked away.

My red hair may be gone on top, but there must still be some in my heart.

I am just not letting her get away!

A photo which appeared in *Guidepost Magazine*:
from the left, Trenton, Jean, Keith, and I.

Dad and I before church.

John-Ryan and his family are on our left, Michael and his family are on our right, during one of our trips to Cancun.

This was taken at Little St. Simons Island. We might have been on our way to dinner with Hank Paulsen and his wife, Wendy.

CHAPTER 11

RACE—A SIMPLE APPROACH TO A COMPLEX ISSUE

"The chapter on race is worthy of a Pulitzer Prize."
Larry Hisle, two sport prep All-American, 13 year MLB player, 2X MVP contender, two-time All Star, Director of Youth Mentoring, Milwaukee Brewers

W hen George Floyd was killed, and protests popped up around the country, I began to think, *If I am going to write a guide for future generations of the Kern family, there really must be a chapter on race relations or discrimination or equality in America.* Immediately, I felt totally unqualified. This subject was not satisfactorily addressed by our brilliant Founding Fathers or the leaders who succeeded them. According to history.com, from 1525 to 1866, 12.5 million people were forced to leave their homeland

and shipped across the Atlantic Ocean. During this time, there was no plumbing or ventilation below deck. Disease was rampant, and women were raped and sexually abused by the crew. Nearly 2 million people did not survive the journey. Netting was stretched around the ship to prevent suicide. Upon arrival, people were sold like animals. The slave trade was outlawed in 1807, but slavery was not banned until 1865. The children of slaves became slaves at birth.

Slave owners beat and whipped their slaves, abused their women, destroyed their families, and prohibited them from reading, much less being taught. A civil war was fought, costing an estimated 620,000 lives. When the slaves were freed, their only choice was to become sharecroppers, unable to cover their living expenses without the protection of their owners or the law. Double standard Jim Crow laws were instituted. Public lynching was legal. When the Supreme Court passed laws requiring equal education, civil rights, and voting rights, those laws were ignored in many places. There was discrimination in every phase of American life, from owning homes to renting apartments; swimming in public pools to going to theaters; attending public colleges to preparing to succeed at those schools. *The Negro Motorist Green Book* was sold from 1936 to 1967, showing a variety of businesses—restaurants, beauty salons, hotels, and drugstores—that African-Americans could patronize while traveling without discrimination or physical assault.

Presidents, senators, congressmen, mayors, police officials, ministers, and civil servants of all types had failed for decades. What did a simple man like me have to contribute?

Maybe That Was It—Simplicity

My parents were simple people, both raised on farms in central Ohio. By that I mean they taught basic values: caring for family and others, hard work, saving money, and giving money and time. They taught the fundamentals of living.

From elementary school to the NFL, I played baseball, basketball, and football for coaches who taught the fundamentals in every sport. They all said that proper fundamentals would help us beat other, more talented teams at times and always allow us to be the best we could be, in competition and in life. I learned that my parents and my coaches were correct.

Race was not an issue or a topic of conversation in our house or the nearly all-white community of Lancaster. In fact, the only comment I can recall is when my father said, "In Lancaster, Blacks had a committee. If a Black family wanted to move into the city, the Black committee voted thumbs-up or thumbs-down."

I was about fifteen or so when he said it, so I immediately took it as gospel. Later I asked myself, *Was it barbershop talk and said in jest between men? Was it because he did not think I was ready for a serious discussion? Was it said in a group, or one-on-one?* There was little or no other conversation to place it into context. But my brother, Keith, recalls a Black teammate of his whose father was on that committee. It was a part of Lancaster, Ohio, where I grew up.

Gregg Brown was my only Black teammate before Ohio State. Gregg was an outstanding running back on our Lancaster High School football team and a great centerfielder in baseball. We roomed together when our American Legion baseball team played in a tournament at Ohio University. He was in the class of 1965 at Lancaster. Gordon Franke signed my senior yearbook in 1967. He did not play sports. They were my only Black peers until the North-South All-Star football game.

I remember the talent level was very high in that game, Black and white. Dave Cheney, a white member of the OSU recruiting class, was my roommate at the game and would become my roommate at Ohio State. His high school teammate at Lima Senior was Randy Cooper, a Black man who went to Purdue as a receiver and running back. The three of us played on the South team with Black OSU recruit Leo Hayden from Dayton Roosevelt and Black players at Steubenville, Mike Palmer and Dwight Simms, who did not attend OSU. Future Buckeye Larry Zelina, white, played for the North. Race was not an issue during practice or the game.

Our record in three years at Ohio State was 27–2; friendships between Blacks and whites contributed to that success. Some stories, from and since that time, might help explain our friendship.

After the deeply disappointing loss to Michigan my junior year, there was an appreciation banquet for the team. At the banquet, captains for the 1970 season were announced: Doug Adams, Jim Stillwagon, and myself—two for defense, one for offense. That seemed wrong to me, so I decided to make a change and hoped to do it lightheartedly. When my turn at the microphone came, I said, "Wait a minute. I've got to deal with Woody and run the offense. I need some help. What about our All-American tight end Jan White coming up here?" To me, Jan was the hardest-working player on our entire team.

That was an audible no one expected, but it worked. Jan was cocaptain and gave us outstanding leadership in 1970, as he did before, as he has since.

That same night, when Jack Tatum took the podium, he said, "Here's one man who treats everybody right." He gestured to me.

Many years later, in 2003, Tate called when Nancy and I were living in Ventura, California. He had diabetes and had had an operation to remove all five toes on his left foot.

"Rex, my daughter, Jestyn, is playing basketball at Santa Barbara City College, and I was hoping you and Nancy could check on her from time to time," he said. "In fact, she's got a tournament at Ventura College this weekend."

I replied, "Tate, we will be at the game and introduce ourselves to her."

We met Jestyn that weekend, and she reported to her father.

"Dad, who is that guy Rex Kern?" she asked.

"He's an Ohio State teammate," Tate replied.

"Dad, that's been thirty-five years," she said in disbelief.

"Honey," he said, "that's who we are—we take care of each other."

In 1969 I had appreciated what he said to the large gathering of Buckeye fans. So many years later, it touched me that the feeling of closeness we had was second nature to him to the extent that he had not thought to explain it to his beloved daughter.

When Jack died far too soon, July 27, 2010, Buckeyes from around the country came to honor him. If you are counting, I remember Black men Tim Anderson, John Brockington, John Hicks, Ralph Holloway, Phil Strickland, and Jan White, and white men Tom Backhus, Randy Hart, myself, Jim Otis, and Jim Stillwagon at the reception Raiders owner Al Davis organized to celebrate the life of his great safety and friend. As always, the colors of the day for us were scarlet and gray. Also, a stranger introduced himself to me that day. When he said his name was Joe Roberts, I was immediately back in fifth grade, staying up late to see cocaptain Roberts and my Ohio State Buckeyes defeat defending champion California for the 1960 NCAA basketball title!

When John Brockington, a Black teammate, needed a kidney, our teammates rushed to see if we qualified to donate. Nancy and I were traveling, but when Ron Maciejowski reached me with the news, I called the hospital in San Diego to talk with the kidney people. The lady I spoke with said, "Mr. Kern, would you please tell the Ohio State people to stop calling? We are inundated with requests for information from people who wish to help."

None of us qualified to donate, but his future wife, Diane Scott, gave him one of hers, and he is doing well.

When Larry Zelina, a white teammate, died prematurely, a golf tournament was organized to provide funding for college for his children.

In June 2020, during the marches and discord following the

murder of George Floyd, I sent Jan White a text that said, in part, "Jan, I have been hurting for you and all our African-American teammates at this time, but always remembering the great times we had together and the wonderful memories we made. *Without you and all our teammates I would have never been the player I was!* You in particular emboldened me as a player (especially when the *Old Man* thought he had a better play before it arrived in the huddle). More importantly, you guys made me a better person!

"If I did offend you or our teammates, I am truly sorry! You are the dearest!"

Almost immediately Jan replied, "Good to hear from u my brother. I cannot think of one time that u ever offended me in any way. I never thought for a moment that u saw color. It's not your nature."

When Dave Cheney heard about this chapter, he said, "I never saw any racial issues on the football team at Ohio State. In fact, our senior year, Bruce Jankowski, Jan White, and I had an apartment together." I had forgotten that. Better still, when Jan read an initial draft of the chapter, he had as well.

My point in telling those stories is that my Ohio State experience put me in close contact with African-Americans for which my Lancaster experience did not seem to prepare me, but the change was smooth. As the song "As Time Goes By" tells us, "The fundamental things apply."

My suggestion about getting along with people of a different race comes from an American movie star, columnist, public speaker, and humorist of the 1920s and early 1930s, Will Rogers, who famously said, "I never met a man I didn't like."

Once, a reporter said to him, "How is it possible to like everyone?"

"Oh, I don't," Rogers replied. "When I meet people, I look for things to like about them. Usually, I find things, and usually the more I know them, the better I like them. Sometimes I find I do not like the other person. Then I avoid him."

Rogers was a Cherokee at a time when many Americans disliked Native Americans. His sense of humor and belief that there was good in almost everyone made him the most popular man of any color in the United States for many years.

Besides looking for the good in each other, I would suggest fairness.

In athletics, three strikes, and you are out, Black or white. Hit the ball out of the park or catch the ball or run faster than anyone, the rules do not specify color. That is a good model to follow—in every way, at every time.

Nothing makes me sadder than hearing Black men or women concerned about how the police will treat their child. In Lancaster in the 1960s, we were taught to find the police if there was a problem. Today Black parents and grandparents teach their children, "If you are stopped by the police, the only thing that matters is that you get home safely. Your job is to get home alive." That is not fair.

The second paragraph of this chapter has many examples of whites being unfair to Blacks, and a comprehensive list might fill a library. There is one example from the sport of basketball that I find particularly compelling.

On September 12, 1927, the Ku Klux Klan was successful in its campaign for separation of Black students and white students in Indianapolis, Indiana. Crispus Attucks High School, honoring the first man to die in the Revolutionary War, a Black man, was opened. Every Black student in the city was to attend. The turnout of 1,385 students was nearly double what city officials expected. The school was overcrowded and understaffed from the first day.

The ramifications of the previous paragraph would make an accurate example of discrimination, but the rest of the story is fascinating. Because the school was not open to whites, Attucks was not considered a public school. Teams representing Attucks were forbidden from playing athletic teams around the state, with the exception of other all-Black schools and Catholic schools. Whites made an unfair rule, then further punished Blacks for the consequences of that rule. It took fifteen years and a world war for the Indiana State High School Athletic Association to allow Crispus Attucks High School to compete in the state tournament. Source: *ATTUCKS* by Phillip Hoose.

Fair is fair; unfair is not fair.

Beyond the dominant issue of fairness to minorities, what about the contributions they could make to our lives if they only had the chance? Some of my best friends today are Black men I played football with at Ohio State. I benefited from knowing them on and off the football field then, and I enjoy them now, whether in person, on the phone, or by text. From a broader perspective, how many outstanding teachers, doctors, financial advisors, accountants, and other contributors to our society have been lost because Black women and men did not have proper academic preparation as children?

The other suggestion I would have for the younger Kerns comes from my father: "If there is trouble, get out of there."

In May, 1970, four unarmed Kent State students were killed by the Ohio National Guard at an antiwar gathering. Demonstrations of all types broke out on campuses, including Ohio State's. I called Nancy, my girlfriend at the time, at her sorority house and said, "Pack a bag. We are going fishing."

We left immediately for one of my favorite fishing holes, then spent a couple of days in Lancaster with my parents.

I mention that because race is an emotional hot button in today's society. Dad's advice is not about race, but it applies if a demonstration gets out of hand.

Just because I believe racial problems can be greatly relieved by eliminating preconceived notions, looking for the best in others, and applying fairness to all does not mean all Americans do. Sometimes you just have to get out of there.

Finally, while researching this chapter, I found a quote attributed to Ruby Bridges Hall: "Racism is a grown-up disease, and we must stop using our children to spread it."

If ever anyone is entitled to an opinion about racism, Ruby Bridges is.

In 1960, at the age of six, Ruby courageously marched to her first day of school. A picture shows her being escorted by three federal marshals on the schoolhouse steps. Out of sight are angry whites, saying things no six-year-old should hear and holding signs no little girl should be able to understand. She looks like a miniature woman on a serious mission, which is exactly what she was.

It was her assignment to be the first Black child to integrate William Frantz Elementary School in New Orleans.

After unbelievable stress the first day, Ruby returned, day after day. Only one teacher agreed to teach her. They studied alone. Students reacted to her in various ways, generally the way their parents had taught them to act. There was not another Black face at the school the entire year. Her father was fired from his job. Segregationists attempted to intimidate the family, particularly Ruby. The family persevered. Conditions improved. They are still improving.

But they are not yet fair.

Some of the "Super Sophs"—Ralph Holloway,
Tim Anderson, myself, and Jack Tatum.

CHAPTER 12

MENTORING AND LEADERSHIP

"You don't really 'win' in business, you succeed in business when both parties benefit."
Jack Havens, former Chairman of Bank One

Both of our sons mentioned leadership being a topic of conversation in our home when they were children. That surprised me because I do not remember mentioning it very often.

Nancy and I did stress being your best, trying as hard as you can and doing as well as you are able in everything, especially school. We also stressed being kind, caring and considerate to people, whether they can benefit you or not, and especially if they helped you in the past. Maybe they equated those thoughts with leadership. If so, I agree. At least the person with these traits would be someone to consider following.

Whatever was behind their comments, it seemed important to include leadership in the book. After all, quarterback is certainly a leadership position on the football team, and I was a quarterback for many years. Captain of an athletic team is a leadership position on a sports team, and I was a captain of several teams. I was player-representative on the Baltimore Colts. I managed a multimillion-dollar Nautilus franchise in California, and I served on about half a dozen corporate boards. I never aspired to be a leader or even considered myself to be one, but I do have ideas about leadership to pass on to future generations of Kerns.

My first thought is that people do not begin as leaders. Those who do make so many mistakes they are fired or replaced quickly. Good leaders have a great deal to learn before they can begin to lead at any level. Mistakes will happen, and they are a wonderful means of acquiring knowledge and experience, but life is too short to learn only by making your own mistakes. Sound decisions come from knowledge and experience, but no one begins with experience. When you start learning about a subject, find people who know more than you do and learn from them. And not just a few people—find a bunch!

Mentors

Having good mentors has been a huge part of any and every success I have had.

What is a mentor? I found definitions like coach, counsel, guide, pilot, tutor, advisor, trainer, counselor, and teacher. They all fit to some degree. I would add religious leader, higher ranking officer, corporate executive, senior physician, and senior members at any job as possibilities. Our first mentors are our parents and our older siblings. These are vertical mentors. We learn from people who are older, wiser, more experienced and/or in a higher position, which seems only natural. Listen to what they say, watch what they do and ask questions.

Some children ask questions not so much to learn as to keep the attention of the parent or adult. When that happens, at any age, a wise mentor will assure the child of his or her attention, then answer the question. Youngsters, give some thought to your questions before asking. Then reflect on the answer. Absorb what was said. You may have another question. More likely, you will have to think about the answer. By telling your mentor how the answer fits the question, you are giving additional feedback, helping him or her help you.

We can also learn from peers, who may be termed *horizontal mentors.* They are at the same level we are—classmates, teammates, same pay grade, fourteen-year-olds, that sort of thing. The reason they serve as mentors is that they have an advanced skill which we recognize. For those struggling with fractions, why not reach out to another student? If you do not understand what the coach is saying on the first day of practice, ask a teammate who played last year. If your first day on a new job is confusing, ask a fellow worker. Are you a first-time parent? Ask for help! All new parents need it. People appreciate being asked to help with important matters, like parenting. Again, learn from the mistakes of others.

A perfect example of horizontal mentoring came from our sons, John-Ryan and Michael, though we did not know about it until long after they were adults.

Michael thought he was being singled out for spankings because his older brother was seldom, if ever, spanked. One day he asked his brother why?

John-Ryan stopped whatever he was doing and said, "It's because you always talk back to them. Listen to what they say. If you say anything, say, 'Yes, ma'am,' or 'Yes, sir,' then do what you want. You may get in trouble again, but talking back always gets a spanking."

Sometimes the obvious answer escapes us. A peer with knowledge of the situation may be able to diagnose the problem, as John-Ryan did for Michael.

Most of us hesitate to ask questions for fear of something—that was not true of Michael, who bordered on fearless! It could be fear of being considered not smart or inadequate in some other way. Remember two things: none of us knows everything, and people feel respected when they are asked to help. So, make someone feel good by asking them questions and learn something, too. It may be difficult at first, but it gets easier.

There is another type of mentoring that is largely unrecognized. It takes place when we learn from mentoring those we intend to help.

The first time I was asked to teach vacation Bible school, I felt unprepared for the assignment. I was in tenth grade; the children were between eight and twelve years old. Who was I to be analyzing the Bible and explaining parables? The answer to my concern was, "Every teacher learns more from teaching the class than the people in the class do."

I took the challenge and found that the answer was true. To prepare myself for class, I researched the material with more diligence than if I had been in the class. I asked myself questions which certain students might ask and was prepared if they came up. Of course, that does not mean I was ready for every question. But that experience taught me the only correct answer when I was unprepared: "I do not know, but I will have the answer next week in class."

People dislike being bluffed or conned, but they appreciate honesty and dedication. If people felt I could be trusted, it was because I did not "blow smoke" to cover the fact that I did not know.

The process of learning through teaching helps us because it brings up so many different points of view, through so many different paradigms of perspective. From the standpoint of mentoring, it might be labeled reverse vertical mentoring. Whereas vertical mentoring is from the top down, in this case the student teaches the teacher. Learning takes place from the bottom up.

Experiences in all three types of mentoring help prepare people to lead, because mentoring is such an important part of leadership.

Another important point is that we all lead. Every parent, every older sibling, every younger sibling, every teacher, every person of authority in any field, every friend, every spouse, every teenager is a leader, and therefore a mentor. The question is not whether we have that responsibility but whether we accept it, learn from it, and take responsibility for it. Parents, the way you teach your child to do homework or wash the dishes will be the way that child approaches life and teaches others. Be careful. Teachers, when a child is disruptive, you will help him or her find a path of interest and growth—or one of continued disruption. Take advantage of this opportunity. Young person, you want friends with similar beliefs and values? What are your beliefs and values? Teach yourself, and people will want you to teach them.

My way of discussing leadership will be to reference many of the people in my life who have mentored and led me. (Some are still trying to do so; thank you for your persistence.) By reading how they have helped me, the reader may recognize ways to mentor or be mentored.

Before doing that, I learned that the accepted word for the person being mentored is *mentee*. That seems forced and awkward. Synonyms included student, apprentice, fledgling, newcomer, protégé, tenderfoot, rook, intern, aspirant, trainee, novice, and new entrant. None of those seemed quite right, although protégé seemed the most applicable. Another which generally applies is simply friend.

Here are my mentors from childhood until today, roughly in chronological order as they appeared in early chapters of the book. My deceased parents are here because they were my first mentors and because their lessons remain with me today.

Living Legends of the Kern Family

My mother and father, Jean and Trenton Kern: They taught life lessons to us and modeled them for us as well as to our friends, who were always anxious to visit the Kern home. We learned that often those boys and girls were there to be cared for and cared about in a way they did not receive at home. Nancy and I always wanted our home to be as welcoming.

When the subject of sports came up, Keith and I always explained, "Mom was the athlete, and Dad was the coach." She taught us how to throw a ball. When our basketball hoop went up, she was out there shooting with us. It makes me sad that she and so many other girls grew up in a time when they were almost invisible as athletes and did not have the opportunity to compete for state championships, make all-state teams, or receive college scholarships. More importantly, they missed many of the life lessons sports provide, like not making a team or missing—or making—an important shot or having a whole city care about your game and on and on.

Dad was the one showing us how to field ground balls and teaching strategy. Both filled important roles in our athletics, which made us closer to them. Though not alive, they do live in my heart.

"What about football?" you may ask. Without minimizing the importance of what I learned about sports from Mom and Dad, I liked learning about football on my own—with many great mentors, of course.

My brother, Keith Kern: He was a life mentor and sports mentor, a vertical mentor and horizontal mentor. Because he allowed me to be involved in his life, his friends became my mentors as well. Three grades can be viewed as a very long time when you are a child, but I never thought that way because Keith treated me as an equal. When I began to play organized sports, I was three years ahead of my teammates based on what I learned from my father, Keith, and his friends. In addition to the coaches, I was able to encourage my peers in many ways. That helped them, made them better (probably my top priority at the time, because I wanted to win) and helped me learn what I was teaching. Also, when I began to gain attention for athletics, Keith was always first to support me. Lesser people might have been jealous, but not my brother, not my mentor.

When Keith and I were in grade school, our neighborhood challenged some kids from nearby Cedar Heights to a basketball game. I was by far the smallest and youngest player on the team, and one of their players started picking on me. Keith immediately shouted, "Leave my brother alone," and tussled with him before pinning the guy. He was my protector as well.

Dick Daubmire: Dick was a great baseball pitcher, with so many good pitches at a young age—fastball, curveball, and knuckleball. When we were kids, I was a catcher, so he taught me how to think like a pitcher when I called pitches for him. The ability to think along with pitchers gave me a tremendous advantage as a hitter, too. With the help of the scouting report, I had a good idea which pitches each pitcher was going to throw on different counts. In our regional final senior year, Dick was in my head. With a 2–0 count, I knew the pitcher had to throw his best pitch, which was a fastball. I shifted my weight to my back foot to get more power, swung as hard as I could, and ended up on third base. When I scored the winning run to send us to the state tournament, Dick had earned an assist! He deserves mention as a great competitor as well.

Bill Grein: Bill could always find something funny to say, no matter how serious the situation. At the same time, he was a dependable athlete and a serious competitor. He broke me in as a Little League catcher and encouraged me to be a leader, even though I was a year younger.

Howard and Rick Bozman: Our next-door neighbors, the Bozmans, were like my younger brothers. I treated them the way Keith treated me: with respect and as equals. They had someone to guide them, and I had two people to guide. The three of us benefited from Keith's mentoring.

Perry Blum: Perry was a superb horizontal mentor on the basketball court. We were the same age but went to different elementary and middle schools. He was from the more affluent side of town, and his teams had better uniforms. In fourth grade basketball, I had a head start due to Keith and his friends. Most of my opponents conceded that to me. It would have been easy to spend time thinking how good I was. But Perry conceded nothing. If I scored a basket, he competed harder than ever to stop me the next time, by any means necessary. That made me mad, but it also made me work harder and demand more of myself. He helped me get closer to my best, which is what any mentor wants to achieve for his protégé.

Greg Woltz: Dad had a nickname for everyone, and Greg's was Salesman Sam. Greg was a talker, and most people, including my parents and myself, liked to listen to him. He has been a dear friend since elementary school, and always will be. He accomplished more in athletics than his size would suggest because he was such a fine competitor.

Nicki Baltz: When I liked her (as a girlfriend), she liked someone else. When she liked me (as a boyfriend), I liked someone else. Fortunately, we have liked each other (as people) for a lifetime. Also, we helped each other through chemistry as juniors.

Mark Baltz: Nicki's husband, Mark, was the trainer on our basketball team and a friend through that time. It has been fun to follow his career as a referee from reserve games in Lancaster to the highest level of the NFL. While watching televised games with friends and family, I enjoyed saying, "I went to high school with that referee."

Tim Bailey: When his name comes up, my heart just melts. I could always depend on Tim in any situation. On the football field, he was 170 pounds of reliability, whether protecting me from a blitzing linebacker or making the perfect overthrow block on a defensive end for a long run. It is easy to lead reliable people, or to be led by them.

Debbie Clark Reid: Our homecoming queen, but no pretense about her. We could sit and talk! She brought some friends up to Columbus to cheer me up after my first back surgery and turned a down time around. We spent a summer working at Anchor Hocking, finding out what we did not want to do for the rest of our lives.

Debbie, I kept those Anchor Hocking work boots we had to buy to protect our feet and took them to Ohio State. They reminded me to go to class or study a little harder more than once.

Dr. John Holland: That's the guy I wanted to be. I admired the way he handled himself, as an educator, a coach, a man. I wanted to be as smooth and confident as he showed. When I was with the Colts we played a game in Houston, where he and his wife, Shirley, were living. I arranged for tickets and got to see them after the game. I was proud to know that they came to the game, and hoped they were proud of me.

Mike Baughman: In the same way Dick Daubmire taught me to think like a pitcher, Mike taught me to think like a receiver. That not only enabled me to pass to him better, but to have a conversation with every other receiver at Lancaster and at Ohio State, to learn how and where they wanted the ball. We played safety together when I was a junior, so he helped me there as well. He started on Indiana's Rose Bowl team and made first-team All-Big Ten in baseball. He was quite an athlete, and indispensable on our fine 1966 basketball team too.

Randy Groff: Randy's name brings a smile to my face. He was sort of loosey-goosey most of the time, but that changed when it was time to compete. Then his competitive spirit rivaled my most accomplished Ohio State teammates. At not even 150 pounds, he gave everything he had. When he got beat up, he came right back. Who could ask for more?

Paul Callahan: He was a quiet captain for our 1966 state tournament basketball team. He played hard and well, and he was unselfish. He demonstrated the principle that leaders should never ask others to do what they were unwilling to do themselves. Paul, Bill Grein, and Dick Daubmire were outstanding pitchers for our 1966 baseball team, which almost made the state tournament. We did not have to score many runs for those guys!

Dick England: Our baseball coach, one of three remarkable varsity coaches I had at Lancaster High School. Keith played for him for three years before I got to the varsity and shared what he learned about the game, so I thought I was pretty knowledgeable. But listening to Coach England teach the game and seeing him prepare us for every situation was a true education.

Coach England made a more important contribution to my life away from the diamond. He and his wife, Connie, had a beautiful daughter named Jennifer, not quite two, who fit perfectly on my lap. She was such a joy, then tragically, she died. It was an inspiration to me to see the way they continued on. By that I mean, while they dealt with their grief they lived their lives, did their jobs, served their community, and loved each other. That impressed me as a teenager and does even more as a grandfather. For more than fifty years, I have remembered the way they reacted to a disaster far more serious than one I might be facing and gained strength from the memory.

Before the 1969 Rose Bowl, I went to the cemetery and placed several roses on Jennifer England's grave. It was my honor to know that her parents, Dick and Connie, would be traveling all the way to California to attend the game and a comfort to think of Jennifer as being with them. For all I know, she tripped O. J. at the line of scrimmage a couple of times.

Paul Kendrick: Paul's injury prevented him from achieving his full potential as an outstanding athlete, and I was impressed with the way he handled that disappointment. As any athlete would want to do, he went on to a successful career and life. That impressed all of his classmates and friends.

Fallen Heroes of the Kern Family

Reverend Larry Hard, minister, the Sixth Avenue Methodist Church: Hearing Reverend Hard preach, or teach, or counsel was like I would imagine it was to hear Jesus. He was a soft, gentle soul with the right words to show us the way.

Fritz Reed: Class of 1966. A joy to have as a teammate, he worked hard all the time, whether he was a star (football and baseball) or a valuable part (basketball). As a freshman, dealing with the academic rigors of Harvard, being away from home and adjusting to college football, he took the time to send me an inspirational letter of affirmation and support. It was unlike a letter one teenage boy would send another, more like something a sixty-year-old man would send a lifelong friend. Fritz had that kind of maturity and wisdom. When I read "I never met a boy who is more of a man than you," I was proud of that high school senior and glad to be writing this memoir about my mentors and guides, like Fritz.

George Hickman: My Sunday school teacher, a humble and loving man who brought the Scriptures to life. A factory worker, he was well suited for this job, as a famous carpenter was for His.

Joe Edwards: We lived about two blocks apart on the west side. In grade school we were not in the same classes and did not have much contact. As teammates on the seventh grade basketball team we got to know one another. We seemed to date girls who were friends so we double-dated and became inseparable in high school.

When I think of him after high school I remember inviting him and his wife to an NFL game in Baltimore's Memorial Stadium my rookie year and the fun we had that weekend. We stayed in touch until he passed away—May 6, 2020.

Earl Jones: Our high school football coach, he graduated from Miami (Ohio), where he played football for four years—two under Woody and two for Ara Parseighian. He played with Bo Schembechler the first two years. That is quite a group of coaching mentors!

As a coach, his game preparation was good, and his teaching of fundamentals was excellent. As a man, one of the many things I admired about him was that he did not swear. When he said, "Cheese and crackers," he was not happy. We shared an intense competitive spirit, which bonded us together. When he asked me to visit Miami (Ohio), I got to know his former teammate, Bo, then Miami's head coach, who remained a friend until he passed away in 2006.

The 1966 Lancaster football team started the season 1–4, then defeated four straight Central Ohio League opponents to win our third straight COL championship. That joyful experience and memory was the direct result of playing for a fine coach and man, Earl Jones. His death, August 31, 2019, was a primary stimulus to do this book.

George Hill: Our basketball coach, who led us to my favorite season in Lancaster sports. He is discussed at length in the 1966 chapter.

Jim Posey: I idolized Jim Posey, my physical education instructor at General Sherman Junior High. Like John Holland, he was the standard of the man I wanted to grow up to become.

Ed Klinker: I smile again when I think of Eddie. He was a breath of fresh air. I loved sports, devoted a tremendous amount of time to them and spent most of my time with athletes, which was great. Eddie served to give me some balance. He loved sports, so I led that discussion for him. I wondered what else was going on in high school, or anywhere else for that matter, and he kept me informed.

Terry Webb: When I was young I had no idea how lucky I was. Does everyone think every life is the same as his? Maybe think is the wrong word. Assume? Not question?

Whatever the case, as we grow we see differences in each other.

She is good in math; he is a fast runner; her parents must be rich; he lives in a nice house, that kind of thing. When I began to notice how Terry seemed to avoid going home, and did not like talking about himself, I wanted to help. Unfortunately, I was too young to know how. When I noticed he enjoyed coming to my home, I made a point of asking him more often.

My other friends seemed to like being in our house. They seemed to like my mom and dad. Slowly I put things together and realized I had something they did not, or at least I had it to a greater degree. I started to notice how my parents showed Keith and me that they loved us, how they treated our friends, how they disciplined us. I began to realize I wanted to provide a loving home for my children, and for their friends.

Many people, young and old, helped me learn those lessons, among them my friend and basketball teammate Terry Webb, a mentor to me and a hero to all who knew him.

Milt Taylor: Milt owned a large Chevrolet automobile dealership just north of Lancaster. I first remember meeting him during that wonderful basketball season we had junior year. He was a friend of Coach George Hill; I seem to remember that Dad cut his hair was well. Milt was kind enough to arrange a dinner with the Ohio University coaches and our family during my recruitment senior year, when they offered me a scholarship with the right to choose any sport(s) I wished. That has always been a treasured memory.

When I was planning to spend the 1970 summer in California to have time with Nancy and her family, I asked Milt to arrange for me to rent a car there. Several weeks later I realized a car was not going to be necessary, so I told Milt. He very graciously explained to me that it had been difficult for him to make the arrangements and that I should be more careful about asking for assistance I did not really need. That discussion was uncomfortable for me, but very necessary. The way he handled the situation went beyond something a mentor would do to something a father would. Not many people are concerned enough about you to endure your growing pains.

Milt also introduced me to his friend, Dr. Jimmy Hull, OSU's first basketball All-American, a well-known dentist in Columbus and a supporter of Buckeye sports. After my graduation, Milt and "Dr. Jimmy" asked my father and me to lunch several times, usually at The Columbus Club on E. Broad St. Even though they always scheduled Thursdays, Dad's day off, he was not always able to attend. He did not seem comfortable as they asked about my goals and mentioned ways I might prepare to meet them. I appreciated successful people taking an interest in my future and never had a hint that they had anything to gain from our lunches, other than enjoying my success.

Milt passed away in 2012, and Dr. Jimmy passed in 1991.

Major Mentors after Growing up in Lancaster

Woody Hayes: Unforgettable.

Tiger Ellison: Our freshman coach, Tiger was a grandfather, mentor, coach, confidant, and friend. I was glad to run into him on the road from Lancaster to the Horseshoe.

George Chaump: He saved Ohio State football. His reward was near-constant abuse from his coach, who wanted to run the fullback off tackle and ignore the forward pass. George persisted, and Ohio State became known for a (somewhat more) modern offense.

In chapter 9, we discussed the failure of the jet cut evaluation despite nine of ten successes at practice. After his explosion, Woody was so angry he ordered wide receivers and quarterbacks to run to the fence and back, a round trip of about a quarter of a mile. I was excused due to back problems at the time, but Woody added, "You run with them, George," penalizing his offensive coordinator for suggesting an effective play, rather than praising him. At the time, George was nursing a sore knee that would later require an operation. As a result of the run, he limped around for the next several days.

After the Gator Bowl incident, George was hired as the running backs coach of the Tampa Bay Buccaneers and assisted with the quarterbacks as well. Their quarterback was Doug Williams, taken in the first round of the NFL Draft the year before. After George's memorial service in 2019, I read an article in the local paper in which Doug was quoted about how much he had been helped by Coach Chaump. I checked the numbers. Williams improved his yardage from 1,170 yards as a rookie to 3,562 yards during the three years George was there. His quarterback rating went from 53.4 to 76.8, and his completion percentage from .376 to .505 as well. In 1988 the media celebrated Doug Williams as the first Black quarterback to win a Super Bowl with the Washington Redskins. He was also named MVP.

I doubt if George celebrated Doug for his color. He coached Black quarterbacks in high school (Jim Jones, who earned a scholarship to Southern Cal, went 22–8–3 as a three-year starter, and set numerous school records), and at Ohio State (two fine ones regardless of color: Cornelius Greene and Rod Gerald), as well as several "white" ones at Ohio State. To paraphrase Dr. Martin Luther King, George judged quarterbacks, and people, by their character, not the color of their skin.

Mace called him "a calming influence in a constant storm" in 2019 at George's memorial service, attended by former players from near and far who wanted to show their respect for a humble and kind man.

Ron Maciejowski: Mace was a great, great quarterback and a true MVP of our team. He would enter the game in dire situations and, as the saying goes, "pull a rabbit out of the hat." He was crucial to our three-year record of success—27–2. Mace and I came to Ohio State as competing quarterbacks, but always worked as a very positive tandem, in practices, meetings, and games. I really felt that Ron supported me, and I supported him. That is just as true today, as we have continued to grow closer as teammates, friends, and couples. I have always been able to count on Mace, and I hope he feels he can always count on me. I bet this is rare on most teams with competing quarterbacks.

Jan White: I have loved and respected Jan since our freshman year at Ohio State. He was an astute, cerebral worker and a great athlete. It was essential to me that he approved the chapter on Race before we could go to press with this book. Knowing he was satisfied, I could be.

Larry Zelina: A dear friend and hard worker, Z was hampered with hamstring issues his entire career. I have always believed those problems began with a hard hit he took in the North-South All-Star Game in 1967. After all this time, he still ranks third in career punt return average at Ohio State. As is the case with other Buckeyes, with more opportunities he would have caught more passes and rushed for more yards. As it was, he was a key part of our 27–2 record.

Dave Cheney: A diligent student on his way to a long and successful legal career, Dave's study habits served as a model for what mine could become. As a roommate, every time he took his shoes off I was reminded to keep my feet clean. Sorry, roomie, but your feet were lethal!

Bruce Jankowski: We were joined at the hip from freshman year— same classes, after class, and extra throwing after practice. Jack Tatum said his name was always in the New Jersey sports pages as a three-sport star athlete. If Jack was impressed, I was.

One story about Bruce comes from an 8:00 a.m. physical activity course we shared in soccer. The teacher was proud of the fact that he had been on the Faculty Council which voted 28–25 against the Buckeyes going to the 1962 Rose Bowl. He was less than neutral toward athletes. One of his class requirements was that we keep a notebook of class notes. He told us, "If you miss a class, just get the notes from a classmate, that's fine." I never missed a class, period. I knew Woody kept track. When Bruce missed a class, I gave him my notes to copy. Our notebook grades were "B" for me, "A" for Bruce. In my book the teacher wrote, "It is apparent you worked with Mr. Jankowski." What we did was acceptable, and his attendance sheet showed I never missed his class. In this case, Bruce was lucky Woody hated passing outside the classroom. The teacher probably did not know he was on the team.

Tom Matte: Tom was an eight-year veteran when I showed up with the Baltimore Colts, so he was clearly a top-down mentor, the wise sage offering wisdom to the rookie. At the same time, he was a horizontal mentor, helping a teammate, friend, and former Buckeye find a place in the NFL. His encouragement to "make yourself valuable to the team," and insistence that the same approach had worked for him, helped me put together a four-year career as a pro at a position—cornerback—I had never played in high school or college.

Bob Vogel: An All-American tackle at Ohio State, the fifth selection in the 1963 NFL Draft, a ten-year starter and five-time Pro Bowler with the Colts, Bob is a better person than he was an athlete. He and his wife, Andrea, cared for forty-eight foster children, he has visited numerous prisons and taken medical supplies to places such as Cuba and Honduras.

We played together on the Colts for two years before he retired. Soon after we met, he asked, "What will you do after football?" He wanted me to be thinking about the future, even before I had a present.

"I want to work toward becoming athletic director at Ohio State," I replied.

"Have you told them about your interest?" he said.

I had not. I immediately realized how obvious it was to initiate that, and I did. It led to an internship in the off-season.

Bob Vogel could have spent his time talking about his accomplishments but wanted to guide me to reaching my own goals. I will never forget his interest or his valuable input.

Gunnar Vogel, Bob's grandson, started at tackle on the Northwestern University football team in 2020 and graduated with a double major in communication and economics. He is in a fine position for future success in a variety of fields. Bob never stopped mentoring.

Nancy Henno Kern: Nancy has been a mentor to me in many ways, but the first and strongest was academics. When it came to school, my father's advice was "figure out who is the smartest person in the class and sit next to him or her." That was not the inspiration I needed. When Fred Taylor and Woody Hayes recruited me, their focus on earning a college education attracted my interest. At Ohio State, their continued emphasis built my interest, but I was still not committed. Then I met this beautiful, funny Rose Bowl princess.

I won't say that my attention to preparing for the Rose Bowl waned, but finding time to spend with Nancy gave it some competition. When I mentioned being satisfied with Bs and Cs, she gave me a ten-thousand-word message without a word, just one look. Her expression said, "Not satisfactory" ... "disappointing" ... "will he change or should I move on?" ... and much more I did not want to imagine. When she agreed to transfer to Ohio State, my choice was clear: be outstanding in the classroom *now* or say goodbye.

Nancy is my inspiration, in and out of the classroom, and my favorite teacher, who will be the guiding light of the Kern family for many generations.

As it came time to put the finishing touches on this book, one sentence came to my mind which absolutely had to be added. When I think of Nancy Henno Kern I think of three traits—bright, courageous, and resilient. She is intelligent enough to contribute ideas to solving almost any problem, and often took over to solve those problems herself when injuries and operations limited my participation. She was courageous enough to follow me to Ohio

State and to show me many things I was unable to see. The trait of resiliency was obvious when she moved to Columbus, more obvious during my four-year NFL career when a player's wife never knows what the next day will bring and continued when operations kept her from knowing how much she could depend on her husband. I could have mentioned date, or mother, or partner, or teammate, besides mentor, but "bright, courageous and resilient" just overshadowed dozens of other qualities.

The Karl Rothermunds: Karl Jr. and I went to Lancaster High School together, but he was two classes ahead, so we were not close then. Plus, he lived on Pill Hill, where the doctors and businessmen lived—the most affluent area of the east side. I remember seeing him at the hotel before the Rose Bowl and inviting him up to my room to watch film and explain how we were going to attack USC. Now we are great friends and have been for decades. I will get back to Karl Jr., but first, Karl Sr. was a major mentor in between.

Karl Sr was a very important mentor at a difficult time in my life. My avocational life was at a low point when I did not pass the physical for the Buffalo Bills. I had just played my best game against the world champion Steelers, and now football was over. My vocational plan, getting in line and working toward the position of Ohio State athletic director, for which I had been preparing for four years, had ended when Hugh Hindman told me the line was closed. I had no job, no plans, no ideas, and Nancy was pregnant.

As a leader of the Ohio Contractors Association, Karl Sr. had arranged for Bruce Jankowski and me to work construction when we were in California the summer before our senior year. That did not work out as we had planned, but his help had always been appreciated.

At this challenging time for our family, Mr. R. came through again. Governor Rhodes was promoting a jobs program around the state. Of course, the Contractors Association wanted jobs for their people, so they were helping in the promotion. Mr. R. said, "We would love to hire you to speak for us. We will pay you $100 but will schedule you as many times as we can for as long as you want."

It was surprising how much $100 was compared to nothing. It not only bought some groceries and put something toward the house payment but it also gave me a purpose and a place to go. At a time when the NFL rejected my body, and Ohio State rejected me, it was nice that someone thought I had value and wanted to help us. It was another indication to me that the world was not divided into groups of rich and poor, but caring and not caring.

Back to his son, Karl Jr. After the Rose Bowl victory, January 1, 1969, Karl was one of the people who met us at the plane. When I said hello, he replied, "We've got to hurry. We've got to get to Lancaster immediately."

I tried to explain that my car was at the university, and I would drive down as soon as I could.

"No," he said, pulling my arm. "There is a celebration tonight for former Lancaster players who played in a college bowl game, Mike Christian (defensive back at Ohio University) and you. Dad said to get you there as soon as possible. We have a plane reserved. Let's go."

I can honestly say that taking a plane to Lancaster was the last thing on my mind at that particular time. I had lived there all my life and had never taken a plane into or out of the city. I wondered how many people who lived in Lancaster even knew it had an airport.

Since it was clear that Karl Jr. was on a mission, I gave in and let him take over. It was fun to be "a favorite son of Lancaster for a part of an evening" and to share a celebration with so many lifelong friends.

Several years later, when $100 checks were not as critical as they were in 1975, and Nancy and I had some money to invest, I turned to Karl Jr., who had become a stockbroker and now lived in California. We are still working together today. While Karl Sr. and I had a traditional vertical mentoring relationship, with him helping me, Karl Jr. and I are more of a team. I have most of the same financial certifications he is required to have, and I have added working knowledge over the years, primarily under the direction of Jack Havens, a superior mentor. Karl Jr. and I have been involved in projects he brought to me, others I brought to him, and more than one that came up in casual conversation. We are truly vertical mentors to each other—in both directions—as well as horizontal mentors. Mostly we are trusted friends.

Jack Havens: Knowing and working with Jack was more educational than an MBA from any college could be, because he combined business skills with character development and genuine caring for others. He taught me to look at a situation and understand it as it was, while also seeing it as it could be. Some people call that "seeing around the corner." But if we never had a professional relationship—and we had several—he would be in this book as a friend.

The last time I saw him I was leaving Columbus for California. I had to see Moose (Dr. Moustpha Abou-Samra) because my back was so bad. Jack said, "No problem, as long as we have the phone and the computer.

I said, "Jack, I want you to know I love you dearly," and kissed him on the cheek.

Ellen Havens Hardymon: Ellen was several years younger than I was when we worked together in California to build the Nautilus business, but her maturity and innate intelligence were immediate assets. We began as a threesome, with her father providing needed guidance, and became more independent of Jack as we learned from him. When we returned to Columbus, she was able to dissect and evaluate all components of a banking system. She knew how to interpret financial statements, both what was there and to notice what was not there. This was particularly valuable in determining the right price to pay for a business.

It could have been difficult working with Ellen. She was a majority stockholder in the company, I was her supervisor, and we both reported to her father. Because we were both conscientious and encouraging, we were always partners, and we remain so today.

Penny Myers: Penny sat in front of me in elementary school. She was a sports fan and carried a picture of John Havlicek in her wallet. The whole state of Ohio was excited about the sophomore class of Buckeye basketball players in 1960, but she had taken the initiative to request a picture from Ohio State. That taught me the importance of contact with fans and the responsibility athletes have to their fans. I have thought of Penny many times over the years and tried to treat every fan as she had been treated. Penny, thanks for your guidance.

Other Close Friends

Bruce Peterson noted the following: "I saw Lancaster in both games of the state basketball regionals in 1966 and thought, *Rex Kern is going to be a good college player*. A friend told me he had set the school record for passing yardage in football. So, when Lancaster played Watterson in football that fall, I went to the game. Watterson had a great team, but the score at the half was very close. Lancaster lost the game, but afterward every Watterson player went over and shook Rex's hand. It showed great respect for his play. During the basketball season, I saw him on TV with Fred and Woody, announcing he was going to Ohio State to play both sports. That spring, I saw Lancaster play Cincinnati Western Hills in the state baseball semifinals in Columbus.

"When I was at Ohio University for orientation, in the cafeteria I recognized the redhead in the American Legion baseball uniform and said, 'You're Rex Kern.'

"He stuck out his hand, said, 'Who are you?' and we ate together.

"That fall my friend, Larry Zelina, invited me to go to the Lancaster–Upper Arlington football game with him and two of his OSU teammates, Dave Cheney and Rex.

"The game was not very interesting, and part way through Rex nudged me and said, 'Hey, Bruce, weren't you telling me about some good-looking girls where you went to high school? Why don't we go meet them?'

"So we went to the Bexley game and talked with some girls. The following year, Larry introduced one of those girls to Ron Maciejowski. She later became Lindy Lemmon Maciejowski. These days they enjoy playing with their grandchildren.

"Back to Rex. The next year, I saw him at the airport when the team left for the Rose Bowl. That spring, he came down to Athens to see the Ohio State–Ohio University baseball game because two of his Rose Bowl teammates, Mike Polaski and Kevin Rusnak, were playing for the Buckeyes. I introduced him to my fraternity brothers, and we sat together. One of the Bobcats hit a ball over a building behind the fence and later hit a rocket for a double. In between, he made several plays at shortstop. Rex said, 'Who is that guy?'

"I said, 'His name is Mike Schmidt. He's one of my fraternity brothers.' Mike went into the Baseball Hall of Fame in 1995. I do not know if Rex would have joined him if he had signed with the Royals out of high school, or even after playing in college, but I once asked OU baseball coach Bob Wren if Rex would have made the majors. Bob's immediate reply was, 'Absolutely! Plus, he would have started for Ohio University immediately and made our 1970 team better before that.' The 1970 team won the MAC with a 14–1 record, won the district with three straight victories, and won two games in the College World Series before finishing fourth.

"Over the years, we have talked about once a month and have seen each other from time to time, more often when he and Nancy lived in Columbus. It was a sad night at the Athletic Club in 1975, at the celebration of Woody's twenty-five years at Ohio State, when Rex told me the Bills' doctor was not going to sign off on his physical, and his NFL career was over. Nancy invited me to their home in Ventura, California, for a surprise thirty-ninth birthday party for Rex in 1988. I remember going with him and our wives to the final game in St. John Arena, where Rex had hoped to play basketball for Ohio State. That was in 1998. Another highlight was when the four of us went to the Kentucky Derby in 2016. The great Pro Football Hall of Fame quarterback Warren Moon sat two tables away and told Rex, 'I patterned my game after yours.'

"But *the* highlight was when he called to tell me he had been elected to the College Football Hall of Fame in 2007. He said, 'There will be several things going on with this, and I want you to be involved with everything. You never asked me for anything, and this will be something for you to enjoy.' That fall he asked me to stand with his family, John Hicks, Dave Cheney, and Jan White on the fifty-yard line of Ohio Stadium, when the university and one hundred thousand fans honored him. Then he invited me to the ceremony at the Waldorf Astoria in New York City. The following summer I was invited to South Bend for the ceremony and parade held there. That entire experience was like one long dream.

"Not many people know this but Woody would not allow the 1970 players to receive national championship rings, because they lost to Stanford in the Rose Bowl. The seniors had their 1968 rings, but Rex and the other captains felt the younger players deserved rings since OSU was claiming the championship. Rex was having trouble getting his calls to the athletic department returned and asked if I had any ideas. I had developed a friendship with athletic director Gene Smith and arranged a meeting. When Rex came in for homecoming, we had breakfast together. Gene said, 'Get me the ring sizes,' and it was done.

"I was shocked to find that Rex had called my brother, Bob, gotten my ring size, and gave me a ring as well.

"Rex Kern is as fine a person as I have ever met. Lancaster, Ohio, never left him."

* * *

Dr. Del Brunner: "Rex and Nancy Kern came to my Sunday school class in Ventura, California. At the end of class, we always asked first-time attenders their names. Having spent eight years at USC as an undergraduate and a dental student, who was in the stadium of the 1969 Rose Bowl, wearing my cardinal and gold, I noticed their name. We talked later in private and have been friends for forty-five years.

"I have a unique way of evaluating friendships: How long could you travel with this friend? With some couples, an hour is plenty. Others, a couple of days, tops. Rex and Nancy have no expiration date with my wife and me. You get very few friends like that in your life.

"We went to many games in Columbus over the years—particularly, to the OSU-USC series and quite a few Michigan games. He was always being asked for tickets, to the point where I thought it would be annoying. He was always gracious, saying, 'Let me look into that for you,' and he inevitably came through for the fans.

"Speaking of Ohio State, Rex has a very deep commitment to the university, but it pains me to say that they feel free to use him for fundraising but feel no obligation to reciprocate. He invited me to New York City when he was inducted into the College Football Hall of Fame. Ohio State had a reception for him, but the focus on his achievements was minimal. It was mostly a fundraiser for the university, which I thought was very inappropriate.

"His athletic achievements are well known; I love him for his other sides.

"For example, I have a redheaded daughter, so I am aware that redheads have a very low threshold of pain. Also, anesthetics do not historically impact their pain. If you are aware of his injuries, operations, and rehab, the pain he has endured has been much worse than you would expect, yet he never complains.

"We went skiing at Mammoth Mountain, where Nancy's parents had a cabin. He had a classic *yard sale*, a skiing term for a fall with skis, poles, everything flying all over. He could not move his wrist, but he pulled his ski glove on and said, 'I'm good to go.' The next day, he blew up again. This time I insisted we go to the emergency room. He had a broken wrist, which required a cast.

"He had several surgeries after leaving Ohio State and was upbeat for all of them. He truly has a warrior mentality. He does not like attention and does not want to inconvenience people.

"One of my favorite Rex stories took place when he went to Columbus for a game with his two sons. He was about fifty at the time. They went to eat at that restaurant in German Village, Schmidt's. They were seated at a table beside a large picture of Rex in a Buckeye uniform.

"When the waitress came to take their order, Rex pointed to the picture and said to her, 'Some people think I look like that guy.'

"She tilted her head to one side, squinted, turned her head to the other side, and said, 'Nah, I just don't think so.'

"He enjoyed telling me that story because he sees himself much more as a regular guy than as a celebrity. Trying to wrap him up in a few words, I would say he does not crave, or maybe even want, attention; that he has a warrior mentality; and that a man could not wish for a closer or more genuinely selfless friend."

★ ★ ★

Ray Ellison: Ray was part mentor, part friend, and like many others, all of each. We met this brilliant, though uneducated, man through church when we lived in Ventura. He developed thrift stores, including the first one in the United States in 1948, with money from his pay as a World War II paratrooper. According to a January 9, 1994, article in the *Los Angeles Times*, he was semiretired but helping his sons, Mark and Matt, operate twenty-eight stores in seven states. Ray was an ultraloyal friend at many times for our family, but two stand out. The first was during a difficult recovery from my back surgery. He stopped nearly every day, to the extent that the door was left unlocked, and he had a chair in my room. From there we solved the problems of the world on a daily basis. When I fell asleep, usually after pain medication, he let himself out. The second was when Arthur Jones, the founder and manufacturer of Nautilus equipment, ran into financial difficulties, which forced us to cease operations. I could see the end but had no idea of the future. Ray came to me and said, "If you want to work with the Fellowship of Christian Athletes and need to raise support, my two sons and I will commit $50,000 a year for three years." When Jack Havens asked us to go to Columbus and work with him and Ellen, that was what I wanted to do, but Ray's generous offer during a perceived time of need will never be forgotten in our family.

* * *

Sue Ellison, Ray's wife, was a close friend of ours as well. When she was caring for him in his later years, I stopped to see them on my way to therapy. I was sorry to see him bedridden but glad to repay some of his earlier kindnesses in a similar way. They left the gate unlocked, and there was always a chair available. I walked into their house, as he had into ours. When he died in 2011, I continued to stop to see her. We would discuss current events, life lessons, and our faith. She had been a marvelous caregiver for my friend and deserved the same. Sue passed away on February 13, 2021.

* * *

Jeff Kaplan: One of Woody's early "brain coaches," Jeff started out as a graduate assistant for football after I graduated, but we became acquainted when I interned in the winter and became fast friends. He was always a reliable, knowledgeable, trustworthy source of information about what was happening at the university. When Nancy and I were in Columbus, we always wanted to see Jeff and his wife, Darcy, for dinner, if possible.

Jeff told me a story that revealed a new side to Wayne Woodrow Hayes.

"I told Woody I was going to take some vacation time to work for Democrat Dick Celeste," Jeff said, knowing Woody supported the other candidate, James Rhodes. "Woody's reply surprised me."

"'Jeff, I congratulate you for supporting our two-party system. I may support the other candidate, but I believe in the system and am glad you are involved, following your principles.'"

★ ★ ★

There is an important point to remember: Someone does not need to be a teammate, a coach, or a lifelong friend to be a valuable mentor. By meeting Ohio State basketball coach Fred Taylor and Ohio University baseball coach Bob Wren in the recruiting process, I recognized traits such as sincerity and high values that I wanted to establish in myself. By merely watching Buckeye basketball games, I admired the effort of John Havlicek and the beautiful jump shot of Mel Nowell, which challenged me to expect more from myself, on and off the court.

Whether you are a close friend, a future relative, or someone I will never meet, you may be thinking, *That guy is so lucky to have those mentors, guides, influences, and friends!* If so, I agree completely with you and would add a question: "If it could happen to me, why couldn't it happen to you?"

There are people on my list of mentors who are remarkable, but many of them are the kind of people we meet every day. I bet you could write a list of five or ten names of potential mentors right now. Want to try?

When you start thinking about your potential list of mentors, do not forget that face in the mirror—yourself. Are you the type of person others would want to mentor?

If you have gotten this far in the book, you know a lot about me. While I certainly received more wonderful mentoring than I deserved, I made contributions, though not always intentionally. Let's review a few.

- As a child, I wanted to play with older, bigger boys. When they refused, I asked again.
- When I shot free throws and made eight out of ten, I was not satisfied. I usually made ten in a row before stopping.
- I regularly stayed after practice, or arrived early at practice, or practiced at home.
- At our sports banquets, when a speaker like Ohio State's Fred Taylor said, "In any job you do, be the best at what you are doing," I listened.
- When a girl named Nancy Henno let me know that Bs and Cs are not good enough if you can do better, I challenged myself in school. When I learned how to get As, I wanted more of them.
- I set goals for myself. First, I wanted to be a coach. Later, I began to think about athletic administration. Because I had goals, people like Milt Taylor and Dr. Jimmy Hull casually pointed out that I should get a master's degree. I had to hear that from people I respected in order to believe it for myself. Many mentors helped me develop self-confidence.
- When Jack Havens forecast that the future of banking included brokerage, he suggested that I pass the Series 7 exam to prepare for the future he saw. I studied intensely for that exam. As much as I wanted to pass the exam, the unacceptable thought of disappointing him was a far, far greater motivational factor. I was more nervous about taking that exam than I was before any athletic event or my Ph.D. exams.

At times I suspected that Dad believed my mentors did my work or arranged for my success by some kind of backroom deals. He could not believe his son could do some of the things I have done. My mentors inspired me, believed in me, encouraged me, directed me, and guided me, but they did not rob me of the responsibility of doing the work. That would have left me unprepared for future challenges, which would have cheated me in the long run.

It is essential to believe in yourself and your potential for success while following your dreams. Keep in mind these examples of athletes who achieved greatness in their sports, though there was a time when few believed they would achieve it.

Many people believe Michael Jordan is the greatest professional basketball player in history. He was cut from the varsity as high school sophomore and played on the reserve team. Others believe Boston Celtic Bill Russell was the greatest. He received one college scholarship offer after high school. John Wooden is widely considered the greatest college basketball coach because he won ten championships in twelve years at UCLA. He coached there sixteen years before winning the first one.

Tom Brady is often mentioned as the greatest quarterback of all time. As a high school freshman, he was not good enough to start for the junior varsity, a team that was 0–8 and did not score a single touchdown. At Michigan, he was seventh on the depth chart initially. He did not start until his junior year and only earned All-Big Ten honorable mention. In the 2000 NFL Draft, he was selected behind seven quarterbacks—199 overall.

It seems that belief in yourself and working hard—and smart—can lead to results others would call impossible.

For those thinking, *Those things happened long ago. It is different now*, how about two examples from today?

March 1, 2021, J. J. Watt signed a two-year contract with the Arizona Cardinals for $28 million, $23 million guaranteed. It is the kind of contract three-time NFL Defensive Players of the Year and five-time NFL All-Pros receive. Yet Watt was a two-star recruit in high school who received a scholarship to Central Michigan. He believed in himself, transferred to Wisconsin without a scholarship, earned a scholarship, made All-Big Ten and second-team All-American, and became the eleventh pick in the 2011 NFL Draft.

He says, "Success isn't owned. It is leased, and rent is due every day." Applying that philosophy has worked for J. J. Watt. Why wouldn't it work for you?

Jason Preston of Ohio University made a name for himself in the 2021 NCAA Tournament. Whether he is just getting started or had the highlight of his life, he is an inspiration to overachievers in any field.

Preston scored fifty points in high school. Can't-miss recruits often do that in a single game; Preston's total came over his two-year varsity career! Obviously, he was not rated as a college prospect.

After an improbable series of events to arrive at Ohio University, Preston led the Ohio Bobcats team to three victories in the 2021 MAC Tournament as a junior, earning MVP honors. Their first-round NCAA Tournament opponent was fourth-seed Virginia, coached by Tony Bennett. Bennett had led the Cavaliers to an NCAA title in 2019 and dominated the Atlantic Coast Conference—and many more well-known coaches—with five titles in the past eight years, including 2021.

Known for his defensive insights, Bennett studied the Ohio offense. Preston had led the team in scoring in each tournament game. He had also led the team with thirty-one points in a narrow early season loss to Big Ten power Illinois, a one seed. Bennett decided to force the ball out of Preston's hands by double-teaming him at every opportunity.

The strategy limited Preston to seven shots and eleven points. But his season-high thirteen rebounds and typical eight assists led both teams in a 62–58 upset, during which he played all forty minutes.

Two nights later, the bubble burst when fifth-seeded Creighton used the same strategy, and Bobcat shooters went cold. But Ohio

University had one of its greatest victories, and Jason Preston just might have more surprises in store for basketball fans, to whom he says, "Believe in yourself!"

Just before this book went to press, Preston was taken with the thirty-third choice in the NBA Draft. It seems that more people are believing in him!

Studies show that those who write down their goals are significantly more likely to achieve them. Have goals, write them down, and find mentors to help you reach them.

If you work hard at achieving your clearly stated goals, I believe mentors will find you, as they did me. If that is not true immediately, you will be closer to your goals when they find you later.

Leadership at Home

In the chapter on family, you read what our sons, John-Ryan and Michael, felt we passed on to them as their earliest leaders. With Nancy's help, I wanted to mention some of the ideas we intended to pass on as parents.

Always remember you are loved, whether or not you feel deserving at the moment.

Think about something before you commit to it, then honor that commitment by completing the task the best you can.

Aim for personal excellence. No one is perfect, but everyone should aim for his or her best. This begins with attitude at home, then grades in school, then chores around the house, and continues for a lifetime.

No one is better than you are, nor are you better than anyone.

When it comes to money, the first fruits, 10 percent, go to God. Then put the next 20 percent into savings. Then live on the remaining 70 percent. Recently, I heard a quote from Warren Buffet that goes, "Don't save what is left after spending; spend what is left after saving." That makes an important point as well.

Try things that might interest you. They could lead to a hobby or a vocation or they might be an interesting experience. Then try more things.

All things are difficult before they become easy.

FAIL: first attempt at learning.

Do not be discouraged if you are less than outstanding at something immediately. Those who work hard often surpass more talented people in any field. The story goes that Thomas Edison failed 1,000 times before figuring out how to design the electric light bulb. He believed that the first 999 times he succeeded in discovering what did not work, each time getting closer to his goal.

If something or someone would embarrass your family or yourself, avoid it or the person.

Your mother and I will not be able to teach you everything. Learn from others too.

Be respectful to others. When someone helps you, say thank you. Be respectful and be loyal.

Help others without expecting something in return. Sometimes helping someone means guiding them so that person can work it out alone. Sometimes it means trusting them to work it out without you.

If you can, avoid judging someone else.

Real wealth comes to the one who learns that he or she is paid best for the things he or she does for nothing.

Case Study: Woody Hayes

Before concluding the chapter, I would like to discuss leadership in a sort of case study. As much as Woody Hayes has been discussed over the years, in conversation and in print, I have never seen or heard the quality of his supervision by Ohio State officials evaluated. I have spent a great deal of time loving the man, quite a bit of time not understanding him, and much of a year being very unhappy with him. In a chapter on leadership, to me it makes sense to avoid asking "Was he a good leader?" All of his qualities have been discussed at length in many books, including his own, and this one. The question I wish to ask is, "Did he receive the help he needed from the men assigned to lead him?"

Before beginning the discussion, there are two obvious points to state. First, Woody would have been very difficult to supervise by traditional means, especially anything pertaining to money. His relationship with money can be described in three words: "I despise money." His players heard those three words many times in many meetings during a Buckeye career. Second, I do not have firsthand knowledge of anything that took place in the football program before my class arrived in 1967. I do know that Woody dedicated his book, *You Win with People*, to Dick Larkins, the Ohio State athletic director from 1947 to 1970, indicating a high regard for his supervisor. Also, this quote of Woody's appeared earlier in the book: "My greatest friends are always people that I fight with. Bo [Schembechler] was one of those. That was true with Dick Larkins. We were always arguing but agreed on everything."

With the benefit of hindsight, here are some thoughts on the supervision Coach Hayes was entitled to receive during his early days at Ohio State. If he had, things might have been different.

First, Woody banned unfriendly journalists from practice because things happened in practice that would not look good in print. This may have been his right. But Woody's supervisors could not be banned from practice, and they should have been there. Dick Larkins was undoubtedly too busy to go to practice every day, but why not pop in every other week? A staff member could have been there daily. If Woody's supervisors did not know what happened in practice, they were negligent.

Practice is where Paul Warfield trained to run pass routes, Jack

Tatum trained to tackle, and Mike Sensibaugh trained to defend passes. They did it by repetition. It is also where Woody Hayes trained to lose his temper. It could—and should—have been where he trained to keep his temper under control.

It is not acceptable to hit football players, yet Woody was allowed to do it daily. He got very good at hitting football players—often when he was under control, sometimes when he was not. Eventually, he did it when he was out of control and in public. That cost him his job.

Second, Woody was allowed to insult coaches, players, and writers at will. He was allowed to damage property without consequences. He led by fear. Yet he thought of himself as a teacher. This obvious disconnect might have been the key to reaching him. In thinking about our favorite teachers, we recall men and women who taught us to dream, to believe, to aspire, to work, to become the best version of ourselves. Woody taught a great deal that was good, but fear was not part of that.

Third, more than winning, more than fame, and much more than money, Woody loved Ohio State University. Helping him see the effect of his actions could have helped him see there were times he embarrassed the school he loved. If he could have seen that and embraced his power to change, he would not have self-destructed on television and would not have been fired.

None of this would have been easy, especially when dealing with Woody. Leadership is not always easy. Helping people face their shortcomings, helping them persevere, helping them grow, none of that is easy.

While Woody is accountable for his life, he could have had more help from his employer—if he could have accepted it.

* * *

So, here we are at the end.

The journey that began on Christmas 2019 with a gift from our son John-Ryan and his wife, Heather, and a request for me to "write down my stories" has come to a close. The dozens of wonderful mentors I have had from Lancaster to the present have been recognized and thanked. The lessons learned, many joyful, some painful, have been discussed and passed on to younger and future relatives. The stories have been told (except for a few more in the back of the book, titled "Ask Rex").

While Lee Caryer helped me achieve my original goals, he asked questions or made suggestions which caused us to get into areas I had not anticipated, such as analysis of particular games and entire seasons; discussion of racial relations in society; how we learn to be leaders; different ways we are mentored; and a look at the many sides of Woody Hayes, as Woody put it, "Warts and all."

I can't thank Lee enough for his wisdom, insight, encouragement and, at times, leadership. Without him, *The Road to the Horseshoe and Beyond* might never have been expanded and completed. Thank you, Lee Caryer!

To the college football fans who joined our family and my mentors in the audience, I hope you have enjoyed a few laughs and learned a bit about college football fifty-plus years ago. To the Ohio State die-hards, I hope you learned many new stories to share with friends at tailgates or gathered in "man caves."

To steal a line allegedly spoken by baseball's Yogi Berra, I would like to "thank all of you for making this project necessary." My wife, Nancy, and I have had so much fun reliving the blessings of our lives, and even debating a few facts. At the same time, writing the book and dealing with the business side of it took away time I would have been spending with her. She was most supportive.

We hope you enjoyed the result as much as we did.

Rex Kern
"Ole No. 10"

I am right behind our Hall of Fame defensive end Ted "The Stork" Hendricks.

My final NFL game, the 1974 playoff loss to the Super Bowl
champion Pittsburgh Steelers. Rocky Bleier is in the foreground.
My right little finger was finally fixed in August, 2021.

Meeting these wonderful children while honorary
chairman of the Easter Seals campaign helped
me remember Who is in charge.

Office of the President

December 29, 1994

Dr. Rex W. Kern
Rexer Corporation
4675 Winterset Drive
Columbus, OH 43220

Dear Rex:

    Thank you very much for your wonderful note. And, I am so pleased that you found my regular letter to our parents to be of help. In turn, know how much we appreciate all that you are doing on behalf of the university. Indeed, we should have you on our payroll for all the good deeds done by "Ole #10."

    Best wishes to you and Nancy for the holidays.

Cordially,

[signature]

A letter from my dear friend Gordon Gee,
President of The Ohio State University.

Catching up with Rex Kern

by Kelly Kaufman

Kern led Woody Hayes' 1968 Buckeyes to the national title as a sophomore and was second runner-up for the Heisman Trophy the next year.

The legacy left behind by the 1968 national championship team can best be described by something Ralph Waldo Emerson, a 19th century American poet, said years before the Buckeyes trounced Southern California in the 1969 Rose Bowl: "Do not follow where the path may lead. Go instead where there is no path and leave a trail."

Thanks to one member of the now legendary squad, that trail will never fade.

For former Ohio State quarterback Rex Kern, the "trail" that has formed since his years as a player (1968-70) has been long, winding and is far from ending.

Kern's connection with Ohio State could have ended with his illustrious playing career. It could have ended when he traded his cleats for wingtips, it did not. His most enduring legacy to Ohio State will involve the countless hours he and his wife Nancy have spent raising millions of dollars for his alma mater's various fundraising campaigns and scholarships.

Having recently spearheaded the drive to fund the Wayne Woodrow "Woody" Hayes Chair in National Security Studies, Kern also was instrumental in raising $1.3 million for an athletics scholarship in honor of the 1968 team. He has served on the Board of Directors of the Alumni Association, the President's Cub Advisory Committee and the President's Club Executive Committee. He and his wife are currently co-chairs of the College and School annual giving drive at Ohio State. In 1997, he received the John B. Gerlach Award for his outstanding leadership and service.

Jerry May, vice president for development at OSU and president of The Ohio State University Foundation, has seen first hand the immediate impact Kern's tireless efforts have made on everyone he has worked with.

"Rex Kern is a stalwart volunteer," May said. "He is one of the most committed volunteers at Ohio State in both development and athletics and is one of the reasons Ohio State continues to be so successful. He is one of my favorite people because he just stays with you. We are so fortunate to have a lifetime relationship with Rex and Nancy because it is the kind of relationship that just keeps on giving."

Kern admits the best years of his life were the ones he spent on the gridiron.

"I will always remember the reason we were recruited to play for Ohio State – to beat that team up north," Kern said. "We had fire in our bellies every time we played Michigan, although we weren't mean about it. They had a great coaching staff and great players. They were always good. It was a tremendous rivalry because we knew that the road to the Rose Bowl always went through Michigan."

Kern was only a sophomore in 1968 when the Buckeyes beat Michigan 50-14 and became the last Ohio State team to win a unanimous national football title. That season he took home All-America, All-Big Ten and Rose Bowl MVP honors. He also was second runner-up for the Heisman Trophy in 1969.

Kern attributes some of his success as a student and businessman to a coach who would never quit and did not let his players quit either.

"In '67 the fans booed Woody and everyone wanted to run him out of town," Kern recounted. "Then in '68, we won the national championship and he was a hero. Coach Hayes placed a lot of emphasis on players graduating. He wanted every player to graduate, go to law school and become an attorney."

Kern did not become an attorney, but he did graduate from Ohio State – three times. When he wasn't playing professional ball with the Baltimore Colts or the Buffalo Bills, the Lancaster, Ohio native was earning his bachelor's in education ('71), his master's in physical education ('73), and his Ph.D. in health, physical education and recreation ('83). His second of six back surgeries forced him to retire from football in 1974.

Kern and his wife, Nancy, a former Rose Bowl princess and 1972 graduate of OSU's School of Education, moved to California in 1976 where Kern was president and chief executive officer of Nautilus of California. The couple returned to Columbus in 1994 with their two sons, John-Ryan, currently a real estate executive, and Michael, now a senior lacrosse standout at Penn State. Kern is currently chairman of the board of First Mutual Financial and is president of Rexer Corporation. ❖

An emotional leader who always made big plays on the gridiron, Kern is now one of the most committed volunteers to The Ohio State University.

January 7, 1976

Mr. J. Edward Weaver
Director, Department of Athletics
223 St. John Arena
410 West Woodruff Avenue
Campus

Dear Director:

I have had the opportunity to visit the
majority of schools here in Ohio that have an All-
Sports Hall of Fame. I am in the process of gathering
all the material and evaluating the proposal. However,
I am going to wait until I visit the Miami University
Hall of Fame on February 20.

Prior to my leaving for the Rose Bowl, I
had an opportunity -- along with Saul -- to visit the
Canton Hall of Fame under the most gracious guidance
of Dick Gallagher, who I understand is a good friend
of yours.

As you can see from the enclosed, Dick has
invited you to be his guest anytime it is convenient
for you. Saul and I may venture back to Canton the
first of the year. If you would like to go along, we
would love to have you ride with us so you will have
an opportunity to see the Hall of Fame firsthand.

Director, I will keep you informed as I am
able to progress on the Hall of Fame. I will most
assuredly have the proposal ready for the Varsity "O"
members by March 1, 1976.

Sincerely,

Rex Kern

RK:nlk

Because it was originally my idea, I was excited
to have the opportunity to develop The Ohio State
University Athletic Hall of Fame.

My youngest son, Michael, and I with two-time winner of the Heisman Trophy, Archie Griffin.

BIBLIOGRAPHY

Dave Hyde, *1968: The Year That Saved Ohio State Football* (Wilmington, Ohio: Orange Frazer Press, 2018).

John Lombardo, *A Fire to Win: The Life and Times of Woody Hayes* (New York: St. Martin's Press, 2005).

William Harper, *An Ohio State Man: Coach Esco Sarkkinen Remembers OSU Football* (Canal Winchester, Ohio: Enthea Press, 2000).

Phillip Hoose, *Attucks!: Oscar Robertson and the Basketball Team That Awakened a City* (New York: Farrar Straus Giroux, 2018).

Bo Schembechler and Mitch Albom, *Bo* (New York: Warner Books, 1989).

Robert Vare, *Buckeye: A Study of Coach Woody Hayes and the Ohio State Football Machine* (New York: Harper's Magazine Press, 1974).

Earle Bruce, *Buckeye Wisdom* (Chicago: Triumph Books, 2014).

Lee Caryer, *The Golden Age of Ohio State Basketball: 1960–1971* (Shippensburg, Pennsylvania: Companion Press, 1992).

Rocky Bleier, *Fighting Back* (New York: Stein and Day, 1975).

Dick Schafrath, *Heart of a Mule* (Cleveland: Gray and Company Publishers, 2006).

Steve Greenberg and Dale Ratermann, *I Remember Woody: Recollections of the Man They Called Coach Hayes* (Dallas: Master's Press, 1997).

Jack Park, *The Ohio State Football Encyclopedia* (New York: Sports Publishing, 2001).

Steve Greenberg and Larry Zelina, *Ohio State '68: All the Way to the Top* (New York: Sports Publishing, 1998).

Monte Carpenter, *Quotable Woody: The Wit, Will, and Wisdom of Woody Hayes* (Nashville, Tennessee: Towle House Publishing, 2002).

George Howe Colt, *The Game: Harvard, Yale, and America in 1968* (New York: Scribner, 2018).

Greg Emmanuel, *The 100-Yard War* (Hoboken, New Jersey: Wiley, 2004).

Bill Levy, *Three Yards and a Cloud of Dust* (Cleveland: World Publishing Company, 1966).

Kevin Daum and Anne Mary Ciminelli, *12 Lessons in Business Leadership: Insights from the Championship Career of Tom Brady* (New York: Skyhorse, 2020).

Michael Rosenberg, *War As They Knew It: Woody Hayes, Bo Schembechler, and America in a Time of Unrest* (New York: Grand Central Publishing, 2008).

Jeff Snook, *What It Means to Be a Buckeye: Jim Tressel and Ohio State's Greatest Players* (Chicago: Triumph Books, 2003).

Alan Natali, *Woody's Boys: 20 Famous Buckeyes Talk Amongst Themselves* (Wilmington, Ohio: Orange Frazer Press, 1995).

Paul Hornung, *Woody Hayes: A Reflection* (Champaign, Illinois: Sagamore Publishing, 1991).

Mike Bynum, *Woody Hayes: The Man and His Dynasty* (Gridiron Properties, 1991).

Woody Hayes, *You Win with People* (Typographic Print, 1975).

Lou Holtz, *Wins, Losses, and Lessons* (New York: Morrow Publishing, 2006).

ASK REX

Here are some of the questions fans have asked me over the years, and a couple of miscellaneous items which seemed too good to omit. Maybe there is one you wondered about.

★ ★ ★

"Rex, I loved the 1968 team. Can you tell something I do not know?"

Most people know about the huge Purdue game, when Heisman candidate LeRoy Keyes was held to 19 yards rushing and 44 receiving. The defense, particularly Jack Tatum, who spied Keyes all over the field, did an amazing job. Tate was named Defensive Back of the Week by one wire service and Defensive Lineman of the Week by the other. That had never happened before. And the defense also did a tremendous job on O. J. Simpson in the Rose Bowl. Although he gained 161 yards rushing, he averaged 170 on the year. Keyes and Simpson were great players.

But the defense was particularly outstanding in two other games that year, against two other great college and NFL backs.

Ed Podolak of Iowa had gained 286 yards in only seventeen carries against Northwestern the week before Ohio State arrived in Iowa City. Podolak gained forty-five yards on fifteen carries against the Buckeyes. Ron Johnson had run for a Big Ten record 347 yards the week before TTUN came to Ohio Stadium. Our defense held him to 91 yards.

Johnson was a two-time All-Pro in his seven-year NFL career, a long time for a running back. Podolak gained more rushing yards in his NFL career than Johnson did. In one playoff game in 1971, he gained 350 yards, rushing, receiving, and returning kicks, then an NFL record.

I do not believe one college team could have done a better job containing four great running backs in one season than our 1968 team did.

*　*　*

"Rex, what did Woody say to you after the SMU game when you waived the punter off the field?"

Nothing. He had told me in the spring to use my judgment.

*　*　*

"Rex, what would have happened if you had not been able to run for a first down on that play?"

Probably two things. First, you would be talking to Ron Maciejowski right now. Second, Mace would be remembered as one terrific quarterback.

*　*　*

"Rex, who was the most underappreciated player on the 1968 team?"

I am going to call an audible and mention the most underappreciated person, our quarterbacks coach, George Chaump. Woody got on everyone, but none more than George, who was responsible for Woody adopting the I formation in 1968.

Three years before, Mike Garrett of USC had earned a Heisman Trophy running in the I. Two years later O. J. Simpson finished second as an I back; that season he won it. Woody vehemently opposed the concept. He called it the lighthouse formation because the defense always knew where the ball was going by watching the lead blocker, the fullback. We had several successful tailbacks at Ohio State, from Dave Brungard to John Brockington to Leo Hayden, but the best was to come later. Archie Griffin won two Heisman Trophies, the only college player to do that, and he did it in the I. Fans should be glad the assistants sided with George and convinced Woody to make that change. Otherwise, our class would not have been as successful, and Archie may have been a blocking back!

* * *

Every time I meet someone who identifies himself as an Alabama fan, I ask this question: "Who played for Woody Hayes and Bear Bryant?"

The answer is Dave Brungard, who played for Woody in 1967 and 1968, transferred to Alabama, sat out in 1969, and starred for Bear in 1970. He was elected cocaptain before playing a down, led the SEC with 5.7 yards per carry, and was one of the leading receivers for a team that tied Oklahoma in the Bluebonnet Bowl.

Dave was a fine player as a Buckeye. He gained more yards than all the other halfbacks combined as a sophomore, and 101 yards for us in the first game in 1968. But his playing time diminished during the year, as John Brockington and Leo Hayden grew into the NFL first-round draft choices they would become.

Woody did not want anyone to transfer, but he understood that Dave wanted to play. "All right then," Woody said, "where do you want to go?" When Dave mentioned Alabama, Woody called Bear and said, "I have a player who wants to go to Alabama, and he will start for you!"

Only one 'Bama fan has gotten the answer right, and he was a trainer on the team.

★ ★ ★

"Rex, I heard a story that your class had a basketball team. Is that true?"

After our senior season, the guys put together a basketball team and traveled around Ohio, playing different school faculties to raise money for charity. Bruce Jankowski provided the following list of our players: Doug Adams, Tim Anderson, John Brockington, Dave Cheney, Mark Debevc, Leo Hayden, Bruce Jankowski, Rex Kern, Dick Kuhn, Ron Maciejowski, Mike Sensibaugh, Jim Stillwagon, Jack Tatum, Jan White, and Larry Zelina.

Some of the guys were serious players, like captains of their high school teams. Bruce played for a future Naismith Basketball Hall of Fame coach, Hubie Brown, in Fair Lawn, New Jersey, who is still broadcasting NBA games at eighty-seven.

I did not get to play as often as I would have liked due to FCA speaking, and I particularly regret missing one pickup game at St. John Arena, when John Havlicek stopped to play. He had been, and would continue to be, one of my idols. Bruce referred to him as "a gazelle."

Several of the guys in our class had excellent credentials in other sports, especially baseball, track, and wrestling.

★ ★ ★

You have commented that you feel better than any time in your life. What suggestions do you have for others?

First of all, do not make the mistake I did initially of thinking nothing could be done. There are many solutions to explore. I was fortunate that my wife, Nancy, took the initiative for me. So, that works, or look for your own answers. Second, be open and forthright about your situation. The first person you speak with may not be able to help, but may help you find the person who can. Third, degreed physical therapists and certified Pilates instructors have been helpful in evaluating my total health and suggesting ways for me to be happier and more productive. Fourth, deep tissue muscle massage has been helpful to me for years and led me to myofascial therapy, which gives nerves more elasticity and energy. If your answers are in that area, I would contact the John Barnes Institute to suggest someone in your area.

It was good that you did not supply specific information because I am not an expert. My advice is that there are experts in many fields, so knock on some doors and make some calls; there may be people who can help if you look for them. Good luck!

★ ★ ★

Here is a story that no one has asked me about, but you may enjoy it.

In 1994 I was asked to speak to the Buckeye football team before the Michigan game. At the time, Coach John Cooper's record in *the* rivalry game was 0–5–1. On the season, the Buckeyes had a record of 8–3. Things did not look promising, but when I spoke to the team, I was fired up.

I mentioned the history of the game. I looked Eddie George in the eye. I listed some of the Buckeye greats who had won the game: Sark, Tate, Hicks, Griffin. I looked Bobby Hoying in the eye and said, "Bobby Hoying, if you see them in the wrong defense, don't be shy—go for it!"

"After losing to them in 1969, we were so wired we had to be controlled before the 1970 game. When I saw them in man-to-man coverage I called 'Gold 98,' a post pass to Bruce Jankowski. He was open, but they had a fire game. I threw the ball, their linebacker hit me in the chest, and drove me to the ground. I heard the Buckeye crowd roar, saw that ugly helmet on my chest, kissed it, and said, 'It. Is. Finished.' Today each one of you is going to say 'It. Is. Finished!'"

Saturday, at the President's Club Luncheon before the game, President Gordon Gee pulled me aside and said, "Rex, if we don't win today, I want you to be the chairman of the search committee to find our next football coach."

I immediately began to think of people who belonged on the committee, and candidates to interview for the head coaching position. I wanted this challenge.

The Bucks led the game from beginning to end and won, 22–6, then lost to Alabama in the Citrus Bowl. John Cooper kept his job, beat Michigan again in 1998, but finished with a 2–10–1 against our rivals. In 2001, Jim Tressell was hired and turned that series around.

* * *

Here is another story you have not heard that is worth checking out.

Imagine if Woody Hayes asked the assistant coaches to critique the team, say, after spring practice, then imagine that the comments were in writing. Then imagine that one of those critiques came from a man who had coached a high school team the previous fall, who had numerous ideas about making radical improvements to the offense, Woody's offense. Finally, imagine that talented offensive weapons would be available the coming fall, sophomores like John Brockington, Leo Hayden, Jan White, Bruce Jankowski, Larry Zelina, Mace, and I.

Do you know what is coming? I bet you do.

George Chaump's observations of the team after the 1968 spring practice were written down, given to Woody, and are now presented for your review, along with Woody's reactions—to the extent they may be printed in a family book.

Staff meetings: "Assistant coaches should be given opportunity to express themselves more often. Both offensive and defensive staffs could meet together one to two hours a week to understand and help each other. Everyone's opinion should be treated with respect."

Practice: "We must work to build more and better morale. I've observed some things that had a negative effect on team morale. No coach should be reprimanded in witness of any squad member. You should spend some time with the defense during practice. It seems like we now have two separate teams."

Personnel: "My only comment on personnel is that we must get the ball to John Brockington more, whether it is on a run or a pass."

Personal interest: "I would like to have the opportunity to do more coaching than I have had this last spring. During spring practice, after the QB individuals, I felt very much like the highest paid manager in the history of football. During games I could help the QBs read the alignment and rotation in the secondary."

Offense: George made some very specific suggestions. On tailback sweeps (18–19), he suggested a sweep pass to put the defensive back in conflict between defending run or pass. Then George described 26–27, fullback off tackle, as "a real good, sound football play, however, vastly overemphasized in our system, even to the point of monotony." Out came the felt-tipped pen with an *unprintable* reply. George even suggested that other plays were more consistent and productive. When George suggested using a pass off the same action as 26–27, Woody replied "Are we anti-FB!" I took that to mean fullback, not football.

Our pass offense: "As such we don't have much. We've got to get busy to work on the development of a simple, effective pass offense. From what I have seen personnel-wise, we have what it takes to run an open formation as well as anyone."

Wondering if Woody adopted these suggestions? I would say no more than 10 percent.

★ ★ ★

"Rex, were you ever late for a team meeting?"

No, but I certainly was close once.

Senior year I spent Sunday with Mom and Dad, lost track of time, and was late starting back to Columbus for a meeting with Woody. While rushing up I-33 trying to make up some time, a patrolman pulled me over. Fortunately it was Smokey Hines, who grew up in our neighborhood. I told him the problem and he said, "Follow me," turned on his siren, and I barely got to the facility on time with an escort.

★ ★ ★

"Rex, didn't I see a picture of you wearing a sombrero during the trip to the 1969 Rose Bowl?"

On a rainy Christmas Day, a graduate assistant named Sam Elliott, a Californian but not the movie star, asked me if I wanted to go to Disneyland. I said sure, and climbed in the car with Dave Foley, Ted Provost, Kevin Rusnak, and Mike Sensibaugh.

After about an hour, I said, "When do we get to Disneyland?"

Silence.

Then Foley, our team captain, said, "We're going to Tijuana and you are our insurance policy (in case we get caught)." I wanted out but they did not stop. I decided to just enjoy myself.

When we left, a Mexican boy wanted to sell me a giant sombrero for $20. I said "no" until he got to $5, then I bought it. I knew Woody was going to Vietnam after the game and figured it would be safe to wear it when he left—if we won. I wore it on the airplane back to Columbus. When we landed, a UPI photographer took a photo. I do not know where it showed up, but the caption read, "Rex Kern wearing a sombrero at a team outing in Tijuana." I checked just before the book went to print and saw the picture on eBay for $13.99 plus shipping. Woody never mentioned the sombrero, but Anne Hayes later told me, "Everyone knew, but nobody told him."

★ ★ ★

Last story! Fittingly, it is about Woody.

In late 2001, early 2002, I was considering writing a book about Woody Hayes and sent letters to people like Jack Nicklaus, Archie Griffin, and John Havlicek, asking them to contribute stories. Just before this book went to press, I came across the response Jack Nicklaus sent. Here are "Jack's Gems."

"Let's begin with how Woody influenced my life.

"I was a young kid, about fourteen years old, and Woody was a regular customer at my dad's pharmacy on Lane Avenue. Woody came into the drugstore one day, and my dad, who had played professional football, said, 'Woody, I want to ask you a question. Jack is a pretty decent football player—'

"Woody said, 'I know that. I have followed him, and he is a nice little football player. But you know he has another talent.'

"My dad said, 'Jack is thinking about dropping football. What am I going to do?'

"Woody said, 'You keep that boy as far away from football as you can. He's got a talent that will far exceed anything that may happen in the game of football. He can play football, but he has another talent that is far greater.' Dad never said anything to me about the Woody Hayes conversation until years later because he wanted me to play football so much. That was when I gave up football.

"As an Ohio State student in 1960, I qualified for the US Open at Cherry Hills in Denver. Woody was out there for a conference and came to see me play a practice round.

"'You mean the Columbus papers didn't send anybody out here?' he said to Dad. 'Here Jackie is, the National Amateur champion, playing in the US Open at the age of twenty, and nobody's here?' So he stayed the rest of the week and called his stories in to the *Columbus Dispatch*.

(Jack did not mention this, but he was second to Arnold Palmer by two strokes and the leading amateur in the Open that year.)

"Woody became a fan of mine. He came to Oakland Hills the next year and was at Oakmont when I did win, in a playoff with Arnold Palmer. He was with my dad through the whole thing with Arnie. He got in almost as many fights with Arnie's gallery as my dad did.

"Woody, to me, was one of the great people in sports. If people only understood how much he cared about people, how much he cared for his players, how much feeling and compassion the man had. The day Woody died he was going to take my son, Gary, to lunch, hoping to convince him to study and play golf at Ohio State. Gary did and became an All-American.

"My favorite Woody story happened on Christmas Day 1969. My Dad was dying of cancer at the time. After what turned out to be our last dinner together, there was a knock on the door. Woody gave Dad a copy of his book with the inscription: 'To the best father-son team I have ever known.' That was pretty special. It still is." Jack Nicklaus

★ ★ ★

You may not believe this, but just before the publisher's deadline, I thought of another Jack Tatum story which had to be in the book. We just got it in under the deadline with the publisher.

When Tate was in Columbus for a fundraiser, having already had part of his leg amputated due to the diabetes from which he was suffering, a man in the crowd approached him after the program.

"I make prostheses and would be glad to make a foot for you," he said while extending his hand.

"That would be fine," said Jack.

The man asked a few questions, then excused himself. Jack and I talked about whether or not anything would come of the conversation.

Later, Jack called and said, "Do you remember the guy who was going to make a foot for me?"

"Sure," I replied. "What happened with that?"

"He sent it to me, and it fit great," answered Jack. "I called to thank him and asked, 'Do you know what color I am?'"

"Of course," said the man, "Remember, we shook hands."

"Then why did you send me a white foot?" Jack laughed when he got to the punch line.

The man was embarrassed at first, then Jack told him he was teasing, which his new friend appreciated. When the man learned that a white foot actually had been sent accidentally, he sent a more appropriate foot which fit just as well.

★ ★ ★

Bill Hosket, captain of Ohio State's Final Four basketball team in 1968, has a trunk load of stories about his Buckeye days, from 1964 to the present. One he heard from former athletic director Jim Jones seemed the perfect way to conclude this book.

At a meeting of Big Ten athletic directors, the suggestion was made to build a Big Ten athletic hall of fame. The discussion went as far as mentioning names for the initial class. The first four athletes were obvious: Archie Griffin for football, Jerry Lucas for basketball, Jack Nicklaus for golf, and Jesse Owens for track and field.

Don Canham, Michigan A.D., stood up and said, "I am not going to discuss any Ohio State hall of fame," and the idea was tabled.

That story reminded me about running into "Hos" when he came back to campus after his first season in the NBA in 1969. He mentioned that the Buckeye baseball team had won the NCAA championship in 1966, the basketball team had gone to the NCAA Final Four in 1968, and at the end of that year the football team won the Rose Bowl and was named national champions.

According to him, I said, "Well, you tried."

That was when I was a redhead, so it may be true.